Tramp Ships

An Illustrated History

Roy Fenton

Seaforth
PUBLISHING

Half title page photo: John Samonas & Sons's *Samjohn Pioneer*, see page 160.
Title page photo: *Irish Plane*, see page 132.

First published in Great Britain in 2013 by
Seaforth Publishing,
Pen & Sword Books Ltd,
47 Church Street,
Barnsley S70 2AS

www.seaforthpublishing.com

British Library Cataloguing in Publication Data
A catalogue record for this book is available from the British Library

ISBN 978 1 84832 158 8

Typeset and designed by Ian Hughes, Mousemat Design Limited
Printed and bound in China through Printworks International Ltd

Contents

Reardon Smith's *Paris City* was delivered by Craig, Taylor and Co Ltd of Stockton-on-Tees in 1920, just as the post-First World War boom in freight rates was ending, catastrophically for many tramp owners who had invested heavily in new ships. Cardiff-based Reardon Smith survived, however, and in 1938 sold *Paris City* to Greek owners who renamed her *Gerassimos Vergottis*. Surviving the Second World War, she was further sold in 1950, but as *Greenville* foundered in the North Atlantic during September 1953.

Preface

Looked down on by some as the lowest form of shipping life, and equally unfairly romanticised by others, a tramp is simply a ship that goes wherever in the world it can find a paying cargo. The term can be applied to coasters, tankers, fruit carriers and other specialised ships, but it is – or rather was – generally accepted to mean an ocean-going, steam- or diesel-powered, dry cargo ship of up to 10,000 tons gross, and these are the subject of this book.

The steam tramp ship evolved in the latter half of the nineteenth century and by 1914, with increases in size and particularly efficiency, it succeeded in rendering virtually extinct its sail-powered forerunner. There followed a long period during which owners and builders debated whether the utterly reliable triple-expansion engine should be replaced with the much more economical but not-entirely-trusted internal combustion engine. But just when the motor tramp had triumphed over its steam forerunner, it too was made redundant by the bulk carrier, itself partially evolving from the tramp and embodying some of its characteristics, although extending the size envelope, in some cases massively.

The tramp ship has been an important engine of industrial development, even of globalisation, providing an economical and predictable means of moving raw materials from mine to mill, and basic foodstuffs from steppe to shop or prairie to plant. It supplied Rhondda coal to power the frigoricos of Argentina, Narvik iron ore to feed the furnaces of the Ruhr, Pacific islands phosphate to fertilise the fields of New South Wales, Ukrainian wheat to nourish the workers of industrial towns in western Europe.

The tramp ship was developed by British shipbuilders and pioneered by British ship owners. For at least half the tramp's lifetime, Britain was the major player in constructing and operating it, and remained an important, if declining, influence right to the end. No apology is therefore needed for British ships dominating this book. Indeed, when yards in continental Europe, North America and Japan built tramps, only in relatively small details could they be distinguished from the British product, and in many important cases the basis was a detailed British design.

The evolution of the tramp ship has been such that, unlike in my previous volume for Seaforth, *Coasters: An Illustrated History*, it has been possible to tell the story in a chronological sequence. However, as with any type of ship there has always been debate as to the optimum design, not the least of which was the steam versus diesel debate. Nevertheless, the story has been told largely in chapters covering discrete time bands, although some cover parallel periods to explore, for instance, the radical and often patented designs of the immediate pre-First World War period, and the simultaneous building of steam and motor tramps until the 1960s.

With the exception of ships used to illustrate the tramp's genesis in chapter 1, the lower size limit for ships in this book has been put at a length of about 270 feet, the upper limit adopted in *Coasters: An Illustrated History*. Consideration of the bulk carrier has been largely confined to the final chapter, so for twelve of the thirteen chapters the upper size limit is about 550 feet.

The photographs have been chosen both to reflect the varied and evolving design of the tramp, and for their clarity. Ships of many major tramp operators and from many builders are illustrated but with such a wide field some have necessarily been neglected, and the author apologises if a reader's favourite ship or owner does not feature. If, after surveying the contents of this book, the reader gains an appreciation of how the tramp ship evolved, and of the often subtle differences which distinguished vessels from individual eras, builders, owners or nations, the author's purpose will have been served.

Roy Fenton,
Wimbledon 2013

Passing under Sydney Harbour Bridge is Denholm's *Hollypark* of 1942. Built at Sunderland as *Empire Tristram*, she was a sister of *Empire Liberty*, on which the designs of the US-built 'Oceans' and 'Liberties' were based.

Introduction

Defining a tramp ship

Very simplistically, a tramp ship is any vessel that takes part in a tramping trade, roaming the oceans in search of paying cargoes. Several types of dry cargo ship, including ageing and redundant cargo liners, have partaken in tramping, and most coasters also fall into this category. As these types have been covered in other books in this Seaforth series, the ships illustrated in this book have been selected largely from the 'classic' tramps that were designed for trading with bulk cargoes, the mainstay of the tramping trade.

Dry cargo shipping can be conveniently divided into liner and bulk trades, and considering the differing needs of the two assists an understanding of just how the tramp was designed.

The cargo liner operated to a regular schedule, providing approximately timed calls at a number of ports. It sailed whether full or not, and offered to carry almost any sized parcel of cargo. Typically its cargo would be mixed, but would mainly comprise higher value manufactured goods or foodstuffs. Importantly, its holds were designed to stow a variety of goods, with two or more decks and multiple compartments to segregate or preserve the separate items of cargo, sometimes including refrigerated spaces. The cargo liner tended to be relatively highly powered, to expedite delivery of perishable or valuable goods and to maintain its schedule despite inevitable delays in port. Cargo gear would be generous in order to speed loading or discharge and minimise time spent in port. Typically the cargo liner carried a few passengers and a comparatively large crew. The past tense has been used here because the cargo liner has been almost entirely superseded by the container ship, helped out by specialised refrigerated and heavy-lift ships.

In the bulk trade, the tramp ship typically loaded at one port and had a single destination. Its operator did not publish a schedule, and remained at liberty to carry whatever cargo gave the best return, wherever it originated and was to be delivered. That cargo would usually be a homogenous raw material, and of relatively low value; typically coal, ore, grain, timber or fertiliser, loaded to the ship's cargo deadweight or cubic capacity. The tramp's hatches and holds would be arranged so that the cargo could be loaded and discharged as readily as possible, so hatches would be as large as could safely be sealed, and the holds extended to the full depth of the ship or with no more than one intermediate deck. As economy of delivery was usually of paramount importance for cargoes of modest value, and which were not likely to deteriorate in transit, engine power was usually sufficient only to provide a predictable voyage time, and for many years 10 knots was considered a perfectly adequate cruising speed for a tramp. Cargo handling equipment would be the minimum needed in the unusual instance of the loading or discharge port not having the appropriate machinery. Accommodation for passengers was very rare indeed, and crew size was the minimum needed to operate the tramp efficiently, perhaps as little as half that considered necessary for a cargo liner.

The ideal ship for carrying bulk commodities is a single-deck vessel, with holds extending almost the full depth of the hull in which the cargo could be loaded and discharged quickly and economically. Although a significant number of tramps met this criterion, the ideal could not always be realised for several reasons. Initially, as iron and steel ships quickly grew larger, there were concerns that a single deck would not provide the necessary longitudinal strength, so an intermediate deck was necessary. This was not a disadvantage with some cargoes, especially the grain and timber commonly carried in tramps, because part could be stowed on the intermediate deck. The additional deck was also attractive when a tramp was chartered to a liner operator. Almost all of the larger tramps in this book completed in the twentieth century were shelter-deckers. As long as a token opening was left, the space between the intermediate deck and the weather deck was not counted for purposes of tonnage measurement, and thus for calculating harbour and other dues, making this design highly attractive to owners. It is perhaps significant that, when this arcane rule was at last abolished by international agreement, the modern bulk carrier – invariably a single-deck vessel – completely supplanted the classic tramp ship.

Although, as discussed later, the tramp operator and the cargo line were very different ship owning animals, the former always had an eye to the main chance. He realised that the cargo line occasionally had capacity issues necessitating chartering tonnage. In the latter days of the tramp, especially, several were designed and equipped to be attractive to cargo lines needing additional ships, with the ability to operate in tramp trades if nothing better offered. Several such examples are featured here, the criterion for inclusion is that they were built for established tramp operators.

As an owner would usually want his ship to carry whatever cargo paid best, the concept of a specialist tramp ship seems an oxymoron. Nevertheless, some owners specialised in certain trades. In some cases this was because they needed to carry a certain cargo used or produced in their industrial process, such as pulp or paper products. In other cases, an owner might eschew flexibility in order to have a ship that would earn well in a particular trade because it could stow the maximum amount of a given cargo. For instance, with timber being relatively light, carrying a full cargo would require a design that would allow the timber to be piled high on deck. At the other end of the density scale, an ore carrier would benefit from hopper-shaped holds to facilitate unloading. Examples of several specialist ships will be found in this book.

Powering a tramp ship

Three overriding considerations governed the choice of machinery for a tramp ship: economy to keep down costs, reliability to ensure completion of what could be world-spanning voyages, and familiarity for those who worked in the engine room. The two latter considerations are the reason why the steam

engine had such a long life in tramps: owners might be persuaded that the diesel cost less to run, but for many years they were not convinced that it offered reliability or that they could readily find men who could minister to its special needs.

In the marine steam engine, steam is simply a medium for conveying the energy released by burning coal to where it moves a piston in a cylinder which in turn rotates the screw shaft to drive the ship. This process is enormously wasteful of energy, so that the overall efficiency of steam machinery is lamentably low: in an 1880s engine as little as five per cent of the energy from the burning fuel was translated into propulsive power. The best way to improve efficiency is to increase working pressure, as the higher the pressure at which steam is generated, the lower the proportion of energy lost. But when improved boiler technology and construction provided higher boiler pressures, these brought their own problems. A high degree of steam expansion is theoretically possible in a single cylinder, but heat losses are severe. By expanding the steam in stages, the compound engine reduced these losses. Steam first entered the high-pressure cylinder and expanded to a certain pressure and temperature, pushing out the piston. Valves then admitted this steam to a low-pressure cylinder where it expanded further until it reached the temperature of the condenser. The two cylinders in a compound engine worked at a narrower range of temperatures and

An old-established tramping company based originally in Whitby, Turnbull Scott & Co built the *Flowergate* of 1952 with the aim of chartering her to liner companies, and she rarely if ever wore her owner's colours. Here the Burntisland-built motor ship is running for Nigerian National Line. Perhaps only after her sale to a Switzerland-based user of flag-of-convenience tonnage as *Amenity* in 1964 did she make any genuine tramp voyages. She returned to Scotland to be broken up in 1977. (*J and M Clarkson*)

With low-density cargoes such as timber, or in this case esparto grass, a tramp ship would only be considered fully laden when its decks were filled as well as its holds. Smaller tramps such as those owned and managed by R W Jones & Co Ltd, of Newport, regularly carried esparto grass from North Africa to be used for making high quality paper, and here is its *Uskside* of 1946 piled high with the vegetation in the Surrey Commercial Docks. *Uskside* was designed for such deck cargoes with its gear mounted out of the way on the forecastle, bridge and poop decks, leaving the wells clear. Laid down at Troon as *Empire Warner*, she was bought by Jones before completion and run until 1965. Sold to Greek owners as *Gero Michalos*, she was lost in May 1968 during a typhoon in the Indian Ocean.

pressures than a single cylinder, and so reduced heat losses. The rise of the tramp steamer with its growing ability to travel far and economically largely paralleled the development of compound and, soon afterwards, the triple-expansion engine, the latter having high, intermediate and low pressure cylinders. Indeed, such was the economy achieved in moving to multiple expansion that earlier engines were often replaced completely or were extensively modified by compounding or tripling.

A few tramps built in the twentieth century had quadruple-expansion engines that utilised the steam in four stages, but a more popular way of squeezing the last available energy from the steam emerging from the low pressure cylinder was to use it to turn an exhaust turbine, itself geared to the screw shaft. Other refinements included reheat, in which heat was transferred from exhaust gases to the steam on its way between the cylinders. In this way, the basic marine steam engine saw its ultimate development, and it was famously estimated that a reheated, triple-expansion engine fitted in a 10,000-ton tramp was capable of moving each ton of cargo one mile on the energy developed by burning half an ounce of coal. In the dying years of the steam engine, some novel types were fitted, notably in German vessels but also in a few British ships. As a result of the robustness of the steam engine, and its familiarity to engine room personnel, it persisted in tramps long after it had been overtaken in efficiency by the internal combustion engine.

The energy losses inescapable with the steam engine led to experiments with burning liquid fuel inside the cylinder itself. Dr Rudolf Diesel developed the compression-ignition engine that bears his name, and in which the air in the cylinder is compressed to such an extent that the accompanying increase in temperature ignites the fuel when it is forced in. The search for higher power output, for fuel economy and especially for reliability has seen the marine diesel engine evolve through several different forms, including two- and four-stroke types, and double- and single-acting types.

In a four-stroke diesel engine, as the piston moves away from the cylinder head, inlet valves open and air is drawn into the cylinder. On the second stroke, the piston compresses the air, and fuel is injected. The high temperature and pressure ignites the fuel, driving back the piston and giving the third or power stroke. During the fourth stroke the exhaust valves in the cylinder head open and the burnt gases are pushed out by the returning piston. The cylinder thus fires once for every two rotations of the crankshaft.

In a two-stroke diesel engine, every second stroke is a power stroke, so that each cylinder fires once for every rotation of the crankshaft. Air is compressed as the piston moves towards the cylinder head, and at the top of the stroke fuel is introduced and

begins to burn. The crucial difference to the four-stroke engine is that, towards the end of the power stroke, the piston uncovers exhaust ports, which are basically holes in the cylinder wall. Further movement of the piston uncovers another set of holes, the scavenge ports, which admit compressed air that expels the burnt gases through the exhaust ports.

The two-stroke diesel is inherently more efficient than the four-stroke, in which energy has to be expended moving the piston four times for every power stroke compared with just twice. The two-stroke engine is also simpler, as no exhaust valves are required. One of the earliest internal combustion engines fitted in an ocean-going tramp, *Eavestone* of 1912, was of this type. However, it effectively demonstrated the disadvantage of the highly stressed two-stroke, and was so unreliable that after just three years it was replaced with a conventional triple expansion steam engine. In the early development of the oil engine the greater robustness of the four-stroke diesel meant that it was preferred. However, as the reliability of the two-stroke engine

The *Hartismere* of J. and C. Harrison was unusual in being powered by a quadruple expansion steam engine whereas most steam tramps, including many of her fleet mates, made do with less expensive triple-expansion machinery. *Hartismere* was built and engined at West Hartlepool by William Gray and Co. Ltd. in 1933, and was photographed loading timber in a port in British Columbia, where Harrisons' ships were frequent visitors. In July 1942 *Hartismere* was sunk by the Japanese submarine I-10 in the Indian Ocean. Fortunately, given the savagery of some Japanese submarine attacks, her entire crew of 47 survived. *(Ships in Focus)*

Designed during bleak times in the 1930s, the Doxford 'Economy' was the design that persuaded many British tramp owners of the advantages of a motor ship. It was built around the Doxford three-cylinder, opposed-piston, two-stroke engine, which offered minimal running costs, burning just 6.5 tons of fuel per day at 10 knots. An example of the thirty built is *Rookley*, completed in 1940 for Stephens, Sutton Ltd of Newcastle, which was the best customer for the 'Economy', taking delivery of nine. In 1948 she was sold to become *Grenehurst*, later carrying the names *La Barranca*, *Westwind* and *Universal Mariner* before being broken up during 1969.

improved, its lightness, simplicity and economy increased its popularity.

The engines described above are single-acting, meaning that the fuel is burnt on one side of the piston only. In a double-acting engine the lower half of the cylinder is enclosed and a combustion cycle also takes place below the piston. In a double-acting two-stroke, for example, every stroke is a power stroke. Double action has important advantages, since in theory twice as much power per cylinder can be delivered at the expense of slightly heavier and – especially in the case of a four-stroke – considerably more complex machinery.

Owning a tramp ship

The owner of a tramp fleet will typically have a tight, highly-centralised organisation. Unlike the operator of a cargo liner, which requires a network of offices or agencies to cover each port served, oversee loading and discharge, and solicit business, the tramp operator will maintain just the minimum staff centrally, and rely on agents and brokers around the world to obtain cargoes. The central administration would have started small, with perhaps a few clerks to cover chartering and disbursement of officers' wages and shareholders' dividends, and perhaps a marine and/or engineering supervisor. The role of the supervisors was relatively limited, because all but the largest and most sophisticated owners relied heavily on the ship builder to design their ship.

Choosing the right officers was often the key to success. Before the introduction of the telegraph, the masters of the earliest steam tramps would have considerable responsibility for finding a homeward cargo. They might even, with the owner's blessing, expect to undertake a lengthy ballast voyage in the expectation of picking up a profitable cargo. The telegraph revolutionised the tramping trade, allowing the office-based clerk to receive current, if expensive, intelligence about freight rates from distant ports, and direct the master to proceed accordingly. The advent of wireless telegraphy further facilitated the process, allowing communication with ships while at sea.

The differences between the organisation of the tramp and cargo liner trade, and the outlooks of those that engaged in them, meant that owners tended to specialise in one or the other. There were exceptions, in that a few tramp operators, such as William Reardon Smith, also dabbled in the liner trades. In later days, when ownership of cargo lines was largely consolidated into a few large groups, these groups found it expedient to buy a tramp fleet to provide a reserve of ships for occasional use in the liner trades.

As with any branch of shipping, an aspiring tramp ship owner needed knowledge of the business, confidence in his ability and the capacity to raise money. This tended to restrict entry to a relatively small group. Perhaps the commonest way in was from an established company, where an ambitious man might see opportunities to branch out on his own, and perhaps capture some of his former employer's business. Less usual was for a master to move directly from bridge to office, although one of the most successful Cardiff owners, William Reardon Smith, made this transition. It was even rarer for an engineer to do so, although Cardiff also provides two example of this in Frederick Jones, proprietor of Abbey Line, and Edward Nicholl. A ship broker would be well aware of what cargoes were moving and how profitably, and might be tempted to buy (or more prudently, perhaps, charter) a tramp ship to enjoy the profit himself. Lastly, a major industrialist regularly chartering ships might decide that, to stabilise freight rates and ensure a dependable supply of tonnage, investment in a fleet was worthwhile. Such a fleet might not be considered as tramps, because they would usually be directed to carry cargoes for the ultimate owner. However, the ships would generally be identical with the true tramp and several in such

Grain was a staple cargo of the tramp, and all of the major grain trading houses have, at times, owned fleets of such ships to supplement the many vessels they chartered. Bunge & Co had its origins with a family from Sweden who moved to Antwerp in 1850, but it prospered largely through involvement in the grain trade out of the River Plate, and moved its headquarters to South America. In 1936, Bunge set up a British shipping arm, Trader Navigation Co Ltd which for the next thirty-five years ran tramps and bulk carriers mainly, but not exclusively, in grain trades. *Welsh Trader* was one of its last group of 'classic' tramps, all Doxford-engined motor ships with the obsolescent feature of a split superstructure. Built by William Pickersgill & Sons Ltd at Sunderland in 1954, the 447-ft *Welsh Trader* was sold to in 1961 to Stephens, Sutton Ltd of Newcastle, which renamed her *Rookley*, but within two years she had moved on again. She then ran under various flags as *London Breeze, Golden Bridge, Songhuong* and had become simply *Song* when she arrived at Taiwan for breaking up in June 1980.

ownership will be met in the following pages.

For at least half its life, and certainly up to the First World War, the tramp ship was predominantly British owned. Around the beginning of the twentieth century, continental European owners began to offer serious competition, especially Norwegians and Greeks, who acquired ex-British tonnage and ran it inexpensively, but also Dutch and German owners turning to products of local yards. This process accelerated between the wars and, after the Second World War, Greek owners took over the position once occupied by the British. Their main challengers were from the Far East and for a time the state-controlled fleets built up by communist governments. The increasingly widespread adoption of so-called 'free flags' after the Second World War allowed owners in high-wage countries (notably the United States and Japan) to use the cheapest efficient crews they could recruit and so operate tramp ships on equal economic terms to those, especially in Asia or eastern Europe, where national wage rates were low.

In the years between the wars, owners in the newly-independent Baltic states of Estonia, Latvia and Lithuania began to compete with established and especially British tramp owners by operating old steamers with crews whose numbers and wages were low. Ironically, the ships had often been built in British yards, for example *Johanne*, which was completed at Sunderland in 1904 as *Arranmoor* for Runciman's Moor Line Ltd. After several sales to Norwegian owners she was bought in 1928 and renamed by Helmsing & Grimm of Riga, which gave her its distinctive 'saw tooth' funnel markings. She was sold to Finnish owners in 1936 and, after adventures which included seizure by Germany and scuttling at Bremen in April 1945, was resurrected and traded until 1961.

Financing a tramp ship

Over time, tramp ships were owned in a variety of ways. Until the mid-nineteenth century ownership of each sixty-fourth share in a ship by an individual was usual, but thereafter became less common because the cost of this proportion of a large steamer grew beyond what the average investor could afford. To comply with government regulations for the registration of ships, one or more of the shareholders would be designated 'ship's husband' or 'managing owner'. This was essentially the person responsible for keeping its registration papers up to date, but who was effectively accountable to shareholders for its profitable operation. In the latter part of the nineteenth century, ownership by a limited liability company became progressively easier, and as a result individual shares were priced so as to be affordable by small investors. Many steamers were owned in this way by a single-ship company, which was usually liquidated when the ship was sold or lost. Ownership of shares was often diverse, the common factor being a manager who floated the company (usually taking a small stake himself), acquired the ship and operated it in return for a percentage of its earnings. Notoriously, most managers extracted their percentage before deciding on the profitability of that year's voyages, so they were guaranteed a return even in a bad year when the average shareholder might receive little or no dividend.

When successful, most managers eventually consolidated registered ownership of ships under a single company, thus reducing the burden of administration, and often taking the opportunity to increase considerably his own stake and hence his expected return.

Selling shares in a tramp required the potential ship manager to either have an established track record, or a network of wealthy family members or associates. So for the novice other methods of raising money were necessary, usually mortgaging the tramp to its builder, a bank or a wealthy individual. The identity of the mortgagee was inscribed in the ship's registration papers, providing the individual or institution with security in case of payment default. At times, and particularly in the years between the world wars, governments stepped in to advance credit to ship owners.

Some of the most financially successful tramp ship owners were what modern business historians describe as asset players. With shipping a notoriously cyclical business, freight rates see-sawed regularly and with them ship values. The ideal was to place orders near the bottom of a recession when builders were desperate for work at almost any price, trade them until the next boom peaked, and sell them at inflated prices. The problem, of course, was to know when markets had peaked and troughed, and very few owners succeeded in becoming significantly wealthy in this way, Glasgow's Burrell family being the best known.

In the 1930s, the British government made an unprecedented move to help the shipping and shipbuilding industries by advancing loans to owners that were prepared to have old ships broken up and build new ships. The 'Scrap and Build' scheme helped owners such as Nailsea Steamship Co Ltd renew its fleet. *Nailsea Court* of 1936 was one of four steam-powered sisters built by Bartram & Sons Ltd at Sunderland. Sadly, many of the ships built under this scheme became war losses, *Nailsea Court* succumbing to a torpedo from *U 229* in the North Atlantic on 10 March 1943.

Building a tramp ship

Although any merchant ship builder with large enough facilities could construct a tramp ship, in practice certain yards specialised in these ships. Tramps were often more standardised than cargo liners, which were often built to an owners' specification, tramps generally being less well equipped. In Britain, for many years the undisputed master of tramp building, many of the yards on the Wear, Tees and in West Hartlepool constructed mainly tramps. The two other great areas of British shipbuilding activity, the Clyde and the Tyne, were proud of their ability to build almost any vessel, from a barge to a battlecruiser, but among these yards some were specialist tramp builders, notably Lithgows at Greenock and Dobson on the Tyne.

Several ship builders owned tramp fleets from time to time, usually when orders were few and they decided to build for their own account, they took older vessels in part exchange for newer models, or took over ships on which owners had defaulted on mortgage payments. The converse, a ship owner running a ship yard, was much rarer. Ropner & Son at Stockton-on-Tees was the best-known example, owned by the West Hartlepool-based Sir Robert Ropner, and notable for building a series of trunk-deck steamers, almost all for Ropner account.

Although the major centres for building tramp ships were in the north east of England and on the Clyde, other areas made occasional contributions. In 1890, the Cornwall-based Richard Chellew was persuaded to patronise the major shipbuilding and engineering yard in his own county, that of Harvey of Hayle. Two orders were placed and *Penwith* and *Penpol* were delivered in 1890–1. At just over 2,000 tons gross these were the largest ships ever built and engined in Cornwall. But the yard failed to win further orders, probably because north east yards could offer better deals on prices, credit and delivery dates.

The larger of the pair, the 276-ft *Penpol*, was a well-deck type that served Chellew until 1921, after which she passed through the hands of several British and Italian owners. Fittingly, she returned to her birthplace in Hayle during 1927 to be broken up by T W Ward Ltd.

Relatively few tramp building yards made their own engines, and usually relied on a small number of suppliers, the foremost being North Eastern Marine Engineering Co Ltd at Newcastle and Sunderland, George Clark Ltd at Sunderland, Richardson at Hartlepool, and J G Kincaid and David Rowan & Co Ltd at Glasgow. William Gray of West Hartlepool was a notable exception, with its wholly-owned Central Marine Engine Works.

Designing a tramp ship

Economy of construction and operation, ease of loading and discharge, and safety were the major considerations when a tramp ship was specified. Essentially, the owner wanted a capacious hull, which was fully seaworthy and was also strong enough to withstand the rough and tumble of loading and discharging bulky cargoes by operatives who cared little for its fabric. Although the tramp was in some ways the simplest of ocean-going vessels, much thought often went into designing a hull with maximum capacity for its dimensions, and yet which could be economically driven and pay the minimum of harbour and other dues. The turret and trunk deck types described in chapter 3 were some of the earliest examples, but in later years effort was expended in achieving true economy of operation (and not just taxation) through such measures as tank testing of hulls. It was axiomatic too that, however much the owner desired cheapness of construction, he had to get his hull insured, and to do that he had to satisfy the often exacting requirements of a classification society, whose overriding concern was strength of construction to ensure seaworthiness.

The equipment of a tramp differed from that of a cargo liner principally in that there were few frills. Cargo handling gear was the minimum that might be needed in ports where shoreside gear was unavailable. Safety equipment such as life-saving gear, anchors, and in later years radio sets would usually be the minimum to satisfy the requirements of the flag state or classification society. Accommodation would likewise be no better than the owner could get away with and still attract a crew, although in the last years of the tramp there were some notable exceptions in, for example, the fleet of Watts, Watts & Co Ltd of London.

Crewing a tramp ship

The crew of a tramp was typically smaller than that of a cargo liner. There was not even the twelve passengers allowed on the latter vessel to be fed and waited on. Cargo loading or discharge was rarely so protracted or specialised that several officers or cadets were needed to supervise it. Machinery was usually quite basic, minimising the need for engineers. Thus there were perhaps three deck officers to navigate and stand watches, and a similar number of engineers below. There might be one or two apprentices in the better-regarded companies, who would undoubtedly see themselves as simply providing cheap labour under the guise of learning the job. The deck gang would include sufficient experienced men to take the wheel or act as lookouts, plus others to carry out basic routine maintenance. Coal-burning steamers would require perhaps half-a dozen firemen, and in both steam and motor ships the engineers would be assisted by greasers and donkeymen, skilled and experienced but not certificated. There would probably be a bosun to run the deck crowd, a lamp trimmer, a cook, and perhaps a steward for officers. The average-sized crew in the heyday of the tramp might not number more than thirty, perhaps less than half those considered necessary to run a cargo liner. So the work was hard and the hours often long: some companies even expected the officers to help with the tasks usually considered the preserve of the deck crew.

In shipping as in most walks of life, and not just in class-conscious Britain, there was snobbery in the workplace. In the perceived hierarchy of shipping companies, the liner operators (especially those with fleets that included passenger ships) would be near the top, and an aspiring apprentice officer would be encouraged to aim as high as possible, and to look down on his opposite number in a mere tramp. In terms of skills and ability required, of course, there was no difference. Indeed, the navigating officer on a tramp might well experience more of the world's trade routes than the liner man destined to plough one route.

And the master of a tramp, especially before telegraphy, might well need more business acumen than his cargo liner contemporary who had offices and agents ashore to help out.

Whether a deck hand or fireman chose a tramp or a cargo liner might well depend on his geographic location. For those from much of Wales, Yorkshire, Durham or Northumberland, the nearest ports would be those homes of the tramp, Cardiff, the Teesside ports, Sunderland and Newcastle, and such a ship would often be a man's first choice. In those rare times, such as the 1950s, when there was abundant employment for seafarers, there would be more choice. The cargo liner would offer a voyage duration that might be approximately predicted and which would better suit the older, family man. However, the tramp might not see home waters for the full duration of the man's articles, offering a voyage into the unknown that might appeal to the younger seafarer. For instance, an apprentice who joined his first Bank Line ship in the early 1950s did not return home for almost four years, by when the 'first tripper' had graduated to fourth mate.

Watts, Watts & Co was, in later years at least, an exception among shipowners in caring about the lot of their seafarers. Edmund Watts read a paper on the subject of crew accommodation in tramp ships to the Institution of Naval Architects in April 1949. He began by painting a picture of conditions in the 1920s. The ratings lived in the forecastle, sleeping in double-tiered bunks, and eating where they slept. Whereas it was not far to carry the captain's and navigating officers' food from galley to saloon, to get it to the engineer's mess a thirty-foot walk was usually necessary, mostly in the open. And the walk from galley to forecastle was, Watts maintained, long enough to ruin any food. He was not impressed with the usual positioning of the galley at the fore end of the engine room casing where the ship

Looking healthy, tanned, mostly young, but not over-fed, are crews of tramp ships snapped by their shipmates in the 1940s and the 1950s. They show, respectively, painting the hull of *Dallington Court* at Freetown, Sierra Leone in January 1946; the crew of *Starcrest*, on charter to Elder, Dempster, going for a swim off Takoradi in March 1952; and a precarious-looking exercise during painting the funnel of *Baron Herries* in Australian waters in 1958. *(K Garrett collection)*

took most water. Watts then contrasted conditions in his own company's recent ships, beginning with *Blackheath* of 1936. In this ship the seamen and firemen's accommodation had been placed in the poop rather than in the forecastle. In the later three ships of the *Tottenham* class, accommodation was moved amidships. This gave the crew better air and light, and placed them nearer to the galley and to their work. However, Watts admitted that the crew did not always like this, and preferred to be in the poop by themselves, and not close to the officers!

Acknowledgements

Even before thanking those who gave permission for their photos to be used, I must acknowledge the Registers of Bill Schell and Tony Starke plus the companion Miramar Ship Index owned by Rodger Howarth, which together give an immense amount of data on ships' histories. In the same breath, the publications of Lloyd's Register must also be mentioned as the origin of most of the ownership, building and construction data. Last, but not least, I thank my wife Heather for proof reading and indexing.

For help with providing photographs I thank John Clarkson, Ian Farquhar, Ken Garrett, Harold Appleyard, Dr David Jenkins, the late Kevin O'Donoghue, Ian Rae, Bill Schell and David Whiteside. Where photographs have no attribution the identity of the photographer is unknown. I apologise if use of these has unknowingly infringed anyone's copyright.

Dimensions and details

Although familiarly used, tonnages are notorious for altering when a ship is re-surveyed or changes flags. They can vary by up to 25 per cent depending on whether the ship is in open or closed shelter deck configuration, and were dramatically increased for many ships when the 1969 International Tonnage Convention came into force. As a measure of size, therefore, I have provided length, which gives a comparison of real sizes. These dimensions are in feet for all but the two ships in the book completed after 1974, and for which Lloyd's Register gives metric units (where 1 metre equals 3.218 feet).

Along with a brief discussion of each ship's significance to the story of the tramp ship, I have included in each caption the date of completion, name of the builder, the owner at the time the photograph was taken and some details of machinery, plus a list of former and/or subsequent names carried and an indication of the ship's fate.

Delivered in November 1940 by Caledon Shipbuilding & Engineering Co Ltd of Dundee, the steamer *Twickenham* (sister of *Tottenham*) was part of a drive by London shipowner Watts, Watts & Co Ltd to improve living standards for crews of tramp ships. All accommodation was amidships, rather than in the forecastle or poop. This was particularly fortunate, because in July 1943 *Twickenham* had her bows blown off by a torpedo fired by the German submarine *U 135*. She then made an epic one thousand-mile voyage to Dakar, and eventually returned to the United Kingdom for permanent repairs. She was sold to India in 1958 as *Jag Mata* and broken up at Bombay in 1963.

Watts, Watts further improved crew accommodation in two series of ships built in the 1950s, but these were essentially cargo liners, built for the company's own short-lived services or for charter to liner operators. *(Ships in Focus)*

Collier into Deep-Sea Tramp

The first practical steamers that could compete with sail for carrying bulk cargoes, the so-called screw colliers, appeared in the 1850s and were specifically intended for the coal trade on the east coast of Britain. They established that steam could capture trades in relatively low-value commodities, largely through adopting three features: economical steam engines, substantial water ballast capacity for unladen voyages, and iron hulls that had ample holds and hatchways to facilitate loading and discharge.

The screw colliers quickly proved capable of making voyages well outside the coastal trade. The Crimean War (1853–6) saw these early bulk carriers pressed into government service, voyaging – albeit in stages – as far as the Black Sea. Coal interests were not slow to realise the potential of the steam bulk carrier, and in 1857 began to build large screw colliers, of 200–250 feet overall, to carry coal to foreign ports. Crew agreements from this period signal that this began long-distance voyages by colliers, with coal despatched to the Baltic, to the Bay ports of France, to the Mediterranean and to the Black Sea, and where possible bringing home grain or a timber cargo. It is easy to see how the design was enlarged to produce ocean-going steam tramps, embodying the principal characteristics of the collier: economy, reliability, capacity and water ballast capabilities.

Screw colliers were not the only influence on tramp ship design. Large, ocean-going iron ships were being built with two (or more) decks, essentially to offer greater longitudinal strength as their length grew. As builders and owners looked to larger ships for tramping, they adopted the two-deck design out of necessity, although the additional deck could complicate loading and discharge of bulk cargoes. In various forms, two-deck ships will be encountered throughout the history of the 'classic' tramp ship.

Tramp steamers are recorded as operating from Sunderland as early as 1860 and in the ensuing decade from London, Newcastle, Cardiff and Whitby. In a significant number of cases, these earliest tramps were constructed by yards that had pioneered, or at least contributed to, the building of screw colliers, notably Palmers' at Jarrow and Howden-on-Tyne, Mitchell at Low Walker on the Tyne, and various Wearside yards. And in a number of instances, men that had owned or managed colliers in the east coast coal trade – such as Lambert, Harris & Dixon, and J & C Harrison – moved into the longer-distance tramp trades.

The early development of the screw collier has been described and illustrated in another volume in this series, *Coasters: An Illustrated History*, and this chapter will discuss how it evolved into the single-deck, deep-sea tramp and then look at some early two-deck tramp ships.

Note: An asterisk in a caption indicates the vessel shown in the photograph.

Large screw colliers

The 1860s saw British coal interests invest in larger screw colliers, equally suitable for the huge coal trade between the Tyne and Wear and the Thames or the developing coal export trades out of the north English rivers. *Tanfield** of 1865 has a direct connection with the pioneer of them all, *John Bowes* of 1852, in that she was built and engined by the same builder, Palmer Brothers, although not at Jarrow but at their second yard at Howden. *Tanfield* shared with *John Bowes* her engines-aft layout, which was not to become commonplace once again in the bulk trades until almost one hundred years later, her length of 203 ft necessitated a navigating position amidships.

Collier ownership in the 1850s and the 1860s typically involved 64th shares spread among various players in the coal trade. On her registration in January 1865, *Tanfield* was half owned by coal merchant Richard Cory, while the coal-owning Joicey family were minor shareholders. In 1896, *Tanfield* became part of the new fleet established under the title William Cory & Son Ltd, which was to remain a major coastal coal shipper for almost as long as the trade lasted. This was a consolidation of a number of fleets in the coastal coal trade, the Cory family's buy-out being conditional on the

owners of the fleets it purchased forsaking the east coast coal trade. This had the effect of launching the deep-sea careers of several owners who became significant players

in tramping, including Lambert Brothers and J & C Harrison. Soon after *Tanfield*'s forty-eighth birthday, her old iron hull was sold to breakers in Boulogne.

Gradually the engines of screw colliers were positioned further forward in the hull, the trend becoming apparent in *New Pelton** of 1871. Having a hold aft of the engine room made the vessel easier to trim when loaded. There were also concerns about the strength of the hull, and positioning heavy masses such as engines and boilers away from the stern was felt to reduce stresses. That the engines-amidships layout persisted in the ocean-going tramp for one hundred years suggests that these concerns were real, because disadvantages of the

engines-amidships layout included the need for an extended propeller shaft, and a shaft tunnel that significantly reduced the capacity of the after holds.

New Pelton shared much with *Tanfield*, including Palmer Brothers as builder and the Cory and Joicey coal merchant/mine owner combination of initial registered owners. Palmers also supplied her machinery, a two-cylinder simple engine that expanded the steam just once. In common with *Tanfield* and many contemporaries, *New Pelton* had her engine replaced or – more probably

– modified in 1878. In her 'new' compound engine, steam from a replacement, higher pressure boiler was expanded in high and low pressure cylinders, extracting significantly more of its energy to turn her screw. At the same time, *New Pelton* was lengthened from 180 ft to 211 ft, and is shown almost certainly after this modification.

In another parallel with *Tanfield*, in 1912 *New Pelton* was sold by her final owners, William Cory & Son Ltd, to the same Boulogne ship breakers. (*C A Hill*)

Early deep-sea tramps

Although built for the coal trade out of British east coast ports, the 200-ft, single-deck *Raithwaite Hall** of 1868 had a long career that took her far away from her birthplace at West Hartlepool. The builder of her iron hull was Denton, Gray & Co, but thanks to the novelty of steam engines contemporary registration documents had no space to record the builder of her original, two-cylinder steam machinery. However, it is known that in 1874, Thomas Richardson & Sons of Hartlepool replaced this with, or perhaps simply rebuilt it as, a compound engine.

The original owners of *Raithwaite Hall* were members of the Pyman family, mentioned several times in this book, and in several combinations they operated her out of West Hartlepool and Newcastle in conjunction with their coal exporting business until 1906. She was then sold to William France, Fenwick & Co Ltd of London, who would have mainly employed her in the coastal coal trade, where steamers of her size were now common.

In 1909 came a major change in employment. The Dwina Ltd bought the old craft and stationed her in the entrance to the Shatt el Arab waterway to lighten incoming ships that could not otherwise cross the 20-ft bar. The shallow *Raithwaite Hall* and two even older steamers would take off sufficient cargo and would accompany the deep-sea ship to her destination. In the photograph *Raithwaite Hall* wears the livery of parent company Frank Strick & Co Ltd.

Work of The Dwina Ltd ended in 1929, when a deep-water channel was dredged through the bar. Now sixty-years-old, *Raithwaite Hall* was sold to ship breakers. *(Harold Appleyard collection)*

The chance of *Nellie Wise** of 1873 being photographed owes much to her misfortune in 1908. Like *Raithwaite Hall*, she was built by Denton, Gray & Co of West Hartlepool, predecessor to one of the great British tramp builders, William Gray & Co. Her original Hartlepool owner was William H Wise, although in 1880 she moved to, and was to remain in, London ownership, a succession of owners honouring the old tradition of not altering a ship's name.

At 230 ft, *Nellie Wise* was only marginally larger than the typical east coast collier, but the engine amidships arrangement was now entrenched, as was the use of two-cylinder compound engines, hers made in nearby Stockton-on-Tees by Blair & Co Ltd. Her total water ballast capacity was a respectable 208 tons, split between fore and aft peak tanks and her double bottom. Although not apparent from the photograph, she has a three-island hull, with forecastle, bridge deck and poop. This is obscured by the high bulwarks alongside the after hatch.

In contrast to the east coast colliers that ventured into the longer distance trades, the career of *Nellie Wise* saw her move in the opposite direction. Her owners since 1887, Green, Holland & Sons, sold out in 1896 to William Cory & Son Ltd, which retained *Nellie Wise* in the coastal coal trade. On a ballast voyage in January 1908 from London to the Tyne she stranded just north of her birthplace, and although refloated was fit only for scrap.

21

Raised quarterdeck design

Despite appearances, *George Fisher** was probably in no danger on arrival at Bristol. Most likely her list is due to her deck cargo of esparto grass having taken on more water to starboard during a storm and adversely affecting her trim.

The well deck of *Nellie Wise* has evolved into a raised quarterdeck design, and from this angle can be seen her 51-ft long bridge deck, beyond which a 73-ft quarterdeck stretches to her stern. This deck increased the depth of the aftermost hold, partly compensating for the cargo space lost to the propeller shaft. This may account for her 25 per cent larger gross tonnage than *Nellie Wise* on a hull just 6 ft longer.

Her builder in 1877 was prolific tramp constructor Richardson, Duck & Co of Stockton-on-Tees and she was fitted with a compound engine supplied by Thomas Richardson of Hartlepool. Owner was Edward Capper of Cardiff, who in 1879 moved to London to enter a partnership with his cousin. As Capper, Alexander & Co, the company survived various ups and downs, with *George Fisher* its only ship for much of the 1890s when she was in the Black Sea grain trade.

George Fisher, which was transferred to the newly-formed Alexander Shipping Co Ltd in 1915, was sold to Hull owners in 1918 and – outclassed in size and economy by newer tramps – retired to the short-sea trades. In September 1920, she sank after striking a wreck on Middle Cross Sand while taking a coal cargo from Sunderland to Boulogne.

Alexander Shipping Co Ltd was acquired by the Houlder Group in 1946 but continued in name until 1961.

No river was to make a bigger contribution to the tramp fleet than the Wear, and few of its shipbuilders could rival the output of J L Thompson & Sons. Built at Thompson's North Sands yard in 1879, *Sybil** shows a late stage in the evolution of the coastal collier to deep-sea tramp. Size has leapt to 266 ft, yet she retains the raised quarterdeck layout of *George Fisher*. Her original compound engine was replaced by triple expansion machinery in 1893. Features of note are the pole on the bridge that holds the compass well above the influence of *Sybil's* iron hull, and is read with the help of a ladder. The emergency steering position on the flat-topped poop is protected only by a flimsy rail.

Original owners were Gordon & Stamp, Sunderland, whose founder was an early investor in screw colliers. Moving to London in 1888, the firm became R Gordon & Sons, owning the capital's largest deep-sea tramp fleet in 1892 with twenty-five steamers. In this year, *Sybil* was tramping to the Baltic and to the Mediterranean, and bringing iron ore from Bilbao to Middlesbrough.

In 1911, *Sybil* went the way of many ageing British tramps when sold to Sweden to become *Goosebridge*. First of many U-boat victims in these pages, *Goosebridge* was captured and sunk with explosives by *UC 46* on New Year's Day 1917 while carrying coal from Port Talbot to St Nazaire. This voyage suggests that, despite her neutrality, she was under some compulsion from the British government.

Two-deck tramps

Clearly, some owners and builders of iron tramp steamers – and their classification society, Lloyd's Register – considered that one of 277 ft, such as *Beaconsfield** needed two decks to provide adequate strength. She was launched in July 1877 by the Tyne Iron Shipbuilding Co at Newcastle for George Cleugh of North Shields and fitted with a compound engine made by North Eastern Marine Engineering Co Ltd at Sunderland. She was unusual for

her time in having no bridge deck, only a forecastle and what appears to be a poop, although the vessel entry in *Lloyd's Register* refers to a 40-ft 'break deck', which was later shown as 40-ft quarterdeck

This photograph at Bristol was probably taken in the 1890s, and she retains gaffs to both masts, a sail just visible, brailed to the foremast, and has more than adequate shrouds. The tall topmasts are something of a

luxury, given her limited remaining rig.

Beaconsfield was sold to an owner in Tromsø, Norway in early 1905, but he either chose not to change her name, or had no chance to do so because she was wrecked north of Kvitholmen in April of that year while on voyage from Blyth to her home port with a coal cargo.

The 260-ft *Netley Abbey** also has two decks, but her entry in *Lloyd's Register* indicates that only one is iron, so the other is presumably of wood. Again, she has a forecastle and poop, but note the tumblehome both to the poop and to the plating alongside the engine casing. Also prominent is the funnel for the donkey boiler, painted in the same yellow and black as her main funnel, but without the chevron top that distinguished the funnel colours of Pyman, Watson & Co of Cardiff. Originating in Whitby, the Pyman family had interests in several major British ports, and the Cardiff branch owned not only ships but also collieries to supply them with cargoes.

Netley Abbey was built by the prolific William Gray & Co of West Hartlepool, and was one of no fewer than eighteen ships launched in 1878, giving Gray the 'blue riband' for the highest output of any British shipyard. This achievement was particularly remarkable because Gray, who originally entered business as a draper rather than a shipbuilder, had assumed full control of the yard only in 1874 following the death of his partner John Denton. Gray was eventually to have his own engineering works, but *Netley Abbey*'s compound engines were built by Thomas Richardson at Hartlepool.

On 4 August 1899, *Netley Abbey* sank following a collision with HMS *Surprise*, near the Shambles Light Vessel in the English Channel while on a voyage from Cardiff to Cronstadt with a cargo of coal.

2

Tramps Mature in the 1880s

The decade from 1880 was one of the most innovative in the history of the tramp, these years seeing builders and owners becoming more confident about designing ever larger and more efficient ships. Tramp building was still almost exclusively the preserve of yards in the north east of England – on the rivers Wear, Tyne and Tees, plus the Hartlepools – although an interesting small example from Dundee creeps into this chapter.

Innovation meant builders and owners exploring a number of different hull forms. The two-deck steamer was built in a number of variations, variously named spar deck, awning deck and shelter deck, but designed to require lighter and therefore less expensive scantlings or to reduce the measured tonnage.

As the decade wore on, the single-deck raised quarterdeck designs became the most popular configuration with tramp builders and owners. Initially, many were to the short raised quarterdeck design, but the long raised quarterdeck, usually referred to as the well-deck design, then became almost ubiquitous.

Iron gave way to steel during this period. The latter was initially more expensive than iron, but stronger and – once the classification societies gave it their blessing – steel allowed the size and thickness of plates and scantlings to be reduced, requiring less metal, reducing costs but also increasing the available space in the hull.

The decade saw another, even more important technical advance, with marine engineering moving on from the compound, two-cylinder to triple expansion, three-cylinder engines. Necessarily coupled with higher boiler pressures, these improvements in engine efficiency extended the range and economy of the tramp, enabling it to compete with sail over longer distances.

This chapter first reviews the multiple deck types built for tramp owners, and the single-deck, raised quarterdeck designs that largely superseded them.

Note: An asterisk in a caption indicates the vessel shown in the photograph.

Two decks

Delivered in 1881, the steamer *Shelley** presaged the development of the three-island hull form, which was to flower for many years. She has two decks and was intended by owner Glover Brothers of London for the grain trade, and was fitted with permanent grain divisions in the spaces between her two decks. The builder was William Gray & Co of West Hartlepool with a compound engine supplied by Black, Hawthorn & Co, Gateshead.

The curved plates alongside the bridge deck of *Shelley* and the turtle-back poop give away her age, but in the *Wordsworth*, delivered to Glover by Gray just fourteen months later, the sides of both bridge and poop were vertical, giving a more modern look. The 285-ft *Shelley*'s foremast would originally have crossed four yards, but by the time she was photographed in the 1890s, these had been sent down.

Glover Brothers' ships were initially owned on the sixty-fourths share system, but in 1898 its six steamers were transferred to a limited liability company, Shakespear Shipping Co Ltd. The name was taken from the 1885-built *Shakespear*, the odd spelling resulting in much comment. The final letter 'e' was dropped because telegraph companies charged for transmitting cables by the word, and any word over ten letters – such as Shakespeare – counted as two words!

Shelley was sold to a Chilean company in 1906 and renamed *Presidente Santa Maria*. Details of her fate are vague, but she is known to have stranded in 1912.

Spar decks

Tramp ship constructors endlessly tried to reduce the cost of ships by decreasing the dimensions of plates, frames and other scantlings to the minimum laid down by classification societies such as Lloyd's Register. One method was to use full-strength scantlings up to main deck level, above which was constructed a lighter structure known as a spar deck. As with other multiple-deck types, these ships were not ideal for bulk cargoes because the spar deck hindered access to the lower hold, but a large number of spar-deckers such as the 251-ft *Cornucopia** of 1882 did work in the tramp trade.

Her first owner was Argosy Steam Ship Co Ltd, managed by Turnbull, Potts & Co, Sunderland, which had ordered her from local builder Osbourne, Graham & Co, with a compound engine from the prolific local engineering company George Clark. For Turnbull, Potts, whose first ship she was, *Cornucopia* ran to the Baltic, Mediterranean and once ventured as far south as Port Nolloth in southern Africa. She was sold to Norway to become *Astrid* in 1895, but unusually returned to the British register, and her former name, in 1900 when J & P Hutchison of Glasgow bought her. It is when in Hutchison ownership that *Cornucopia* was photographed at Preston not long before her demise. On 15 December 1910 she was abandoned in the Bay of Biscay when her cargo of Swansea coal, bound for Genoa, shifted in bad weather. She foundered about five days later. *(J and M Clarkson)*

Photographed in Livorno (Leghorn, no doubt, to her crew) is the small Dundee-owned and built *Ruby**. She was completed and given her compound engine in 1883 by W B Thompson, a builder which changed its name to Caledon Shipbuilding & Engineering Co Ltd in 1896. As the yard's major output was cargo liners, both small and large, and as the owners of *Ruby* styled itself Dundee Gem Line Steam Ship Co Ltd, the steamer's credentials as a tramp may be doubted. The company did have a regular trade with fruit and vegetables from Spain, but records from the 1890s also show a variety of short-distance tramping voyages, mainly from east coast Scottish ports to the Baltic, the Iberian peninsula, North Africa and Italy. In Livorno, a gin is rigged from *Ruby*'s mainmast gaff, suggesting Scottish coal is being worked out of her into the lighter alongside, while a local sailing vessel is moored forward.

An interesting small feature is the flag almost above her funnel, a Union Flag defaced with the initials MSG, showing her master to be proud of his membership of the Merchant Service Guild.

The 235-ft *Ruby* served all her days with Dundee Gem Line, and was broken up in Sunderland in 1909, the year before her owners went into voluntary liquidation.

Awning decks

The name awning deck was given to an upper deck that was even lighter than a spar deck, and it was this that developed into the shelter deck. As with the spar deck ship, suitability for carrying bulk cargoes was limited, but the two ships illustrated here belonged to fleets with impeccable credentials as tramping companies.

The 295-ft, steel-hulled *Meraggio** was built by Raylton Dixon & Co at Middlesbrough in 1889 as *Hibernia* for the grandly-named International Line Steamship Co Ltd, managed in Whitby by Christopher Marwood. In 1906 she was sold and renamed *Meraggio* by Maclay & McIntyre, one of Glasgow's largest tramp operators. Maclay & McIntyre in turn disposed of her in 1914, but her new owners in Syra, Greece had little service from the ship they renamed *Empros*. On 13 November 1916 she was abandoned off Brest after colliding with Ellerman's steamer *City of Cairo*. The Dracopoulos family, which part-owned *Empros*, memorialised her name in a ship-owning venture entitled Empros Lines Shipping Co Special SA, which continues in a modest way to this day.

From another Teesside yard, that of Richardson, Duck & Co of Stockton, the 1889 steamer *Start** was remarkably similar to *Meraggio* – both of around 296 ft in length. Both are described as 'part awning decked' and this structure is, presumably, forward because the two after hatches in both ships are one deck lower (more apparent in this view of *Start* in the Avon). According to the vessels' entries in *Lloyd's Register*, they both had a quarterdeck of 92 ft, the 178-ft awning deck clearly extending beyond. Both had a short poop deck and, as was by now the norm, triple-expansion machinery.

Owner of *Start* was Farrar, Groves & Co of London, which favoured names of lighthouses for its considerable fleet, which, in 1903, was transferred to Fargrove Steam Navigation Co Ltd. *Start* was sold in 1912 to an Emden owner who renamed her *Grete Hemsoth*. She was mined and sunk north of Cape Arkona on 1 April 1915.

Short raised quarterdeck, three holds

The most popular hull configuration for a tramp in the 1880s was the raised quarterdeck. The extra depth this gave to the aftermost holds helped compensate for the loss of carrying capacity due to the shaft tunnel. It also helped, especially in smaller ships, provide sufficient height for the tall, marine steam engine, the cylinders of which were placed vertically above the crankshaft.

At 185 ft, *Hartside** was at the small end of the spectrum of tramps, and was most suitable for short voyages: she is seen here in a Dutch port. In 1892, she was confined to the Elbe to Brest limits of the home trade, whereas most of the fleet of owner Charlton, McAllum & Co of Newcastle was trading to the Mediterranean, the Black Sea and across the North Atlantic.

Hartside's builder was D Baxter & Co of North Sands, Sunderland, which fitted her with a two-cylinder compound engine made by R & W Hawthorn of Newcastle. Lasting just four years, Baxter's short-lived yard has largely escaped the notice of chroniclers of Sunderland iron shipbuilders, but with *Hartside* it built to last. In 1908 Charlton, McAllum sold her to Aberdeen owners who renamed her *Glen Tilt*, continuing to run her in North Sea trades until 1925 when sold to Italy as *Rocco*. Under her fourth name, *Quadrifoglio*, the fifty-seven-year old steamer was requisitioned by the Italian Navy in 1942. On Italy's surrender, she was seized by the Germans, but sank after her boiler exploded in February 1944. Even this was not quite the end, because she was raised and broken up in 1955, seventy-two years after she emerged from a Wearside shipyard. *(Martin Lindenborn)*

Look closely at *Lynton**: she is perilously near rocks and not underway, but neither is she anchored. The back of the photograph reveals that she is ashore near Penzance in 1895. She got off, however, and was to enjoy a remarkably long life.

The builder of *Lynton* was John Readhead & Co at its Lawe Shipyard, South Shields, which fitted its own compound engine. The 240-ft iron steamer was delivered in 1881 to Chapman & Miller of Newcastle, which put its initials on the flag painted on her funnel. These were subsequently removed when Miller left the partnership, the company eventually becoming Chapman & Willan Ltd.

With tramps increasing in size, and adopting the more economical triple-expansion machinery, *Lynton* was becoming obsolescent in the Chapman & Miller fleet, and in 1899 was sold to Swedish owners as *Valkyrian*. Over almost six subsequent decades she was to carry this and the further names *Johanna* and *Hermes* under seven different owners, including an Estonian exile and the young Sven Salén, who was to go on to have a large fleet of tankers and fruit ships. Under the Panama flag since 1948, the iron hull of *Hermes* – still with its 1881 compound engine – arrived at Hamburg in December 1957 and was broken up in 1958, at age seventy seven. The Penzance grounding seems not to have done any lasting damage.

The builder of *Raglan** in 1883 was Palmers' Shipbuilding & Iron Co Ltd, whose Jarrow yard also supplied her two-cylinder compound engine. As builder of the pioneering *John Bowes*, Palmers' provide another link between the tramp and screw collier.

Owner of the 211-ft *Raglan* was John Cory, originally an investor in sailing ships in Padstow, but who in 1872 crossed the Bristol Channel to build up an impressive steam tramping fleet in Cardiff.

In July 1901, *Raglan* stranded while entering Workington with a cargo of iron ore from Castro and broke her back. Declared a constructive total loss, she was yet sold to a Liverpool owner, who had her repaired and returned to service, as the only non-coaster in his fleet.

Sold on in 1910, the ageing steamer then had several Italian owners as *Mongibello* and two further French owners as *Minerva* before she was broken up at La Seyne in 1926. *(World Ship Society Ltd)*

Short raised quarterdeck, four holds

Considerably longer than *Raglan* at 258 ft, *Gardépée** has two of her four hatches on the long raised quarterdeck abaft her superstructure, and the mainmast is significantly further aft to serve both hatches.

Gardépée was completed in 1882 by William Pickersgill & Sons of Sunderland for a single-ship company managed and set up by Morel Brothers of Cardiff. Her distinctly un-Welsh name reflects the French origins of the Morel family, Huguenots who moved to Jersey following religious persecution, perhaps as far back as the sixteenth century. From Jersey, members of the family moved to South Wales in the mid-nineteenth century and became ship brokers, from 1876 ship owners and from 1882 ship builders with an interest in the short-lived Bute Shipbuilding, Engineering & Dry Dock Co. Despite this interest, only two of Morel's ships were built at Cardiff (out of just three completed there), and the company continued to order from the north east of England.

The 1,633-grt *Gardépée* was sold to London owners in 1915, but on 10 October 1916 was captured by the German submarine *U 43* north of North Cape and sunk by explosive charges. She was on voyage to Archangel with a cargo consisting of an unlikely-sounding mix of zinc spelter and herrings.

Unusually, the Bristol photographer has ventured away from the River Avon where he captured *Raglan* and many other images to take this photograph of *Gardépée* arriving in the City Docks.

Edward Hain's career as a tramp ship owner was remarkable on at least two counts. First, Cornwall's biggest and most successful shipping entrepreneur, he set up business in the distinctly un-industrial port of Truro, although his ships loaded most of their outbound coal cargoes at Cardiff, where Hain had an office. Second, was his unremitting loyalty to just one shipbuilder, John Readhead & Co. There were other owners who favoured one particular builder, but the unbroken sequence of seventy-four steamers delivered to Hain from Readhead's South Shields yard between 1878 and 1918 is unique. The thirteenth product of this association was *Tremayne** of 1886, 259 ft long and powered by a compound engine built by Readhead.

Tremayne was sold in 1905 to owners in Helsingborg. She remained under the Swedish, and briefly the Finnish, flags as *Helios*, *Helny* and lastly *Frigg* until she sank after striking a wreck near Kiel on 28 April 1944 while carrying coke from Emden to Sundsvall in Sweden.

The First World War was disastrous for Hain. As well as losing eighteen ships from his fleet and one hundred lives, his only son, who was being groomed to succeed him, was killed at Gallipolli in 1915. Sir Edward Hain never recovered from this loss and on 20 September 1917 died at his home near St Ives. His company was almost immediately acquired by P&O, and maintained a moderately independent existence until the 1960s.

Rivalling the Hain name for longevity is that of the Bolton family, of which the London shipbroker Frederick Bolton entered ship owning with *Raphael** of 1885. The builder of this steamer was the well-established J L Thompson & Sons of Sunderland, who fitted the 271-ft raised quarterdeck steamer with a compound engine made by Thomas Richardson & Sons of West Hartlepool.

Bolton initially traded his ships to the Black Sea, with the classic combination of coal from Cardiff or the Tyne outwards, and grain from Nicolaieff, Odessa or Varna back to western Europe. The reason why *Raphael* is dressed overall on arrival in the Bristol Avon is not known, although possibly the large sheeted items on her decks might give a clue.

In the first decade of the twentieth century, Bolton must have received a good offer for his ships from owners in Chile. *Raphael* was sold to Valparaiso in 1906, and was subsequently renamed *Presidente Bulnes*. Further names carried were *Ercilla*, *Antofagasta* and *Fresia* until she was sold to Brazilian owners in 1920 and eventually became a hulk at Rio de Janeiro in 1930.

A significant change occurred between the delivery to Frederick Bolton of *Raphael* in 1885 and *Rembrandt** in 1886 – the adoption of triple-expansion machinery. Such an engine had first gone to sea in *Propontis* of 1874, but like other developments was slower to be adopted by tramp ship owners and builders, who were always fearful of extra expense.

The same combination of builders and engineers who had completed *Raphael* was responsible for

Rembrandt, whose hull was identical in size to that of her forerunner. Visible in photographs of both ships are the framework for awnings over both forecastle and poop, and the large, white-painted 'lighthouses' on either side of the forecastle which housed the port and starboard lamps.

Rembrandt also went out to Chile, sold in 1905 and a few years later taking the name *Presidente Prieto*. Precise details of her fate are unknown, but she appears to have

been badly damaged in 1912 and condemned.

Boltons continued in shipowning for many years, continuing to use names of artists beginning with the letter R, at least until they became involved with a series of ore carriers that were given place names in the north east. They survived to own bulk carriers, and the company that made the leap from compounding to triple expansion in the 1880s even had a ship experimentally propelled by gas turbines in the 1960s.

Well decks

Extension of the raised quarterdeck as far forward as the hatch on number two hold had the effect of leaving a short well forward, and Lloyd's Register referred to these ships as having well decks. One attraction of the type was that it reduced the possibility of water filling the well, which could make the ship bow heavy if not quickly drained through the freeing ports.

The design became more popular as the decade progressed, although Dewsland* was completed in 1883. The entry in Lloyd's Register indicates that this 275-ft ship has a well deck, although this is not apparent in this photograph. A well would be expected where the group of five seamen are stood forward, preparing to throw lines ashore but undoubtedly discussing the delights of Bristolian night life. There is a well aft, and there is a poop, although Lloyd's Register does not mention the latter. She is definitely the correct ship, because the funnel carries on its white band the shield of owner John Marychurch of Cardiff – red with three inverted yellow chevrons. Dewsland had been built by J L Thompson & Sons, which went to George Clark, also of Sunderland, for her compound engine.

Dewsland was sold in 1900 to J & P Hutchison of Glasgow, owners that, unusually, operated both short-sea liner services and did some tramping. On 1 June 1916

Dewsland was captured, shelled and sunk by the German submarine U 39 north of Algeria while bound to Cardiff

from Philippeville with a cargo described as comprising lead and shumac.

The firm of Hine Brothers was something of an institution in its small home port of Maryport, and owner of a fleet comprising both ocean-going sail and steam ships, with some pretensions to grandeur in the name Holme Line it adopted. Indeed, some of its larger steamers operating on the North Atlantic had passenger accommodation. However, the mainstay of its business was intermediate and long-distance tramping, and one of its most important outgoing cargoes was railway rails manufactured locally at Workington.

The 277-ft Nether Holme* of 1888 was another Sunderland combination of a steel hull by J L Thompson & Sons and a triple-expansion engine by George Clark. Arriving in the Bristol Avon, she looks particularly well cared for (note how the rails alongside her long quarterdeck have been neatly painted white). Also noticeable are the 'lighthouses' for the lamps, relocated from the forecastle to the fore end of the quarterdeck. There is also a gangway linking the forecastle and quarterdeck, useful in the event of heavy seas making it impossible to access the forecastle via the well deck. What is perhaps surprising is the minimalist accommodation amidships.

Nether Holme stranded near Linney Head, Pembrokeshire in fog on 3 November 1907 while on a ballast voyage from Maryport to Swansea when her master assumed the newly-built light on St Govan's was on Lundy Island. Although refloated, she was broken up at Milford Haven in March 1908.

In 1888 Hurworth* was built and registered at West Hartlepool, a town which was almost the spiritual home of the long raised quarterdeck tramp, because so many were built and owned there. Indeed, the busiest local shipbuilder, William Gray & Co, claimed ownership of this design. The triple-expansion engine for the 2,372-grt Hurworth came from Blair & Co Ltd, Stockton-on-Tees.

The owner of Hurworth was Robert Ropner, a German who ran way to sea, only to settle in West Hartlepool where in 1860 he joined a local ship owning company, T Appleby & Sons. He evidently impressed the company, which made him a partner six years later. On dissolution of the partnership in 1874, Ropner began on his own account, and was to build up one of the biggest tramping fleets under the British flag. Like Gray, he will be met again in these pages.

Hurworth was sold out of the Ropner fleet in 1913 and joined the growing Greek tramp fleet, which, in time, was to overtake its British counterpart. Renamed Thrasyvoulos, she survived the First World War and joined a different Greek company in 1927 to be renamed Kydaris. On 2 March 1929 she went ashore near Lemnos and, although refloated, her forty-one-year-old hull was fit only for scrap.

No apology is offered for presenting yet another fine view of a tramp in the Bristol Avon. Indeed, without the now widely-dispersed York collection of negatives, photographic coverage of early tramp steamers, especially in this chapter, would be much poorer.

The 290-ft Dalmally* came from the yard of E Withy & Co in West Hartlepool during 1889. Her triple-expansion machinery was made locally by Thomas Richardson & Sons. Owner was George Horsley & Son, who also had a wood importing business, so coal out and timber home were staple cargoes. Its ships were initially owned on the time-honoured sixty-fourth share system until 1899 when the Horsley Line Ltd was floated and ownership of the fleet transferred.

Dalmally was sold in 1912, new owners based in Riga renaming her Truvor. Although the owner's name was the Germanic G W Schröder, Truvor was evidently in Allied service during the First World War. On 3 May 1917, she was torpedoed and sunk by the German submarine U 45 in Arctic waters while carrying a cargo of Tyne coal to a north Russian port.

Liverpool was the home port of some major cargo liner companies, and is not usually thought of a base for tramp ship companies: these were predominantly located in Newcastle, Cardiff and London. As a result of attention to the Mersey port's liner companies, the tramping sector has been neglected, but there were some significant fleets here, including that of Joseph Hoult, a ship owner from 1873 to 1918. His ships had names beginning Ben-, including Benwick*, built of steel by Schlesinger, Davis & Co at Wallsend in 1889 and given a triple-expansion engine by Black, Hawthorn & Co, Gateshead.

Symptomatic of the steady growth in size of the breed, at 302 ft, Benwick is the first tramp illustrated here to exceed 300 ft. This view of Benwick in an unfortunate position clearly shows the gangway over her well deck. The entry in Lloyd's Register indicates that she had both a raised quarterdeck of 98 ft and a bridge deck of 124 ft, although these appear to make one continuous structure. Note also the short, 17-ft poop deck, mostly occupied by a cover to a companionway.

Benwick changed hands twice in 1899, first to W Holzapfel and then to Thompson, Elliott & Co, both of Newcastle. In the latter ownership, she was on a ballast voyage from Antwerp to Swansea on 4 February 1903 when she struck the Runnelstone. With Benwick in sinking condition, her crew got away in two boats, while the ship drifted towards Porthgwarra where she drove ashore and had broken up within a month. When photographed aground off Porthgwarra, her rudder had already gone.

Benwick.

CHAPTER
3
Design Diversity 1890–1914

The two decades before the First World War saw British yards continue to dominate tramp ship building, with an increasing range of builders entering the business, although yards in the north east of England were still the largest contributors.

There was considerable diversity in design during these decades, although definite trends can be traced. Two types popular in the 1880s declined or disappeared in the early 1890s. The short raised quarterdeck was now largely confined to smaller (under 300ft) ships intended largely for the middle-distance coal trades, while the long raised quarterdeck (annotated as 'well deck' in *Lloyd's Register*) barely survived the 1880s. Effectively, these designs were replaced in the early twentieth century by a variant described as long bridge deck, differing visually in that there was an extra well deck just forward of the poop. Thanks to an anomaly in Lloyd's Register's rules, this design was to prove surprisingly durable.

Emerging and growing strongly in popularity throughout the period was the three-island design, with separate forecastle, bridge deck and poop. But even this came in several varieties, with the single-deck variant the most common, followed by spar-deck, awning-deck and two-deck forms. Again, the three-island design was to prove extraordinarily long-lived.

Two-deck types continued to be built in some numbers during the 1890s, and these included awning and spar deck vessels. These had either three-island hull forms or appeared to be flush decked, although most actually had a raised quarterdeck and a poop deck. The true flush-decked vessel was rare, and the only example in this chapter was built at the end of the period.

Within these broad types there were some external variations in bow form and, of more practical significance, in mast arrangements. These are referred to in detail in the captions.

This period saw the rise, and in most cases also the fall, of the patented tramp designs, including the important turret and trunk deck types, which are covered in the next chapter.

Note: An asterisk in a caption indicates the vessel shown in the photograph.

Three islands, single deck

One of the newer designs that was to become and remain very popular with tramp owners was the three-island configuration. Mostly, these were single deck ships, such as *Wenvoe** of 1894, built by William Gray & Co Ltd of West Hartlepool. This yard was one of the aristocrats among tramp ship constructors, which invested in its own machinery-building works, and *Wenvoe* was given a triple-expansion engine by Gray's Central Marine Engine Works. Owner of the 325-ft tramp from 1897 was Longueil Steamship Co Ltd. The combination of a Welsh place name (Wenvoe is a few miles from Cardiff) and a French-style title for the single-ship owning company identifies the manager as the Cardiff-based Morel family, already met in chapter 2.

The First World War completely distorted the pre-war pattern of ship owning, and one of its oddest effects was that the French government set up a London-based ship owning company, Bay Steamship Co Ltd. The British government had made it virtually impossible for ships to leave the British flag, even on sale to its allies, so France

simply had to resort to leaving under the British flag the ships it expensively bought in the United Kingdom. At least they were allowed to rename them, a practice denied to most British owners, and *Wenvoe* became

Bayvoe in 1916. She was not to see out the war, because *U 84* torpedoed her off the French coast in January 1918 with a cargo of wheat loaded in Portland, Maine and destined for Bordeaux.

So tall are the bulwarks alongside the aftermost hatches of *Radley** that it requires an elevated viewpoint to confirm that she has the 33 ft-long poop deck mentioned in register books. Although the bulwarks might have made the after deck drier, they could allow water to accumulate on the deck and adversely affect the ship's stability. Unusually for a ship from 1896, builder J Priestman & Co of Sunderland has fitted an enclosed wheelhouse. However, the higher steering position – although roofed over – is open to the elements.

The original owner was a one-ship company managed by Galbraith, Pembroke & Co, a partnership that was operating steam tramps out of London as early as 1868, and was also an early independent tanker owner. It favoured a mix of ship types, and in the year that *Radley* was completed its fleet comprised a two-decker, a trio of three-island ships, four well-deckers and three tankers.

Radley was a 1915 sale to a Glasgow partnership who renamed her *Palmgrove*. But it had little benefit from her, because in August 1915 she was captured by *U 38* and sunk by shellfire near Bishop Rock while outward bound from Glasgow with coal for Porto Vecchio.

Comparison of *Radley* with *Rustington** – completed in 1897 by Osbourne, Graham & Co, Sunderland – shows how two builders can make ships with the same hull form look different by their treatment of the superstructure on the centre castle. That on *Rustington* appears to be little more than an engine room casing, plus a couple of cabins below the open bridge, with possibly an enclosed chartroom behind the open steering position. Another contrast with *Radley* is the much lower bulwarks around the aftermost hatches.

Although financially conservative when it came to paying dividends, owner Southdown Steamship Co Ltd, managed by Bell, Symondson & Co, London, believed in keeping its fleet up to date, and *Rustington* was sold in 1906. As *Portsmouth*, she was in Cardiff ownership until 1912, when she went first to Sweden as *William* and then to Norway as *Gustav Vigeland*. She was trading to Great Britain during the First World War, and was wrecked in September 1916 near the Longstone while on voyage from Archangel to London with a cargo of timber.

Three islands with bunker hatch

During the downturns in the economic cycle that shipping suffers, ship builders that are short of orders might build for their own account, if only to keep a nucleus of skilled workers employed until conditions improve. One such was John Readhead & Sons Ltd of South Shields, which formed Cliffe Steamship Co Ltd in 1904 during the depression that followed the Boer War. A secondary purpose was to provide work for John Readhead's son, George Tindle Readhead, who became the steamship company's manager.

Built and engined by Readhead in 1909, the 335-ft *Highcliffe** was the second of seven ships that carried Cliffe Steamship colours, its funnel and house flag carrying a red letter R for Readhead. All but one of the ships were delivered to the company, the exception being *Ulidia*, built by Readhead in 1903 for an Ulster owner and taken back in 1916.

The intention was undoubtedly to trade the ships until market conditions improved and sell them at a profit, but in three cases, including that of *Highcliffe*, war intervened. In September 1918 she left Glasgow with a cargo of coal only to be torpedoed and sunk in St

George's Channel, thirteen miles south east of Tuskar Rock, by the German submarine *UB 87* which – even at this late stage of the war – had been allowed by the Royal Navy to operate in home waters.

At the time her photograph was taken on the Thames in the early 1950s, the 347-ft *Dabaibe** was nominally owned (and registered) in Panama but her disponent owner was the London-based Captain E J Jakobson, an Estonian exile and also her master. She had been built in 1909 by J L Thompson & Sons Ltd, Sunderland for London owners as *Kingsgate*, and then had a succession of Belgian, British and Estonian owners, as *Scottier*, *Lundy Light* and *Koidula*. During the Second World War she was first expropriated (along with Estonia) by the USSR, then grabbed by Germany as *Uhlenhorst*, only to emerge as *Dabaibe* in 1948. But misfortune had not finished with her. In May 1959, while on her way from Calais to Yokohama with a cargo of scrap metal and bound herself for the scrap yard, she sprang a leak in the South Atlantic and cheated her breakers by sinking.

The trio of three-island ships in this section demonstrate how, in the first decade of the twentieth century, the bridge deck was lengthened so that, between the navigating bridge and the engine room casing, a hatch was worked in to serve the coal bunkers below.

The 355-ft *Portreath** was photographed approaching Avonmouth between 1919 and 1932 while in the ownership of a single-ship company managed by W E Hinde & Co of Cardiff. She had been built in 1911 by Craig, Taylor & Co Ltd as *Amicus*.

Portreath was sold to Greek owners in 1932, at a time when many British owners were struggling to keep ships employed. As *Theoskepasti* she was declared a constructive total loss following grounding off Nova Scotia in 1943. But any ship was valuable at that time in the war, and she was sold and put back into service under the Panama flag as *Cygnet*. But war had not finished with the ageing steamer. In March 1950, almost five years

after hostilities had ceased, she was seriously damaged by a floating mine in the North Sea off Terschelling while carrying scrap from Emden to Hull. There was no

reprieve this time for the forty-one-year-old steamer which was sent to the Tyne to be broken up.

Three islands with extended bridge deck

Around 1900 a development of the three-island design appeared with the bridge deck extended to over 80 ft, giving a platform ahead of the bridge on which were mounted two king posts and the associated winches. Tramp ship designers thus broke away from rigid adherence to a basic foremast/mainmast arrangement, presaging the many variations of cargo handling gear which persisted throughout the life of the tramp.

Daleby* of 1900 was part of one of the great tramp fleets of the north of England, and the most successful of those who embraced shipbuilding, Robert Ropner & Sons of West Hartlepool. Ropner bought the Stockton-on-Tees shipyard of M Pearse & Co in 1887 and gave it his own name. It henceforth built ships mainly, but not exclusively, for the Ropner fleet – R Chapman (later Chapman & Willan) also ordered extensively from the yard. Interestingly, Daleby was a conventional three-island tramp built when, as the next chapter will illustrate, the Ropner yard was otherwise turning out the idiosyncratic trunk-deck design. This once again illustrates that there was little consensus as to which of the many designs of ship apparent in this chapter was the optimum for the tramp trades.

The 331-ft Daleby was one of a depressingly huge number of ships lost during the First World War, torpedoed in the western approaches by U 70 in April 1917 while carrying to Garston a cargo of copper and silver ore from Huelva. Sadly, twenty-five of her crew were lost, including Daleby's master.

The other great 'R' fleet of the north east was that of Walter Runciman of Newcastle. The founder had served in east coast collier brigs, becoming a master at the age of twenty-four, and writing a classic account of the coastal coal trade under sail. He bought a twenty-year-old steamer in 1885, and continued to buy and run ships frugally, to the extent that seamen who had a choice tended to avoid the ships of his Moor Line Ltd, formed to consolidate his ship ownership in 1897.

The 314-ft Marstonmoor* was completed by John Blumer & Co of Sunderland in September 1906, and was engined by the Sunderland shops of North Eastern Marine Engineering Co Ltd. Yet another victim of unrestricted submarine warfare, in April 1918 she was sailing north about round Britain when torpedoed well to the north of Cape Wrath by U 107. Her intended voyage from Milford Haven to Murmansk with mail, coal and general cargo suggests she was supplying the British forces that were attempting to aid the White Russian opponents of the Bolsheviks.

Long bridge deck

What can be regarded as the ultimate development of the single-deck three-island design was the long-bridge deck ship, which enjoyed a remarkable popularity. An early example was the 300-ft *Southgarth**, delivered in 1891 by John Readhead & Sons of North Shields to an owner who was based just across the Tyne at North Shields, W D C Balls & Son. Her entry in *Lloyd's Register* indicates that, as well as a forecastle and a poop, she has a 78-ft quarterdeck and a 130-ft bridge deck, but from the photograph it is by no means clear where the quarterdeck ends and the bridge deck begins.

Her exceptionally tall masts are well depicted in this photograph taken beneath the Clifton Suspension Bridge. Note also the white-painted pole for her compass, and how a neat white ring separates the 'mast-colour' of the lower main mast from its black-painted upper part which would soon be coated with soot from the funnel. 'Mast colour' was the suitably vague name for a hue ranging from yellow to brown, and which could even be varnished wood.

Southgarth was captured by *U 39* and scuttled with explosives charges during May 1916 while on a ballast voyage from Marseilles to Benisaf.

The prevalence of west country place names among the fleets of successful Cardiff ship owners reflects the number of men from Devon and Cornwall who crossed the Bristol Channel to set up tramp shipping businesses in the coal metropolis. Among these were the Anning Brothers, who migrated from the Exeter area where they had operated sailing ships in coastal trades.

Close examination of the 340-ft *Exmouth**, shows that her cargo-handling gear has been modestly enhanced by a pair of short kingposts and associated derricks on her poop. The fourth hatch is served by an adequate derrick, and the extra equipment may be to help in loading stores.

Exmouth was built in 1899 by Richardson, Duck & Co of Stockton-on-Tees with an engine by the local but ubiquitous engineering company Blair & Co Ltd. The registered owner was the eponymous Exmouth Steamship Co Ltd with Anning Brothers as manager, a firm that was hardly modest about putting its initial on her funnel. She served them for a creditable twenty-five years and was sold in 1924 to Neapolitan owners who renamed her *Nimbo*. However, in November 1929 she stranded at Portobello, near Brighton, during a ballast voyage from Hamburg to Cardiff. Although refloated, she was declared a constructive total loss and sold for scrapping at Grays, Essex where she arrived in January 1930.

The sweep of the long bridge deck is readily apparent at the angle *White Wings** makes to the camera. There is a substantial chart room, with above it a steering position that appears exposed, but could be at least covered by a canvas awning. The white pole visible on her forecastle also allows an awning to be rigged to give those working here some protection from the tropical sun.

She had been built in 1900 in the yard of J Blumer & Co, Sunderland as *Claverley*, managed in London. In 1906 she passed to Norman Hallett of London, who gave her the slightly fanciful name *White Wings* while registering her in the ownership of his Wing Steamship Co Ltd. Another member of the Hallett family, George, had earlier given his Cardiff-based fleet equally odd names such as *White Jacket* and *Blue Jacket*.

In 1914, the 325-ft *White Wings* was to carry her final name, *Woolston*, under which she was to have two distinct owners and three different managers, all in the space of four years. In May 1918, she was setting off from Syracuse to deliver a cargo of sulphur to Messina when she was torpedoed and sunk by *UC 52*.

Although seen in an unhappy situation – note the crew member being rescued by breeches buoy – *City of Cardiff** exemplified a trend in cargo gear development, and signalled the beginning of a significant Cardiff tramp fleet.

The long bridge deck steamer has but a light and rather stumpy mast forward, while derricks are worked from pairs of kingposts, including a third set on the poop. Multiplying the number of derricks that could be worked at any one time was becoming popular with cargo liner operators, but the Ropner-built, 331-ft *City of Cardiff* of 1906 was extremely unusual at the time in being so equipped for tramping.

The man behind her was William Reardon Smith, a former master mariner who had built up property and other investments in Cardiff. He registered his first ship in the name of Instow Steamship Co Ltd, commemorating a village near his birthplace in North Devon. *City of Cardiff* traded extremely successfully to the River Plate, and Reardon Smith was to quickly build up one of South Wales' biggest fleets. He even turned to his advantage the loss of *City of Cardiff*, which fetched up at Mill Bay, two miles from Land's End, in hurricane force winds during March 1912. While staying in a hotel in St Just when attending operations following her stranding, Reardon Smith met local worthies whom he later persuaded to invest in his new venture, St Just Steamship Co Ltd.

Around 1910, Robert Ropner & Son, having ended its affair with the trunk-deck design described in chapter 4, enthusiastically embraced the long bridge deck type. Ropner's Stockton-on-Tees shipyard had flirted with it as early as 1904, when it built *Teesdale* for another West Hartlepool owner (and later acquired the ship itself). Indeed, so fervently did the company take to this design that it was still accepting them into its fleet in 1930. The

first built for Ropner was the 376-ft *Levenpool** of 1911, engined by Blair & Co Ltd, also of Stockton-on-Tees.

According to Ropner's history, the long bridge deck type's popularity was due to a loophole in Lloyd's Register rules. These forbad a vessel's length being more than twelve times its depth and, because depth was a dimension ruling which ports a ship could serve, it severely constrained length and hence carrying capacity.

However, if a continuous 'superstructure' covered 70 per cent of the vessel's length (*Levenpool*'s forecastle, bridge and poop covered 76 per cent), the vessel's length-to-depth ratio could be increased to fourteen to one. With a length of 376 ft and a depth of 26 ft, *Levenpool*'s ratio was actually just over the magic figure.

Levenpool was a survivor, and was not despatched to breakers, in this case at Troon, until June 1934.

Gradually, the building of tramp steamers extended beyond the rivers Tees, Wear and Tyne. In 1912 the 352-ft *Withernsea* was completed by Earle's Shipbuilding & Engineering Co Ltd of Hull for local owner Brown, Atkinson & Co Ltd, and with a local name. She passed through the hands of several other British owners, who successively renamed her *Bathampton*, *Ardenhall*, and *Northborough* before she became the Greek *Vassilios Destounis* in 1933.

During 1940, *Vassilios Destounis* was attacked by Luftwaffe aircraft off Spain and abandoned by her crew, only to be boarded by a bold set of Spanish fishermen who took her into Aviles. They were no doubt delighted to be awarded £80,000 in salvage money. But her owner would have been even happier in April 1941. Denied the opportunity of obtaining British ships, the newly-formed Irish Shipping Ltd, Dublin, was desperate to buy tonnage at almost any price and in whatever condition, and acquired the wreck for a massive £142,000. With some difficulty she was manned, repaired and entered service as Irish Shipping's first vessel, *Irish Poplar*: she might even have received her enclosed wheelhouse at this time.

When the war was over, Irish Shipping ordered new tonnage and the veteran *Irish Poplar* was duly sold to Turkey in 1949. She first took the name *Taskôprü*, becoming *Mehmet** in 1952 when she painted up the

funnel colours of the Cerrahoglu family, in which she is seen. She survived until 1961 when delivered to Yugoslav breakers.

Two decks

Ships with two decks continued to be built for the tramp trade into the 1890s, although in decreasing numbers. The extra deck contributed to the ship's longitudinal strength, and thus allowed for longer ships with increased capacity. Externally, however, most two-deckers were indistinguishable from single-deck, three-island designs.

In the case of the 360-ft *Queensland** of 1890, owner William Kish of Sunderland might have chosen to build a two-deck ship to make her attractive to charterers in the liner trade, a supposition supported by the provision of four derricks at each mast. Certainly her owner from 1898, R M Hudson, also of Sunderland, had a small but remarkably varied fleet, which at various times included a short-sea passenger ship plying the British east coast, a reefer and conventional cargo ships which he chartered out, as well as coastal and deep-sea tramps.

Built by J L Thompson at Sunderland, *Queensland* gave remarkably good service to Hudson, who kept her as his sole ship from 1915. In the 1920s, after a few voyages to the Black Sea and eastern Mediterranean, *Queensland* struggled to find work – a reflection of her age and relative unsuitability for tramping. In 1928 Hudson accepted the inevitable and sold her to an owner in Riga. But even as *Everita*, cheaply crewed and operated under the Latvian flag, she lasted only four years until sale for breaking up in Savona. (*J and M Clarkson*)

Scottish builders seemed more comfortable building two-deck ships than single-deck tramps, and *Saint Ninian** of 1894 came from the Glasgow yard of D & W Henderson & Co, who also provided her engine. Smaller than *Queensland* at 320 ft, she boasts a particularly tall funnel, even for a period when natural-draught for the boilers was usual. The grey hull colour was, if not unique, also out of the ordinary.

She was the first steamer owned by Alexander Mackay & Co of Glasgow. Mackay had previously operated sailing ships in the Canadian timber trade, but put *Saint Ninian* on longer voyages, including the River Plate grain trade and the Indian rice trade.

Saint Ninian was torpedoed and sunk by *UB 34* in February 1917 off Whitby in the very last few miles of her voyage to the Tees with iron pyrites from Port Kelah. Her loss put an end to Mackay's shipowning business.

Spar deck

Ships with the light upper deck known as a spar deck continued to be built for the tramp trade into the twentieth century.

Frederick Bolton, whose single-deckers *Raphael* and *Rembrandt* were featured in the previous chapter, chose this design for his *Romney** of 1893, staying loyal to builder J L Thompson & Sons of Sunderland for her modest, 316-ft hull. Just ahead of her bridge deck are two light derricks with short king posts, probably used for stores.

Romney served Bolton well, transferring to his Bolton Steam Shipping Co Ltd in 1897, and was not sold until 1916. She would then have been made considerably more than her initial cost. With her value continuing to inflate she changed hands several times. Although she remained registered in London, the names of her various managers indicate that they were foreign nationals who, unable to change the flag of a ship in wartime, had set up shipowning companies in the United Kingdom.

Romney was not renamed until 1920, when she became *City of Amiens*, the new name giving another clue to the nationality of her beneficial owner and operator. As this she remained in the Mediterranean trade until September 1922, when she was wrecked at Camariñas on the north-western tip of Spain while on voyage to Algiers with a cargo of coal from Barry.

Thomas Dunlop & Sons of Glasgow was unusual in operating both sail and steam tonnage in parallel long after most owners had concluded that sail was obsolete. Indeed, it was not until 1911 that its last sailer, *Clan Graham*, was sold. Dunlop's steamer ownership began in 1883.

Dunlop divided its contracts between Clydeside and Wearside shipyards, the 344-ft *Queen Eleanor** of 1896 being from the decade when Bartram & Son of Sunderland was winning most of the Glasgow company's orders for steamers. Like Dunlop's other steamers, she traded far and wide, voyaging to the Far East and making Pacific crossings. She was sold to owners in Genoa in 1913 and renamed *Luigi*.

She became a total loss in March 1918 after she was shelled and driven ashore by *U 152* near Cape Juby, West Africa while on voyage from Marseilles to Dakar.

This fine portrait of the spar-decked *Earl of Carrick** was taken while on her trials in the Firth of Clyde. She is stationary in the water, the trials party having congregated on the starboard side of the bridge deck. It is interesting that a ship delivered as late as 1905 still has a rudimentary sail – a jib is furled on her forestay.

Suggesting she has just been handed over to her owners, she flies at her mainmast the pennant of Glasgow-based Marshall & Dobbie: red with a white shield bearing a blue cross. At her foremast can be discerned her name pennant, a flag flown during trials but hardly ever again during a ship's life. From a wire above her bridge is the defaced saltire of her builder Russell & Co. A famous constructor of standard iron and steel sailing ships, Russell & Co was now concentrating on achieving a similar position as a builder of tramps. This it achieved, and under its subsequent title of Lithgows Ltd,

the Port Glasgow yard mounted the Clyde's biggest challenge to the supremacy of the Wear's tramp builders.

The 345-ft *Earl of Carrick* was sold in 1913 to successful Welsh shipowner William Thomas, Sons & Co

Ltd. Renamed *Maritime* by Thomas, she disappeared off South America in April 1914 while on voyage from Barry with coal for Campana in Argentina.

Part awning deck

Unlike the other two-deck tramps, those with a part-awning deck appear to be flush-decked forward, with a well aft. Understanding this is helped by reference to the lengths of various decks published in *Lloyd's Register*, and the diagrams of typical vessels included in the introduction to these volumes.

In the case of the 330-ft *Haxby** of 1892, the awning deck extends 189 ft back from her bow, and on which sits her superstructure. From here to the poop is a 98-ft quarterdeck, which is *lower* than both the awning deck and the poop, giving the effect of a shallow well aft in which sit the two after hatches. *Haxby* was owned by Robert Ropner & Co and built by the associated Ropner & Son shipyard at Stockton-on-Tees, yet again illustrating how this successful company hedged its bets by building steamers to a variety of designs in the 1890s.

Haxby was photographed near the giant ore gantries in Rotterdam, unloading supplies from the United States for the inhabitants of Belgium who, like much of German-occupied Europe, were suffering from shortages due to the Allied blockade. The ship's normal funnel colours have been painted over for the occasion.

Haxby was sold in 1919 to another major tramp fleet, that of Watts, Watts & Co Ltd of London, who renamed her after the London suburb of *Finchley*. In the depressed years that followed the immediate post-war boom, an ageing awning-decker would be at a particular disadvantage, and *Finchley* was duly sold for breaking up at Gateshead in February 1926. *(Martin Lindenborn)*

The shallow well aft — in which the hatch tops are the same height as the poop deck — can also be seen in the 314-ft *Horsa** of 1894. Although from a different yard to the slightly longer *Haxby*, that of William Gray & Co Ltd at West Hartlepool, she is remarkably similar in hull form and erections, although her masts are significantly shorter. The surprising variation in length between similar ships, even those from the same builder, may in part be explained by differences in length of building berths (even in the same yard). British yards were often on sites of restricted size, their expansion prevented by surrounding housing or other industry. Much later, this was to be one of the factors in the closure of many yards.

Horsa had a very straightforward career. She was built for local owner Herskind & Co, and is recorded as running from the UK to India with coal and returning home with Burmese rice, and voyaging both to the River Plate, with Cardiff coal out and grain home, and to the Gulf of Mexico. In April 1917, she was torpedoed by *U 93* well out in the Western Approaches while heading to Cardiff with iron ore from Port Briera.

The third part-awning-deck tramp, the 315-ft Cluden* of 1896, comes from yet another yard, John Readhead & Sons of South Shields. But again she is very similar to Haxby and to Horsa, although in this view she appears to lack the lighthouses forward.

Her London owner was the well-established Steel, Young & Co. Little discernible policy is apparent in the names chosen for their fleet, which had expanded to

seventeen with the arrival of Cluden. One very distinctive feature of their ships was the hull colour, because only the two upper strakes were black, and the area between these and the boot topping was painted a lighter colour, probably grey but just possibly red.

Cluden's career was also terminated by a German submarine; U 39 sank her off Algeria in October 1916 while she bringing wheat from Karachi to Cardiff. (J and M Clarkson)

Chapman variations

All three examples of full-awning-deck tramps come from the Newcastle-based fleet of R Chapman & Son, better known in its post-Second World War form as Chapman & Willan Ltd. In an era when nineteen out of twenty tramps had the standard foremast and mainmast arrangement, the different rigs given to the Chapman ships, and other aspects of their appearance, justify three photographs of its ships. All three were built at the Ropner yard at Stockton-on-Tees and engined locally by Blair & Co Ltd.

Chapman concentrated very heavily on the grain trades, and with cargoes of wheat, barley or maize the awning deck of his ships was not the disadvantage it was with other bulk cargoes, because the upper deck held bagged grain.

The 3,438-grt *Riverton** is very unusual for an 1899-built tramp in having three holds forward of her bridge and in having a pair of kingposts mounted between numbers one and two hatches. She gave Chapman excellent service, and after a quarter century was sent to a scrapyard near Venice in July 1924.

Delivered six years after *Riverton*, *Carlton** of 1905 was much larger, just hitting the 400 ft mark. She too had five holds but reverted to having conventional masts to serve them, and the forward pair of kingposts on *Riverton* has been replaced. On her full-length awning deck has been placed an 89-ft bridge deck. The very low and rudimentary navigating bridge of *Riverton* has been enhanced with a docking bridge, which is manned as she approaches Avonmouth in this photograph.

Carlton was not as fortunate as her predecessor. In late May 1918, she was torpedoed and sunk by *U 90* while recently having set out from South Wales for Chile where she would load a cargo of nitrate for military use. She was in ballast, whereas in normal times leaving the coal port of Cardiff in ballast would have been unthinkable. *Carlton*'s crew got away in three boats, one reaching Corunna in Spain after eight days and the other two found by a British steamer two days later.

*Nurtureton** of 1912 appears to have a three-island configuration, but the raised bulwarks forward, alongside her superstructure and aft prove deceptive. The vessel's entry in *Lloyd's Register* indicates that she had a main deck above that was a continuous awning deck. In yet another rearrangement of cargo gear, kingposts now replace the mast between holds two and three. The large second funnel, to serve her donkey boiler, is if anything even more apparent than in the photographs of her two fleet mates.

The 415-ft *Nurtureton* had two sisters, *Grainton* and *Demeterton*, and a further clue to Chapman's specialisation in the grain trade is the names chosen. *Demeterton* was named after Demeter, the Greek goddess of produce from the earth and particularly corn.

Nurtureton survived the war, and in an example of how the conflict had affected ship values, in 1920 she was sold for £240,000 compared with the £58,376 she had cost to build eight years previously. Not surprisingly, her new London owner did not prosper, and two years later she passed to West Hartlepool Steam Navigation Co Ltd, which renamed her *Siltonhall*. In September 1929, she caught fire and sank in the Indian Ocean while on a long, coal-laden voyage from Immingham to Adelaide.

True flush-decker

This view of the new 390-ft Welbeck Hall* of 1914 in Avonmouth clearly shows her flush-deck configuration, particularly rare in single-deck tramps such as this. Both Edward Nicholl of Cardiff, who managed the single-ship company that owned her, and her builder William Doxford & Sons Ltd of Sunderland, had been heavily wedded to the turret design (see chapter 4). But with changes to the way dues were calculated, orders for turrets had dried up and Doxford and its customers were looking at new designs. Nicholl also took Welbeck Hall's Doxford-built sisters Bland Hall and Albert Hall.

Usually referred to as the Cardiff Hall Line, although it was a purely tramping concern, Nicholl's fleet began to be registered in London in 1912. This was in reaction to the bad reputation that Cardiff-based tramps were acquiring following several cases in which ships had been deliberately lost either because their recession-hit owners wanted the insurance money or because third parties had taken out insurance policies on the ships. Nicholl himself took part in a conference held by the Board of Trade and this resulted in it being made illegal to 'gamble' on ships being lost.

Welbeck Hall was to become a victim of unrestricted submarine warfare, torpedoed in May 1918 by UB 53 in the Mediterranean while on a ballast voyage from Piraeus to Port Said. By 1917, however, Nicholl had sold his interest in the Cardiff Hall Line to a Sven Hansen, a wise decision on Nicholl's part given how losses had inflated ship prices.

Clipper and teapot bows

Not all features of tramp ship design were driven by practicality. Concern with aesthetics or tradition perpetuated the building of hulls ornamented with clipper bows well into the last century. Oddly, several examples were found in Sunderland fleets – those of Anderson, Horan & Co, F & W Ritson, Taylor & Sanderson, and James Westoll – although those in three of these fleets were built by Short Brothers, suggesting it might be builder rather than owner that clung to this practice.

Robert Eggleton* was built for James Westoll in 1890, Short Brothers fitting a triple-expansion engine made by Thomas Richardson & Sons. The 285-ft, single-deck, steel steamer had a three-island hull.

Despite her anachronistic design, Westoll ran Robert Eggleton for twenty-seven years, and might have done so longer had not the German submarine U 91 finished her career with a torpedo in December 1917. The U-boat had cheekily penetrated the Irish Sea, and caught Robert Eggleton off Bardsey soon after leaving Glasgow with a cargo of coal for Livorno.

Photograph collectors and authors have much to thank the photographer at Bristol responsible for what is known as the York collection, and to the Bristol Museum, and Art Gallery plus various individuals and societies who have preserved the negatives.

The spar-decked *Abbey Holme** of 1899 has not only a clipper bow but also a figurehead, which must have been a nostalgic exercise for builders J L Thompson & Sons Ltd of Sunderland, whose story began in the sailing ship era. Owner was Maryport-based Hine Brothers, who also had a long heritage in sail. Trading as Holme Line, the owners had shown great loyalty to Thompson, ordering seventeen sailing or steam ships from the yard.

The 342-ft *Abbey Holme* was sold to French owners as *Rigel* in 1908, soldiering on until 1927 when broken up at La Seyne. It would be interesting to know if, after twenty-eight years, her clipper bow and figurehead were still in place.

There is an intriguing connection between *Abbey Holme* and a later ship with a clipper bow, *Holly Branch**. Late in 1907 Hine Brothers sold their clipper-bowed *Isel Holme* to F & W Ritson of Sunderland, and she was renamed *Myrtle Branch*. It may be a coincidence that Ritson's next two newbuildings, *Cedar Branch* of 1910 and *Holly Branch* of 1911 from Bartram, both had clipper bows. Had *Isel Holme* inspired Ritson to adopt the feature, perhaps encouraged by the Sunderland builder that was also currently building clipper-bowed steamers for Ben Line of Leith (and who took delivery of ships with this feature up until 1914)?

Despite this anachronism, Ritson and Bartram were somewhat innovative in placing the engines of *Cedar Branch* and *Holly Branch* further aft than was customary, thereby increasing usable cargo space.

We are lucky to have this clear trials view of the 391-ft *Holly Branch*, because she did not survive long. On New Year's Day 1917, she was captured by the German submarine *UB 39* off France and sunk with explosives. She was nearing the end of a voyage from La Plata to Le Havre with a cargo of bagged oats.

There are echoes of the clipper bow in a decorative feature perpetuated in ships of the Pyman family, the beaked or 'teapot' bow. The beaked bow was in evidence at least as early as 1888 when William Gray incorporated this feature into the steamer *Cranford*. It still featured in the Gray-built *Welcombe* of 1930, the last ship built for Pyman.

The 340-ft *Runswick** was managed by Pyman Brothers from London, but her North Yorkshire name harked back to the family's origins in Whitby, as did the name of her owning company, London & Northern Steamship Co Ltd. The long bridge deck steamer was a 1904 product, again of William Gray & Co Ltd and its Central Marine Engine Works.

Pyman sold several ships to William Reardon Smith during the First World War, including *Runswick*, which in 1917 went to St Just Steamship Co Ltd – referred to earlier in this chapter. Alas, her service here was short, torpedoed during April 1918 by *UB 109* off Trevose Head in the Bristol Channel, having just sailed from Newport with a coal cargo. *Runswick* was beached, but was declared a total loss.

Tramp reefer

Given the high cost of refrigeration machinery and the associated insulation, and the unsuitability of ships so equipped for other trades, refrigerator ships were mostly built by established liner operators that had a captive trade in frozen or chilled meat. But tramp operator Turner, Brightman & Co quickly spotted an opportunity here, and began to build some ships suitable for hire to such liner companies. They were either guaranteed charters from the likes of Houlder Brothers or the River Plate Fresh Meat Co Ltd, or gambled that such

companies, desperate for specialised tonnage to shift meat, would pay a premium for suitable ships.

Unusually, Turner, Brightman had different funnel colours for its conventional tramps and for its refrigerator ships. The former had a broad white band between two narrow red bands, and this was reversed for the refrigerator ships. Both types had a white 'Z' on black below the bands, reflecting the use of names beginning with this letter.

The 348-ft *Zuleika** was built by the versatile J L Thompson & Sons Ltd, Sunderland in 1899, and engined by Blair & Co Ltd of Stockton-on-Tees. In this trials view, note the walkways across the well decks, the substantial steam pipe behind the funnel, and the full set of furled sails and gaffs on each mast. *Zuleika* survived the First World War only to be wrecked off Las Palmas in October 1920 while on voyage from Campana to London with meat and general cargo.

CHAPTER

4

'Patent' Tramps

More and more builders entered the market for building tramp steamers in the 1890s, all conscious that the 1880s had been a period of depressed freight rates, idle ships and sparse new orders. Competitive pressures saw several radical hull designs developed and patented by British yards and designers. These were usually marketed to potential owners as offering increased capacity, savings in building costs or better sea-keeping qualities. But in the two most numerous types, the turret deck and trunk deck designs, the major attraction was a significant reduction in net tonnage with concomitant decreases in the harbour and canal dues that were calculated on tonnage. When the authorities who imposed these dues woke up to the anomalies and instituted a more rational basis for their fees, orders for these ship types quickly dried up.

For a time at least, the turret was particularly successful and catapulted Doxford into the front rank of tramp ship builders. The trunk deck seems to have been Ropner's attempt to get round Doxford's patents, and fewer were built, with Ropners themselves taking a significant number. Other builders were even less successful with their own patents, with just three orders booked for tower deck ships, and none at all for other suggested designs.

The arch deck design emerged when turret and trunk building ceased, and had a much longer life cycle, built over a period stretching into the late 1920s. But the record for longevity, at least of effort, must go to the Monitor design, which was marketed for over twenty years, well into the motor ship era, although without conspicuous success.

In fact, the interwar years saw a revival of interest in novel hull designs, with builders once again desperate to win what few orders were forthcoming during a severe depression and owners equally keen to reduce building and operating costs. The story of 'patent' tramps in this chapter is continued in chapter 7.

Note: An asterisk in a caption indicates the vessel shown in the photograph.

Turret deck

By far the most successful patented designs in terms of sales was Doxford's turret ship, with 176 built at Sunderland plus six completed elsewhere under licence. Inspiration was the whaleback steamers originating on the Great Lakes of North America, whose cigar-shaped hulls carried 'turrets' on which were placed the superstructure and deck fittings. Borrowed from these was the idea of a narrow upper deck, about half the width of the hull proper, and about 5ft above the main, or harbour, deck. Advantages claimed included greater longitudinal strength, better seaworthiness thanks to the reserve buoyancy provided by the upper part of the hull, and savings in steel and hence construction cost. There was also a degree of self-trimming in that the narrow, upper part of the hull acted as a feeder for bulk cargoes.

It took hard work for Doxford to convince owners, classification societies and underwriters of the benefits and safety of the design, and only after the modest-sized prototype, *Turret* of 1892, had proved itself did orders start rolling in. Runciman of Newcastle was a belated but ardent convert, accepting a total of ten between 1897 and 1911, including the last built by Doxford, *Orangemoor*. All but the final pair were around 342 ft in length, including *Aviemoor** of 1902, Runciman's third. She was sold to owners in Bombay in 1916, later renamed *Naderi*. Sale to Japan in 1924 saw her become *Ise Maru*. Following stranding off Shinyasaki in April 1940 she was broken up.

This view of *Garryvale** entering Preston in April 1930 demonstrates the cross-sectional shape of the hull. Its bizarre form helps to explain why basically conservative ship owners and underwriters needed much convincing of the type's practicality.

The hull form necessitated some special features. Davits had to be able to swing the boats beyond the harbour deck. Note also that the mooring bollards have to be placed on this deck, which with its tumblehome hardly looks a secure place for crew members to work, with no railings, although some turrets certainly had them. The ladders giving access to this deck appear vulnerable to heavy seas, although one of the selling points of the turret design was that the narrow upper part of the hull tended to turn back the seas and kept the water off the upper deck and hatches. Despite the vulnerability of anything placed there, it is said that the harbour deck could be used to carry a deck cargo such as timber, although photographic evidence of this happening is lacking.

The 350-ft *Garryvale* was completed in 1907 for Vale Steamship Co Ltd, managed by Crawford, Barr & Co of Glasgow, who named their ships after Scottish river valleys beginning with the letter G, which in itself guaranteed a modest fleet. By the time this photograph was taken, *Garryvale* had been sold to Finnish owners who, in several cases, were content to keep a British name. *Garryvale* stranded off the mouth of the River Tees in January 1939 and was so badly damaged that she was despatched to breakers at Inverkeithing. (*J and M Clarkson*)

Like the majority of turrets, Countess Warwick* of 1906 had machinery made by Doxford, who had added an engine and boiler-making facilities to their Sunderland yard in 1878. The smoke leaves no doubt that she was a coal burner. In this trials shot note also the bowler-hatted worthies on the wing of the lower bridge, a mix of men from Doxford and her managers, Williams & Mordey of Cardiff. This photo also shows how the upper part of the deck was faired into the bow and how the cross trees consisted of a triangular frame. Close examination confirms that she has a forecastle and poop but no bridge deck, despite the bulwarks alongside the superstructure.

The 350-ft Countess Warwick moved from Cardiff to Newcastle ownership in 1915 on sale to A M Sutherland, who renamed her Kincardine. Owners in the north of England and London seemed keener on the design than the numerous tramp owners of South Wales. However, the most enthusiastic user was a cargo line, Clan Line Steamers Ltd operating some thirty turrets. A significant factor for this fleet serving India was the reduction turrets enjoyed in Suez Canal dues, which at the time were calculated on breadth at the upper deck. Unlike most turrets built for tramp concerns, those for Clan Line had two decks.

Kincardine did not enjoy a long career with Sutherland. During March 1917, she was torpedoed and sunk by U 70 in the North Atlantic while outward bound from Cardiff to Genoa with coal.

The outward appearance of the turrets was not as uniform as the three previous photographs might suggest. W J Tatem ordered two, Wellington* and Torrington, both delivered in 1905, which had a profusion of goal post masts, including a pair serving the fourth hold on the bridge deck. At the time of her completion, Wellington was, at 390 ft and 5,600 grt, the largest ship registered in Cardiff. The girder-like form of her hull would give such a long single-deck ship longitudinal strength, while the provision of a 104-ft bridge deck would also stiffen the structure. Other features of note are the enclosed wheelhouse and the light railings which gave some security to anyone working on, or boarding her from, the harbour deck.

In September 1918 Wellington was torpedoed by the German submarine U 118 175 miles north by west from Cape Villano while on voyage from Newport to Naples with a cargo of coal. Her near sister, the 390-ft Torrington, had also been sunk by a submarine in the Western approaches during April 1917. (National Museum of Wales)

In another iteration of the turret design, *Haigh Hall** of 1908 has what was for the time a rather unusual layout. Of her five cargo holds, one splits the bridge and accommodation around the engine room casing, while abaft of this is what would appear to be a bunker hatch. Like *Countess Warwick*, she has a forecastle and poop but no bridge deck. Manager was Edward Nicholl & Co, whose Cardiff Hall Line was the only South Wales concern to take more than two turrets, a total of seven plus two more sold before completion.

Opponents of the turret design – largely other ship builders jealous of Doxford's success – pointed to cases where the ships had either capsized or gone missing, and claimed that their design made turrets fundamentally unstable. However, an analysis of losses made by John Lingwood, historian of the type, indicates the loss rate from these causes among turrets was no higher than among more conventional ships. The single largest cause of turret losses were the hazards of the First World War, which accounted for seventy-seven out of one hundred and eighty two. The 360-ft *Haigh Hall* was one such loss, torpedoed on 30 June 1917 by the Austro-Hungarian submarine *U 28* forty miles east of Malta while on voyage from Bombay to Naples with a cargo of wheat. *(World Ship Society Ltd)*

A good number of turrets were ordered by non-British owners, including five which ought to be classed as specialist ore carriers – the engines-aft *Maud Cassels** of 1897, *Skandia* of 1899, *Grangesberg* of 1903, *Blotberg* of 1907 and *Admiraal de Ruijter* of 1907. They were built for W H Muller's Algemeene Scheepvaart Maatschappij of Rotterdam, and were intended to bring iron ore from Swedish mines to Rotterdam, where much of it would be unloaded into barges to be sent up the Rhine to German steel mills. In the case of the 369-ft *Maud Cassels*, cargo gear consists of a mix of conventional derricks at masts and kingposts plus two pairs of cranes. Such provision is somewhat surprising, as there was certainly shore-side unloading equipment at Rotterdam, and undoubtedly at ore loading ports in Sweden and Norway. The later *Grangesberg* had an even more extensive outfit similar to the goalposts of *Wellington*. At 6,749 grt and 440 ft, *Grangesberg* had the distinction of being the largest single deck ship in the world on completion. Several more turrets were built for Swedish operators.

Maud Kassels was wrecked on 23 February 1906 off the Swedish coast while returning from Rotterdam to Oxelösund for another cargo of Swedish ore. *(World Ship Society Ltd)*

Trunks

The trunk deck design must be regarded as an attempt to get round Doxfords' patents on its turret ship; Doxford certainly thought so as they brought legal action for patent infringement. The first was *Trunkby**, completed in 1896, four years after the first turret but at the time Doxford's type was gaining momentum. The patentee was Robert Ropner junior, who could both build the ships at his Stockton-on-Tees yard and operate them as part of his own fleet, which took exactly half of the forty-four built up to 1909.

The major difference from the turret was that the sides of the trunk which ran almost the full length of the ship were at almost right angles to what in the former type was dubbed the harbour deck, rather than faired into it with curved plates. This made the harbour deck a safer place to stow a timber deck cargo, although Ropner's boast that the design could be cheaply adapted to carry cattle on this deck should be treated with caution. Similar claims about enhanced seaworthiness and self-trimming abilities were made as for the turrets.

The 300-ft *Trunkby* had a forecastle, poop and bridge deck, the last named extending to the extremity of the lower hull, and allowing the lifeboats to be carried on conventional davits. Like so many contemporaries, she was a U-boat victim, captured and sunk with gunfire by *U 34* in the Mediterranean during May 1916 while carrying coal from Newport to Cette.

At 352 ft, *Teespool** of 1905 was a size larger than *Trunkby* and almost as big as Ropner trunks got. Like all but two of the forty-four built, engines came from Blair & Co Ltd of Stockton-on-Tees. A prominent feature amidships is the chute for discharging ash from her furnaces. She has a forecastle but no bridge deck, and the problem of launching the lifeboats has been solved by providing a platform alongside the trunk aft of her funnel, supported by stanchions and with conventional davits.

Teespool had a long life with Ropner, surviving until 1935. She was then sold through an intermediary, but the sale was cancelled and instead she passed to the Joseph Constantine Steam Ship Line Ltd of Middlesbrough. She was still destined for the breakers, this time on the Tyne, but Constantine traded her in as a means of securing a loan to build its new ship *Windsorwood* under the British government's 'Scrap and Build' scheme. It was not in the spirit of the scheme that owners could buy life-expired ships (some even from abroad) and claim loans but, as often is the case, the ship owners proved cannier than the civil servants who drafted The British Shipping (Assistance) Act. *(J and M Clarkson)*

Several owners of turrets also bought trunks, including Runciman from Newcastle and Williams & Mordey of Cardiff, and it is likely these owners wanted to compare the two types. Runciman had the 337-ft *Lowmoor** built in 1902, to the same three-island configuration as *Trunkby*, but took no more of the type.

Lowmoor had a respectably long career, although for one owner she was part of a dismal story. Runciman was canny enough to foresee that the post-First World War boom in freight rates would not last. In 1919, he accepted an offer of £1.8 million for his entire fleet of twenty-five steamers from Edgar Edwards, who renamed *Lowmoor* as *Lowmead*. The Welsh optimist had massively increased the capital of his successful Western Counties Shipping Co Ltd in anticipation of equally huge post-war profits. But at the end of 1920 freight rates fell by 75 per cent, and the debt-ridden Western Counties was compulsorily wound up and its ships sold at a fraction of the price Edwards

had paid, many of them – although not *Lowmead* – bought back by Runciman.

Lowmead then passed through several hands, and

was renamed *Nicholaston* by Swansea owners in 1922 and finally *Dimitrios N Boulgaris* by Greeks in 1924. She was broken up at Spezia in 1933.

Cardiff owners showed more enthusiasm for trunks than they did for turrets. One of the largest operators after Ropner was Evan Thomas, Radcliffe & Co, who ordered four. The 352-ft *Clarissa Radcliffe* was completed in 1904, again to the forecastle-only design. With the height of the upper deck above the water, and the provision of a forecastle, it was considered unnecessary to give her any sheer, and as a result she looks almost hogged.

Indecision as to names saw her becoming *Llanover* in 1913 and *Llangorse* in 1917. More renamings were to follow, because in 1924 she was sold to become *Laleham* of the Britain Steam Ship Co Ltd managed in London by Watts, Watts & Co Ltd, another enthusiast for trunks. At the depth of the interwar depression she went to Greek owners as *Marionga D Thermiotis**, and survived the Second

World War to undergo a fifth renaming as *Antonios K* in 1947. When she arrived at Milford Haven to be broken up

in May 1952 she was survived by just one trunk, the former *Coningsby* of 1897, scrapped in Brazil during 1953.

Tower deck

Among other builders that hoped to emulate the success of the turrets and trunks were T R Oswald of Milford Haven, the Sunderland Shipbuilding Co, Sir William Raylton Dixon of Stockton-on-Tees, and John Priestman of Sunderland. The last named produced the tower deck design, of which only three were built, *Enfield** of 1897, and the Norwegian *Universe* and *Kilmaho*. Yet again there was a narrow upper deck, but the plating then sloped diagonally to the edge of the lower hull. There was no harbour deck as such, only a narrow walkway, and no chance of using the sloping plates for deck cargo. In this photograph in the Avon a ladder can be seen just abaft of the engine casing, presumably to allow the pilot to climb on board. Lifeboats are mounted on platforms as with the trunks.

The 288-ft *Enfield* was initially owned in Newcastle by the single-ship Enfield Steam Ship Co Ltd, which over twenty-three years had several managers. After several changes of owner she came into fleet of John Cory & Sons of Cardiff, which obviously had some regard for or

experience of the type as it had managed *Kilmaho* from new until she became a war loss in 1917. When Cory sold her in 1932, *Enfield* had three years as the

Panamanian-registered but London-owned *Sancta Rita* until she was broken up in Italy during 1935.

Monitors

In 1903 Arthur Havers, Doxford's chief draughtsman, left his post and successfully sued his former employer for loss of patent rights on the turret design, of which there is no doubt that he invented. He then joined William Petersen – also involved with the early turret story – in developing a novel corrugated hull form. This had a longitudinal groove below the loaded waterline which was claimed to reduce resistance. The outcome was a hull form with two bulges which was dubbed the Monitor type. The theory was that the concave space between the bulges would channel water towards the propeller, improving speed with no increase in fuel consumption. Lack of proof of this theory did not stop Havers and Petersen from setting up the Monitor Shipping Corporation to exploit the idea, which they attempted to do for over two decades.

The first Monitor was completed by Osbourne, Graham & Co at its Hylton, Sunderland yard in 1909 as *Monitoria*, which became a war loss in 1915. Her owner,

Ericsson Shipping Co Ltd of Newcastle, took a further example from the same yard in 1911 as *Hyltonia*. She is depicted as the 280-ft *Maindy Hill**, a name she took soon after sale to Maindy Shipping Co Ltd of Cardiff in 1919. The

upper bulge can just be discerned in this photograph of the unladen ship in the Mersey. She kept the name after sale to a Scottish owner until she sank in a collision with a US ship off the east coast in March 1940. *(J and M Clarkson)*

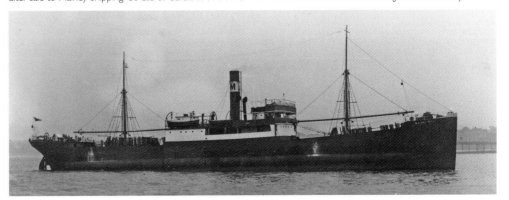

Havers and Petersen kept plugging away at their Monitor concept, and in the 1920s Petersen ordered two motor ships with this hull form from D & W Henderson & Co Ltd. To be named *River Ottawa* and *River St Lawrence*, they were intended to be part of a fleet offering non-conference services to Canada, with the help of a subsidy from the Canadian government. But before the ships were completed, Petersen died and the Canadian government got cold feet about the political implications of the deal and pulled out. The motor ships were completed in 1925 as *King James** and *King Malcolm* for associates of King Line, which paid just £25,000 for the two ships. The engines placed well aft, the three masts and the minimal sheer added to the hull bulges to ensure that the ships looked most unusual. The corrugations are only apparent in photographs of the ships in unladen condition, as in the second image.

In practice the performance of the Monitor hull was disappointing. The anticipated service speed of 11 knots was not achieved, and in wartime *King Malcolm* was hard pressed to maintain station in convoys steaming at 8 knots. In addition, the corrugations on her hull were prone to damage from wharves and from pilot vessels or others which were put alongside.

King Malcolm was torpedoed and sunk in the North Atlantic during October 1941 by *U 374*. *King James* survived the war and was sold in 1950 to a London-Greek owner who put her under the Liberian flag as *Sophoclyve*. In August 1960 the thirty-five-year old motor ship, still plodding along with her original Harland & Wolff-built Burmeister & Wain oil engine, sprang a leak and was abandoned in the Indian Ocean while on a voyage from Mormugao to the Netherlands with an ore cargo. The loss of *Sophoclyve* may well have been a result of her unusual construction, because the corrugations made the lower part of her hull much stiffer in a seaway than the upper which was in part conventionally plated.

The stresses this imposed had previously resulted in cracks in the hull. The Monitor hull not only did not deliver the savings it promised, but it also contained the seeds of its own destruction. *(World Ship Society Ltd)*

Arch deck

The Ayre-Ballard arch-deck ships involved a radical rethink of the hull structure to significantly reduce the quantity of steel needed. Its major characteristic was that the upper part of the hull was radiused inwards. The frames terminated at the point where the deck would be placed in a conventional ship, and were joined to the deck beams by arched brackets. Stringers joined the arch brackets along the length of the ship, the combination acting like a girder and giving exceptional longitudinal strength.

Second to emerge, from the Blyth Shipbuilding & Dry Dock Co Ltd in 1912, was *Sheaf Arrow** for the fleet of W A Souter & Co, Newcastle, who were to take a total of seven of the type. Although shown on the Bristol Avon, the 279-ft *Sheaf Arrow* was mostly employed carrying east coast coal, and was once described in a technical paper as the fastest collier in the trade, although competition would not be great. She remained with Souter until broken up at Inverkeithing in 1933.

In the case of *Sheaf Arrow*, the designer took advantage of the extra freeboard of the arch deck design to adopt reverse sheer, which is why she appears broken-backed. Reverse sheer supported the weight of cargo, engines and deck erections better than in a ship with normal sheer. It was possible to adopt this novel feature and maintain the vessel's sea-keeping qualities because the ship was some seven feet higher amidships than a conventional vessel of the same size. (*J and M Clarkson*)

Unlike other patented designs, the twenty-seven arch-deck ships were built at six different yards: Blyth Shipbuilding & Dry Dock Co Ltd was the most prolific with ten, including *Irene M** of 1912. An impressive forty-five years old when demolished in 1957, she was the second longest lived of the type, and first in terms of number of names carried and national flags worn, eight and six, respectively. When photographed between 1952 and 1955 she was in the ownership of Mina Shipping Co Ltd, a British-flag subsidiary of a London-Greek shipping agency.

The arch-deck design seems to have found its niche among modest-sized colliers such as the 240-ft *Irene M*. The largest, the 320-ft *Tullochmoor*, built for Runciman, who was always prepared to try novel designs. Arch-deck ships were completed over a period of seventeen years – longer than turrets and their imitations – and gained an excellent reputation. They were said to be dry on deck, to handle easily and be sea-kindly. The shape of the hold helped to trim a coal cargo and it was more easily discharged as there were no pillars in the hold. The arch decks were at least 10 per cent cheaper to build than conventional ships as their great longitudinal strength meant less steel was required. The limited take up of a successful design resulted from the innate conservatism of those who operated small tramps, and the limited demand for such ships in the interwar depression.

CHAPTER
5
Competition for British Builders

Although British builders of steel tramp steamers maintained their dominance – with their ability to compete on design, price, delivery and quality – up to and beyond 1914, other shipbuilding nations were beginning to offer competition as early as the 1880s. They could count on local support, and slowly non-British owners, including those from Greece, began to order elsewhere than from the United Kingdom.

Where builders in Scandinavia and Germany first competed in the tramp building business was for smaller vessels, up to about 250 ft and suitable for European trades. The types of ship discussed in chapter 4 were mostly replicated by continental European yards, with spar deck, part awning deck, three-island and short and long bridge deck designs represented in this chapter. This may have been out of respect for the effective designs worked out by British builders, or because the major British classification society, Lloyd's Register, had approved the designs and was to subject the ship to ongoing survey while building. In most cases the continental-built ships were indistinguishable from equivalent types built in Great Britain. Distinctly national designs had not yet emerged.

On the highly unscientific basis of finding examples of deep-sea tramps that had been photographed, it appears that Germany was the leading builder outside of the United Kingdom, followed by Denmark (but with all examples coming from one yard). Belgium, Netherlands and France lagged behind, while Norway and Sweden – both of which specialised in smaller ships – were yet to become significant builders of larger tramp steamers, relying for these mainly on British yards or on second-hand purchases. But as with much else, the forthcoming war was to begin changing this situation.

Note: An asterisk in a caption indicates the vessel shown in the photograph.

Belgian-built

Antonios Vrondisis* was unusual in being built for Greece and remaining Greek-owned for over thirty years. Builders in 1904 were Chantiers Navals Anversois at Hoboken, who turned to North Eastern Marine Engineering Co Ltd at Sunderland for her triple-expansion engine. She was completed as *Rosina* for A Embiricos of Andros, a member of the most important Greek shipping dynasty of the day, who still have substantial shipping interests.

A recurring theme of this chapter is that the ship was little different in concept from those building contemporaneously in British yards. This is not surprising as the 318-ft *Rosina* was built under the survey of Lloyd's Register. Her long bridge deck extended 200 ft almost to her stern: note the short well aft crossed by a light walkway. There is also a short kingpost and derrick aft for stores.

Rosina survived the First World War and in 1925 was sold to Greek owner J A Vrondisis, who renamed her *Antonios Vrondisis*, probably after his father, or his son, or perhaps both, because forenames were frequently recycled in Greece. The ship struck a rock near the Solovetsky Islands in August 1936 while on voyage from the port of Kem on the White Sea to Hull with a cargo of timber. Although refloated a few days later, taken to Archangel and beached, she was declared a constructive total loss and abandoned. She was probably broken up but there is no record of when and where.

The 360-ft *Berkdale** was another example of a long-bridge deck, single-deck steamer from Chantiers Navals Anversois at Hoboken with a triple-expansion engine made by North Eastern Marine Engineering Co Ltd at Sunderland (left hand photograph). However, her outfit of cargo gear is distinctly different from that of *Antonios Vrondisis*, with four sets of kingposts serving her four holds, and the single mast having little more to do than to carry a navigation light, support a radio aerial and fly some flags. Both have tall funnels, which suggests their furnaces have natural draught.

She was completed as *St Johann* in 1908 for Robert M Sloman & Co of Hamburg. By 1919, when she was surrendered to the Allies as war reparations, she had already carried the further names *Oswiga* and *Wotan* and was with her fourth German owner. The name *Wotan* sufficed for her first British commercial owner, but in 1927 she became *Berkdale*, managed by King, Warriner & Co of London. When in 1933 her British owners decided she was superannuated, she went to Fricis Grauds of Riga as *Everolanda*, but her career was far over.

In 1940 *Everolanda*, along with the rest of Latvia, was expropriated by the USSR, and was soon at war with Germany. In July 1941, she was mined and sunk in Kunda Bay, but was refloated later that month, towed to Leningrad and beached, to be eventually repaired and returned to Soviet service.

Renamed *Janis Rainis** in 1945 (right hand photograph), in post-war years she looked very different, with a completely new bridge, superstructure, funnel and masts, although these could not disguise her original hull form with its straight stem and counter stern. In the early 1950s, it is believed she received a triple-expansion engine of 2,500 ihp, thought to be originally from a 1942-built Liberty ship; this might well have occurred in 1952 when she received new boilers.

She was an occasional visitor to British ports, and the author remembers seeing her at Liverpool in October 1968. This may well have been her last voyage, because by December 1968 she was reported in a breakers' yard at Tallinn, although scrapping did not begin until mid-1969.

Out of Helsingør

The yard of Helsingørs Jernskibs & Maskinbyggeri at Helsingør (Elsinore) appears to have been the busiest tramp producer in Denmark during this period. In 1897 it built and engined *Skanderborg* for the Dannebrog company of C K Hansen, a major Copenhagen owner, who since 1883 had divided his orders between domestic and British yards.

Of a modest 280 ft, *Skanderborg* was quite capable of long voyages, and is recorded as steaming from Algiers to Santos in 1919. Unfortunately, after repairs to her steering gear during this voyage it was found that her engine would not start. After she had been towed to St Vincent it was found that the trouble was simply due to lack of lubrication in the stern tube. No doubt the chief engineer had to answer some difficult questions.

Sale in 1933 saw her move to Finland, taking the name *Wanda** for Herbert Janhonen, who put the initial of his first name on his funnel. *Wanda* is seen at anchor on the Thames in the early 1950s, awaiting a berth in the Surrey Commercial Docks to unload her timber cargo. Bridge and superstructure have been enhanced in the half century since she was built, and her original masts modified to incorporate separate topmasts. One further name change was to come, to *Ridal* in 1957, and during 1958 she was broken up at Grimstad in Norway.

Also seen under the Finnish flag delivering timber to London is another Helsingør product, the 290-ft *Dagmar** of 1900. Unusually, and apart from a short spell after the First World War, she kept her original name until broken up at Bruges in 1959.

Original owner was the Russisch-Baltische DG, a company based in Riga managed by Helmsing & Grimm. At the time Riga was in Russia, and in 1916 *Dagmar* was requisitioned by the Imperial Russian Navy as a transport in the Baltic. Following the Bolshevik revolution in 1917, she was renamed *Sotsialist*, but by 1920 she had reverted to *Dagmar* and was again owned in Riga, now part of independent Latvia. Sale to Finland in 1935 saw her retain the name, which was kept through several changes of owning company and manager. When photographed she was owned by Fraenk Lundqvist of Mariehamn.

Both *Wanda* and *Dagmar* clearly have poop decks, although their entries in *Lloyd's Register* indicate that they have only forecastles, quarterdecks and bridge decks.

In 1902 Helsingørs Jernskibs & Maskinbyggeri built the 2,260-grt Marie for A Andersson, a Swedish owner based just across The Sound at Helsingborg. Once again classed by Lloyd's Register, her hull had a combined quarter deck and bridge deck with a short forecastle and no poop. At 302 ft, she was quite capable of ocean voyages, although when photographed as Atos* in the 1930s she was trading more locally and is seen bringing baled wood pulp to Preston. Owner by now was O A Börjesson, of Helsingborg. The name Atos was taken in 1924, following a period working as Uppland from 1917 for Axel Broström of Gothenburg.

Atos was torpedoed by U 57 and sunk in the North Sea during August 1940 while on voyage from Glasgow to Petsamo with general cargo. Her neutrality had not saved her, as trading with Great Britain made her a legitimate target for the German submarine.

Although some Danish yards continued to build 'traditional' steamers not unlike Marie well into the 1920s, the country also produced the world's first successful ocean-going motor ships in this period, and Danish

influence on the design of tramps will become much more apparent in later chapters. (Harry Stewart/J and M Clarkson)

A slightly later and more sophisticated product of Helsingørs Jernskibs & Maskinbyggeri, the 292-ft Boscia was built in 1906 for a Copenhagen owner, who unfortunately went bankrupt, so that his ship was taken over by a bank in 1910 and renamed Ørkild. But despite this inauspicious start she was have a long and successful life.

The name Najaden* was adopted in 1928 when she moved to her fourth Danish owner, a company managed by the enormously successful J Lauritzen, later known for his polar vessels, reefers and bulkers. Lauritzen sold her to Finland in 1939, and this might have contributed to her long survival, because the Finns successfully kept many older ships in commission during what for them were the very lean post-war years. When photographed, Najaden, as she remained, was owned by O/Y Finska Ångfartygs of Helsinki, who fitted its trademark cowl-topped funnel as seen in this photograph. It probably also modernised her bridge and fitted a closed wheelhouse, although she retained her Helsingør-built triple-expansion engine. Her awning deck suited her to the owner's general cargo services, although her almost invariable outward cargo from Finland would be pulp or paper products.

Her end came following grounding on the Finnish coast in January 1960 while on voyage from Helsinki to Ellesmere Port. Although refloated and returned to Helsinki, she was beyond economical repair and was sold to local shipbreakers.

Three islands from France

Photographed in the English Channel in the 1950s, *Cor Jesu** was another survivor from before the First World War. As *L'Erdre* she had been completed in 1908 by Ateliers et Chantiers de la Loire, Nantes, for the local Compagnie Nantaise de Navigation à Vapeur. The 376-ft, single-deck steamer (her hull builder also provided her engine) was of the three-island design with bunker hatch on the bridge deck, an arrangement which was also very popular in the United Kingdom.

The name *Cor Jesu* came in 1925 when Genoa owners bought her. As an Italian cargo ship during the Second World War, she was a target for Allied attacks, and was bombed and sunk during June 1943 in the Golfo di Aranci. After the war she was refloated, repaired and returned to service, probably gaining the enclosed wheelhouse seen in this aerial view. It is also likely she was converted to oil firing at this time, because the derricks which would have served the bunker hatch have gone.

A more radical change came in 1957 when an eight-cylinder Nordberg diesel was fitted, extending her life by another fifteen years. At the very respectable age of sixty-four she was broken up during 1972 at La Spezia.

From a different French yard, but to a similar three-island design, was *Loiret*. The builder of the hull and engine was Forges et Chantiers de la Méditerranée, Le Havre, also in 1908, although she was somewhat smaller than *L'Erdre*, at 300 ft in length. Her owner, Compagnie de Navigation d'Orbigny of Paris, sold her in 1912 to Norway, where she had a succession of names: *Evanger* (for Westfal-Larsen of Bergen), then briefly *Tosca*. In 1916 she became *Braa**, under which name she was photographed at Preston in 1930 under the ownership of Nilssen & Sønner of Oslo.

She took her final name, *Varangnes*, in 1939, but did not retain it long. She came under German control when Norway was occupied, and in March 1941 was in a convoy off Esbjerg carrying a cargo of iron ore from Finneid in the north of Norway to Hamburg when she sank after colliding with a German vessel identified as *V 1106*. (J and M Clarkson)

German variety

Although small at just 225 ft, *Hammonia** is a fine example of an early, single-deck cargo ship produced in a German yard. She was completed of iron in 1882 as *Mathilde* for A C de Freitas & Co, Hamburg by Germania Werft, Kiel and given a two-cylinder compound engine by Märkische AG of Berlin. As with so many contemporary British ships, the hull arrangement of forecastle with a combined bridge and quarter deck was adopted.

The name *Hammonia* – still carried when seen visiting Preston around 1930 – came in 1910 when she was transferred to owners in Danzig, and this may have saved her from confiscation as reparations by the Allies, because Danzig was not part of Germany under the Treaty of Versailles. The cabs at either end of her bridge wings were probably a recent addition.

In 1931 she was sold to Italy, and changed names several times, first to *Alba*, then *Naty* and finally *Avionia*. She caught fire on 26 June 1942, while discharging drums of petrol at Heraklion, was towed out of port, shelled and sunk. *(J and M Clarkson)*

Part-awning-deck steamers very similar to those from UK yards were also built in Germany. Although considerably modernised in this photograph, the 302-ft *Olivia** has the typical appearance of this type, with a long awning deck forward merging into her quarterdeck with a short well before her poop.

She began life in 1900 at the busy and successful yard of AG 'Neptun' at Rostock, which also provided her engine, and completed her for Rabien & Stadtlander of Geestemünde as *Westfalen*.

Westfalen had the misfortune to be at Petrograd on 1 August 1914 and was captured, soon entering service for the Imperial Russian Navy as the transport *Zemlya*.

Although her owners recovered her after the war, as a result of the demands of the Allies for reparations she was delivered to the United Kingdom in 1920, and quickly sold back to Germany as *Spessart*.

She was bought by Finnish owners in 1932, initially becoming *Kemi* until sold to Gustav Eriksson as *Olivia* in 1941. Again she was in the wrong place – Boston – at the wrong time – December 1941. Finland being nominally allied to Germany made her enemy property, and she was requisitioned and renamed *Isolator*, and was not returned to Eriksson until 1947. Resuming the name *Olivia*, she lasted until breakers at Rosyth began to cut her up early in 1957.

The introduction to this book noted that not all ships built to carry bulk cargo were necessarily tramps, and *Drottning Sophia** is an early example of such an exception. Her owner, Axel Johnson of Stockholm, had won a contract in 1896 to ship 80,000 tons of Swedish iron ore to Rotterdam annually, and he ordered special ships to achieve this, including three from Howaldtswerke in Kiel. The second of these emerged in 1901 as *Drottning Sophia*. She was given a trunk deck, probably to assist in trimming the ore cargo, but possibly also to add strength, because at 407 ft she was exceptionally long for a single-decked ship of the period. However, it is very unlikely any royalties were paid to Ropner for the use of its trunk deck design.

After the First World War, *Drottning Sophia* was sold to German owners, first as *Heinrich Hugo Stinnes 7*, and later as *Emsland*. She was sunk by British aircraft off Stadlandet, Norway in January 1944.

The photograph of *Drottning Sophia*, beneath the ore unloading gantries at Rotterdam, also shows one of the impressively large inland craft that would take her cargo up the River Rhine to German steelworks. *(Martin Lindenborn)*

The 291-ft *Oituz** not only provides an example of a German-built shelter-decker that ended up carrying bulk cargoes such as timber, but also was highly unusual in having been torpedoed and sunk twice by submarines of opposing navies, and raised on both occasions.

The Rostock yard of AG 'Neptun' completed her as *Hornsund* in May 1906 for H C Horn of Lübeck. In 1911 she was sold to Deutsche Levante Linie as *Leros*, and found herself at Constantinople when the First World War broke out. In a legendary and daring exploit, the British submarine *E-11* penetrated Turkish waters in December 1915, and sank *Leros* at Haydarpasa.

At some point she was salved, and by 1919 found herself with the Romanian State Maritime Service as *Oituz*, as seen arriving at Preston with a cargo of deals. In 1943 she came into German hands and was used by the Kriegsmarine as a transport. But as the fortunes of war swung away from Germany, she was captured by the Soviets in August 1944, and at the end of that month was torpedoed and sunk in Constantza harbour by the German submarine *U 23*. Raised again, she was then used as a floating warehouse until withdrawn and broken up in the 1950s. (*J and M Clarkson*)

The 307-ft *Clara Blumenfeld** was a single-deck steamer with a short bridge deck, plus a forecastle and poop, the latter barely visible. Completed and engined in 1908 by Bremer Vulkan, Vegesack for Bernard Blumenfeld of Hamburg, she has several details of interest. The lower crosstrees on both masts are features usually associated with the coal trade, although the separate topmasts,

which overlap the lower part of the mast, are unusual.

Inevitably for a major German ship, she was confiscated in 1919, and handed over to Belgium, where she was later renamed *Borinage*. In 1930, she passed to Estonian owners as *Sulev*, but was evidently in British-controlled waters when the Soviet Union annexed Estonia in 1940, because she passed into the hands of the

British Ministry of Shipping. It retained her until 1950 when, as *Pacora*, she was put under the Panamanian flag. Her beneficial owners, domiciled in Stockholm, were Estonian exiles and the former principals of a Tallinn shipowning concern. *Pacora* was broken up in Milford Haven during 1954. (*Schiffsfoto Jansen*)

Dutch-built

The paucity of photographs of Dutch-built tramps in the period up to 1914 strongly suggests that local owners interested in deep-sea shipping preferred investment in liner traders. The example shown here was built and engined in 1912 by Rotterdam Droogdok Maatschappij for Van Nievelt, Goudriaan & Co, also of Rotterdam. She was originally named *Alcor*, her owner liking names of stars.

On 31 July 1914, *Alcor* was on voyage from Rotterdam to Kronstadt with a coal cargo when intercepted by Russian torpedo boats and ordered to Hangö, where she was sunk in the harbour entrance as a block ship. The legality of the action against a neutral ship was highly questionable, although her later sale to Finland suggests that Russia had perhaps settled with her Dutch owner. Refloated in November 1918, she then enjoyed a lengthy spell under the ownership of J W Paulin of Viborg as *Imatra**. Only in 1955 was she sold to further Finnish owners, first reverting to *Alcor* and finally *Sonja*, before going to breakers at Grays, Essex in 1960.

The 342-ft *Imatra* again demonstrates the popularity of the elongated bridge deck (hers was 100 ft long) with the bunker hatch abaft of the bridge structure, a structure which had been considerably extended in Finnish ownership.

The outbreak of the First World War effectively stopped non-British owners ordering from UK yards for the duration of the conflict. With few other options, and the prospect of sky-high freight rates, they turned to their national yards, which previously had struggled to compete on price with British builders. *Rozenburg** was completed by NV Werf vorheen Rijkee & Co, Rotterdam for NV Halcyon-Lijn, also of Rotterdam, in September 1918, in time to profit from the boom that continued until the early 1920s. She was a small, three-island tramp, just 293 ft in length. Her triple-expansion engine was also built in the Netherlands, by Werkspoor of Amsterdam.

Rozenburg came under Allied control during the Second World War. Close proximity in convoys, lack of navigation lights and the extinguishing of lights on shore added to the hazards of enemy action. *Rozenburg* sank following collision with another Dutch vessel, the motor tanker *Murena*, near Halifax in August 1941. She was on voyage from the Tyne to the Caribbean with a cargo of coal.

Norwegian misadventure

Norwegian shipbuilders were some way behind Norwegian owners when it came to tramps, and those they built before the First World War were mostly small. The 277-ft Ærø was at the top end of the scale, but was not a fortunate venture for the yard that began her, Sørlandets Skibsbyggeri at Fevig, and which failed before she was completed in 1912. She was finished by Fredriksstad Mekaniske Verksted, which was an outstandingly successful Norwegian yard, to the extent of having a distinct type of timber carrier named after it. Ærø conforms to this type, with three islands (only just visible as her bulwarks are particularly tall) with masts and kingposts arranged at the extremities of its decks.

In 1915 she was sold to owners in Christiania, later renamed Oslo, and became Asturias*, a name which was to serve her for over forty years. This name survived a sale to Finland, under whose flag she was photographed in London's Surrey Commercial Docks on Christmas Eve, 1953. She had only a few more years of life left, and in March 1957 she sank after colliding with another Finnish steamer in fog while entering the Baltic when on voyage from Lisbon to Oxelösund with a cargo of scrap iron.

Southern Europeans

Italian builders were not slow to adopt innovations from elsewhere, and in November 1901 Cantiere Navale di Muggiano delivered this awning-decked steamer as *Il Piemonte*. Although built in La Spezia, British engine builders were still the first choice, and a triple-expansion engine was supplied by Richardsons, Westgarth & Co Ltd from Hartlepool. The awning deck ran the entire length of her hull, giving her a flush-decked appearance.

Il Piemonte remained in Genoese registration for her entire life. For a year's charter in 1908 she was renamed *Presidente P Montt*, and after sale to others in Genoa in 1917, became *San Rossore*. The 389-ft steamer is seen relatively late in her career, under the name *Emilia Pellegrina**, which was carried during 1925–28 when owned by Società Anonima Finanzaria Camogli. Just one final name, *Janua*, was bestowed on her before she was broken up at Savona in 1931.

As was the case in other countries, the First World War stimulated yards in Spain to help meet the demand for ships. In 1917, the Bilbao yard of Astilleros del Nervion completed *Mar Rojo*, destined for ownership by Compania Maritima del Nervion, also of Bilbao. She was a 336-ft three-island type, with just one strength deck. Main machinery was purchased in the United Kingdom, a triple-expansion set made by J G Kincaid & Co Ltd at Greenock, giving a service speed recorded as a modest 8 knots.

Like many Spanish ships, she remained with the same owner for many years, her work interrupted only by the Spanish Civil War, which saw her laid up at Hartlepool from July 1937 to March 1939. Very near the end of her career in 1961 came the one change of ownership, followed the next year by renaming *Bicaba*, still registered in Bilbao. But the writing must have been on the wall for the ageing steamer, notwithstanding her conversion to oil firing, and she was sold to shipbreakers at Valencia in 1965.

6

First World War Standards

The First World War was ultimately to have a profound and not always beneficial effect on the shipping industry, not least on British participation in tramp shipping and building.

The immediate effect of the war was to emphasise how vitally important merchant shipping was to Great Britain. This was not only in terms of moving armies and war materiel but also in importing the raw materials needed for the war industries, for feeding the nation, and supplying its massive military forces overseas.

Historically, commerce raiding had been a regular feature of warfare. But in this conflict it became a major strategy, facilitated by the submarine and Germany's ability to build and deploy this radically new weapon in significant numbers, and the British Admiralty's inability to effectively counter it.

Several years into the war, the British government was finally convinced of the importance of merchant shipping, and accepted that – rather than build even more warships – victory and even survival depended on a massive construction programme of merchant vessels. As the projected needs were beyond the capacity of the British shipbuilding industry, itself undisputedly the world's largest, the government turned to the Empire and, even more so, to neutral countries. Orders placed in the United States and Japan, in particular, did much to, respectively, re-establish and actually encourage ship building in these nations, with profound long-term consequences.

However, despite massive building of tramp-type tonnage, there was relatively little innovation in ship design, although there certainly was in terms of ship construction, with prefabrication introduced in both the UK and the United States. If anything, the need to build ships rapidly and in industrial quantities resulted in a reduction in the variety of designs built, with three-island types of various sizes predominating.

Economic warfare, including the highly effective blockade of Germany by Great Britain, had major effects on shipbuilding in Europe. For Germany there was little point in building ocean-going ships, because they dared not venture beyond the Baltic. But for the neutral countries of Europe, the Netherlands and those of Scandinavia, the war presented exciting opportunities for their ships to earn money, although at very considerable risk from mines, torpedoes, shells and the tendency of the British to invoke archaic laws in order to requisition foreign ships. Inevitably, with a strong demand from owners that British yards were not allowed to meet, shipbuilding in these countries, and especially the Netherlands, enjoyed a strong stimulus. In the long term, this also helped erode British dominance of the industry.

The chapter begins by examining the standard ship types built in British yards, concentrating on the single-deck vessels most suitable for bulk cargoes and which in the main gravitated to tramp owners following the war. It then moves on to the British orders placed in the United States – where the ships were denied to Britain once this country joined the conflict – Canada, and in the Far East. The story is taken beyond the British orders to examine the later ships built for the governments of the United States and Canada.

Note: An asterisk in a caption indicates the vessel shown in the photograph.

British A type

To replace the increasingly devastating losses to mines and torpedoes, the principle of building standard ships was accepted in December 1916, and a variety of designs from various builders were finalised in order to maximise the capacity of British yards. The first and most numerous to be built were the 412-ft A and B types, of similar dimensions and external appearance, but the former a single-decker and the latter having two decks. Thirty-nine shipbuilders turned out A and B types, many building vessels of both classes,

which was somewhat contrary to the principle of standardisation and its advantages of streamlining production.

The lead yard for the A and B types was D & W Henderson & Co Ltd, Meadowside, Glasgow, which completed six As and three Bs. All but two were delivered too late to see wartime service, and indeed *War Lilac* was launched as this in July 1919 but never carried the name in service because she was completed for Hain Steamship Co Ltd as *Trecarrell**. She was one of

five Henderson-built A-types bought by this company, as well as several As and Bs from other builders.

Casualties among the many surviving First World War-built ships were particularly heavy during the Second World War. *Trecarrell* – still with Hain, although now part of the P&O group – was torpedoed by *U 101* west of Cape Race in June 1941 while on a ballast voyage from Hull to the St Lawrence. Four of her crew of forty-three were lost. (*J and M Clarkson*)

Although the three-island hull design of the A type was hardly original, this and other First World War standards did see some moderately novel features. In this photograph of *King Alfred** at Cape Town, clearly visible are her lattice derricks, a feature that would save weight and steel. She was launched in June 1919 by William Doxford & Sons Ltd at Sunderland as *War Azalea*, but completed for King Line Ltd in September.

King Alfred also demonstrates that individual builders were allowed considerable latitude in details of design. Note, for instance, that the hances –where the bulwarks dip at the ends of forecastle, bridge and poop decks – are straight rather than curved as in *Trecarrell*. In addition, the crosstrees are lower, and stanchions support the bridge deck rather than this area being plated in. The latter was unusual, even among the A types built by Doxford.

King Alfred was another Second World War loss, torpedoed by *U 52* in the North Atlantic while on voyage from Halifax to Liverpool in August 1940. She broke in two and the bow section sank, but the stern remained afloat only to be sunk by gunfire from escorting warships. (*Ships in Focus*)

British C and D types

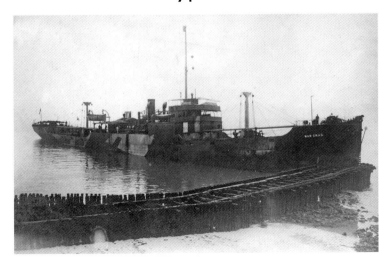

To use the building capacity of yards with berths too short for the A and B types, the C type was developed by the Tyne Iron Shipbuilding Co Ltd at Willington Quay-on-Tyne. Of 342 ft overall, it was intended for bulk cargoes such as ore and coal, and was of the single-deck design favoured by most tramp owners.

War Crag* was delivered to the British government's Shipping Controller by William Gray & Co Ltd, West Hartlepool during August 1918, in time to see brief war service. When completed she was dazzle-painted in an effort to confuse U-boat commanders as to her outline, range and speed.

War Crag was sold and at the end of 1919 new owner T G Berg of Cardiff expended little effort in renaming her Wye Crag* (second photo). There also seems to have been

little expenditure on paint, and in the second view she appears to be in almost uniform grey, relieved only by extensive areas of rust. Neither has she been much modified, because she retains the tall signal mast on her bridge and as yet has no topmasts. Registered in the name of Wye Shipping Co Ltd, Wye Crag was the last ship in the small Berg fleet, which had originated in 1915 and did not survive the recession that quickly followed the war. In 1924, she began a string of further renamings, first to Orbe, then Margari and finally Redstone. By 1940, she was obviously in poor condition because, despite Britain's desperate need for ships, she was bought by the Admiralty and sunk in May to block one of the entrances to the Home Fleet's base at Scapa Flow. This was not quite the end of her story, because the hulk was raised in 1948 and broken up at Cairnryan.

Many British war-built standard ships, particularly the smaller models, were either sold to or ended up with foreign companies. What was to become one of the most famous of these was War Highway, completed by John Blumer & Co Ltd at Sunderland in May 1918. She was sold in 1919, going to Hartlepool owners first as Seatonia and later as Bracondale, before passing to the Soviet Union in 1934 as Beresina.

In 1959, when she was already forty-years old, she was transferred to Romania's Navrom, which modified her name slightly to Berezina. She was rebuilt, emerging in 1962 as Eforie*, still with her original hull lines and counter stern, but with a new superstructure. Her original triple-expansion engine, supplied by J Dickinson & Sons Ltd of Sunderland, by now had been converted from coal to oil burning. Eforie certainly visited the United Kingdom,

contributing to her fame as one, if not the, last First World War-built ship still in active service. She is recorded as broken up at Constantza in 1978, but she seems to have been simply stripped of anything reusable and left to slowly rust away on the banks of the Danube near the port of Braila. (Michael Cassar)

Existing yards could not cope with the demand for replacement ships, and as a result several new shipbuilding companies were set up during the First World War. Some were disasters, but one of the most successful was Burntisland Shipbuilding Co Ltd, who began to lay out a new yard on the Firth of Forth in May 1918. By August 1918, its first four berths were ready, and on three of these were laid the keels for vessels of a modified C type.

War Brosna was the first to be launched, in June 1919,

and the delay was largely attributed to the lateness of delivery of essential plant, although, with a national shortage of skilled shipyard workers, the new yard needed to train its workforce. The photograph shows her running trials during October 1919, completed as *Sunbank** for Sun Shipping Co Ltd, and managed by Mitchell, Cotts & Co, London. Her engines came from the Kirkcaldy works of Douglas & Grant Ltd and drove her at 12 knots.

Sunbank was sold in 1928 to Japan, which was busy

building up a merchant fleet in line with the country's industrial and imperial aims. Renamed *Daishu Maru*, she shared the fate of so many Japanese vessels during the Second World War, and was sunk during the US submarine campaign which, unlike that waged by Germany, made a significant contribution to winning the war. The boat responsible for her torpedoing was USS *Seahorse*, which sank her on 22 November 1943 approximately 50 miles north of the Goto Islands.

The 298-ft D type was designed by S P Austin & Son Ltd to suit even shorter building berths than could accommodate the Cs. These were essentially large colliers, a type in which the Sunderland-based designers specialised, and those that remained in British hands after sale by the Shipping Controller were used mainly in the coal trade from the Tyne and Wear to the Thames.

War Dart was completed and engined by Caledon

Shipbuilding & Engineering Co Ltd at Dundee in December 1918 for the Shipping Controller. In 1919, she and her Dundee-built sister *War Dagger* were bought by Cory Colliers Ltd of London to become *Corstar** and *Corwen*, respectively. Any derricks that were initially fitted were removed because these were not essential and would merely add to maintenance work, because loading and discharging of coal cargoes would inevitably have

been done by shore-side equipment.

After plodding up and down the east coast, and surviving a further war, in which colliers were in the front line, *Corstar* was sold to Turkish owners as *Nefiye* in 1952. She is most likely to have continued moving coal, but now from Zonguldak on the Turkish Black Sea coast to Istanbul. *Nefiye* was broken up at La Spezia, Italy in 1961.

British H type

The H type was the last design of conventionally-built war standards and, like the E type, the drawings were made by S P Austin & Son. A size larger at 313 ft overall, the Es were also to a single-deck design. Despite Austin's input into design, this builder produced just two, both with a very non-standard long bridge deck.

War Orange was built and engined by Dunlop, Bremner & Co Ltd and, despite being the first of the four this Port Glasgow yard launched, was not completed until August 1919. By then she had been sold as *Backworth** to a company managed by R S Dalgliesh & Co of Newcastle, which took not only the four from Dunlop, Bremner but also a further hull from Ardrossan Dockyard Co Ltd.

Backworth's career was long and not without drama. Sold to Cardiff owners as *Ogmore Castle* in 1939, she went out to South Africa in 1946, initially as *Bokkeveld*. She traded as far as Matadi in the Belgian Congo, but is reported to have struggled to get up the Congo River

because of the limited power of her triple-expansion engine. After her owner's company collapsed in 1951, she passed to another short-lived outfit, which renamed her *Roodewal*. Her final owner from 1954 was an eccentric

South African senator who refused to pay harbour dues while his underused ships rusted away in Cape Town. The derelict *Roodewal* was burnt out there in September 1961, and her remains sold for scrap.

Of the eight yards that built the H type, only William Gray & Co Ltd succeeded in getting vessels into service before November 1918. The tardiest builder was Monmouth Shipbuilding Co of Chepstow, whose first hull did not reach the water until March 1920, while its third became the last H type completed anywhere, not entering service until November 1920 as *War Fig*. She was one of last standard ships to remain with the Shipping Controller, the registered owner for the majority of British war-built ships. Her slow sale might well have been due to the steam turbines fitted to the three Chepstow-built Hs, because this machinery was almost unheard of for small, single-deck tramps such as *War Fig*. She was, however, sold in 1921 to Watkin James Williams of Cardiff, but service with him was cut short because she sustained severe grounding damage near

Antwerp in December 1921.

Following repairs, a buyer was found in 1922, when she became the Cardiff-owned *Silverway* and three years later she moved to another Cardiff company, Charter Shipping Co Ltd, managed by Lewis and Grove Williams, as *Charterhague**. In 1929 the firm fitted a conventional triple-expansion engine, which gave her an unimpressive 8.5 knots, down from the 10 knots that she had achieved on trials in 1920. She was quickly sold to H Lundqvist of Mariehamn, who saw no need to rename her, and she was in his ownership when photographed leaving Liverpool. The year 1939 saw her sold to other Finns as *Jäämeri*, but she was a victim of war in the Baltic. She was mined and sunk on 26 April 1944 off northern Germany while on voyage from Bremen to Danzig. (*J and M Clarkson*)

The prefabricated N type

The most interesting, if also the most ugly, First World War standard ship produced in Britain was the prefabricated N type, the N standing for 'National'. The idea was that inland engineering works, which built structures such as bridges and thus had little of their normal work during wartime, would produce parts that were sent to shipyards for erection. To simplify construction, the design was very much based on straight lines and most plates were flat, even the stern appearing to be cut off, as in this photograph of *King Bleddyn** at Cape Town. The vessel's entry in *Lloyd's Register* describes this transom as a 'cruiser stern'.

Designed at Harland & Wolff, Belfast, the 425-ft N type steamers were shelter-deckers. Several of those erected at Belfast served as cargo liners in the fleet of Elder Dempster, but many – and eventually most of the Elder Dempster ships – gravitated to tramping. *King Bleddyn*, which was completed as *War Music* in December 1918, was the sole N type in the fleet of King Line, bought in 1920 after she had been briefly owned by Glen Line Ltd as *Glenspey*.

The Ns were not generally long lived, but sold to Netherlands in 1937 as *Stad Maassluis* and post-war to Italy as *Francescu*, this Harland & Wolff-built and engined example lasted until April 1954, when she stranded and broke in two in the River Schelde while inward bound from Bona for Antwerp with iron ore.

*Essex Lance** was photographed while anchored in the River Plate off Montevideo in 1932, undoubtedly waiting to load a grain cargo for Europe. The 'coal out, grain home' pattern of trade was one of the mainstays of firms such as Meldrum & Swinson, which managed *Essex Lance* on behalf of Essex Line Ltd. The failure of the South American grain harvest in 1934 was a particularly hard blow to the tramping industry, already hit by the worldwide depression.

In October 1918, the ship had been completed and engined by Sir W G Armstrong, Whitworth & Co Ltd as *War Courage*. She was bought a year later by Glen Line Ltd, which paid £250,991 for her. It is an indication of how inflated were ship values in the wake of the First World War that, nine years later, *Glensanda* as she had become, passed to Meldrum & Swinson for just £35,000.

Not all Ns made it into the Second World War, because several were scrapped in the 1930s. *Essex Lance* survived only to succumb to a torpedo from *U 426* in the North Atlantic during September 1942. Old and slow, she was a straggler from a Milford Haven to Halifax convoy, laden with 4,000 tons of anthracite. Fortunately, her crew of forty-four and eight gunners were rescued.

United States-built Lakes

With British yards unable to build sufficient ships to counter war losses, the British government turned to the United States. Although the country had excelled at building wooden ships in the nineteenth century, its iron and steel shipbuilding industry was eclipsed by that of the United Kingdom. Even before British orders were placed, US shipbuilding capacity had increased as domestic owners and others sought to build ships to fill the gap left by the withdrawal of so many British ships. Scandinavian owners, who would normally have built in Britain, also placed orders in the United States. However, when the United States entered the war in April 1917, the ships under construction were requisitioned, and only one of the many ordered entered service with Britain.

The British government followed the Norwegians in ordering ships from builders on the Great Lakes, and over seventy single-deck steel ships from twenty-one yards were allocated 'War' names. However, with US takeover of the ships in August 1917, these were replaced with 'Lake' names, *War Rifle* ordered from Toledo Shipbuilding Co becoming *Lake Bridge**. She emerged in November 1917 and was later requisitioned for overseas service as a mine carrier for the US Navy. Photographed in July 1920, she later found buyers in San Francisco, who put her into the lumber trade as *Cascade*. In 1940, under the Panamanian flag she went out to Asia, where in August 1941 she was destroyed by fire not far from Calcutta while carrying timber from Rangoon. *(Eric Johnson)*

Several 'Lakes' had their lives significantly extended by conversion to motor vessels. Ordered by the United States Shipping Board and completed in August 1918 by Detroit Shipbuilding Co at Wyandotte, Michigan, *Lake Ormoc** was fitted with a conventional triple-expansion engine manufactured by her builder. In 1925, *Lake Ormoc* was sold to the Ford Motor Co of Detroit, who fitted an oil engine that had been built in the United States to a

Sulzer Brothers' design. The rebuild extended to her superstructure, which was originally little more than a few cabins around the engine casing, and to her funnel. Ford bought several Lake types, but most were scrapped (the steel was used to build cars) or converted to barges. Unusually, too, *Lake Ormoc* kept her name and survived the Second World War.

In 1947 *Lake Ormoc* was sold to Sweden, initially as

Signefjord and later as *Gunny*. The latter name was not changed when she passed to an owner in Naples in 1955, although he replaced her Busch-Sulzer engine with a German unit. In December 1962, *Gunny* sank in the Mediterranean after hitting a reef while on a voyage with phosphates from Casablanca to Venice. *(Both: Eric Johnson)*

Wooden ship

The story of North American shipbuilding at the end of the First World War would not be complete without brief mention of the many wooden hulled steamers constructed. Although less acute in the United States than elsewhere, a shortage of steel and skilled steel shipbuilders, encouraged this folly. With so many steel ships available after the war, the wooden ships' lives were miserably short. For instance, of the two that were actually delivered to British account, one caught fire and burnt out after a year's service, while the other sprang a leak and sank in the North Atlantic having been afloat for just a few months. And as builders of steam vessels had found in the early nineteenth century, wood was too tender a material to construct a hull in which to install heavy steam machinery.

The 265-ft *Adway** was ordered by and delivered to the United States Shipping Board. She was built by Nelson & Kelez Shipbuilding Co at Seattle, where there was plenty of timber available. However, her triple-expansion engine was shipped from Milwaukee where it had been built by Nordberg Manufacturing Co. Completed in June 1919, *Adway* was dismantled towards the end of 1923, because no commercial operator was interested in her. *(Eric Johnson)*

US-built multi-deck ships

The great majority of the larger vessels built during the First World War by US east and west coast shipyards, whether ordered by Britain or the United States, were multi-deck vessels. Some were classed as shelter-deckers, many as two-deck ships, and a few had three decks. This probably reflected the experience and capabilities of shipyards that had built predominantly for domestic US owners, which mostly needed vessels for regular liner services. Although few of the war-built ships that had active lives could be accurately classed as tramps, this massive shipbuilding effort cannot be ignored, so two representative ships are illustrated.

The shelter-decker *Antinous** was completed in July 1920 for the United States Shipping Board by G M Standifer Construction Corporation at Vancouver, a town in Washington state. The 412-ft steamer remained with the Shipping Board until 1931, when sold to Waterman Steamship Corporation of Mobile, in whose colours she was photographed in the

Mersey. A 1919-built General Electric steam turbine replaced her original triple-expansion engine in 1934.

Like so many ships of her time, *Antinous* was eventually torpedoed and sunk, although it took two submarines and several torpedoes to finish the job.

Attacked by *U 515* on 23 September 1942 off Venezuela she was disabled and during rescue attempts the next day *U 512* arrived to finish her off with a further torpedo. She was carrying a typical tramp cargo, bauxite ore, which was loaded at Port of Spain. *(J and M Clarkson)*

When the United States Shipping Board began its own programme of building, it ordered a 424-ft, two-deck, design, to which it allocated a series of 'West' names, because they were contracted to yards on the Pacific coast. A relatively early delivery of what was designated Emergency Fleet Corporation Design Number 1013, but

still just too late to aid the war effort, was *West Kyska** from Northwest Steel Company's yard at Portland, Oregon in November 1918. The class included examples with both triple-expansion and steam turbine machinery, *West Kyska* having direct geared turbines supplied by General Electric Co of Schenectady, New York

Waterman Steamship Corporation purchased her in 1931, using her on routes to Europe, as evidenced by this photograph taken in the Mersey. In 1943, she returned to state ownership, now in the form of the United States War Shipping Administration. She was broken up at Oakland in 1947. *(J and M Clarkson)*

Hog Islander

The US equivalents of the British fabricated N type were the vessels built by the American International Shipbuilding Corporation at Hog Island, Pennsylvania.

The shipyard at Hog Island was completely new, and for this to get underway the first task was to clear a green field, or rather green swamp, site and install a ship assembly plant. This was achieved on a monumental scale with the installation of fifty building ways. Two types of ship were to be built, a 401-ft, two-deck freighter assigned Emergency Fleet Corporation Design Number 1023, and a larger troop transport (448 ft) to Design Number 1024, both sheerless and turbine-driven.

Work began on the site in September 1917 and, remarkably, the first hull was laid down in February 1918. Progress then slowed, and *Quistconck* completed her trials only four days before the Armistice was signed. Like many of the 110 others of the types eventually completed, her employment in the 1920s was patchy, although after sale to Lykes Bros Steamship Co in 1930 it became more regular. Sold in 1940 to a British government again desperate for ships, she became *Empire Falcon*. Her 1946 purchase by tramp operator Rowland & Marwood's Steamship Co Ltd of Whitby as *Barnby** justifies the inclusion of this two-deck, turbine steamer in a book on tramps. From 1952 she carried one more name, *Mariandrea* under the Panamanian flag, until broken up at

Troon in 1953.

The Hog Island affair resulted in 122 ships completed too late for war service at a cost of at least twice that anticipated. However, as an apologist pointed out, in 1917 no-one had a schedule setting out when the war would end.

Canadian deliveries

The Canadian shipbuilding effort during the First World War was impressive, as prior to the conflict the industry was tiny. It was not only the British and Canadian governments that stimulated demand, but also Norwegian, French and Japanese owners who turned to Canada when other options were not open to them. But Britain led, ordering some forty steel ships and – anticipating steel shortages – forty-six of wood. The largest ships built in Canada – ten by J Coughlan & Sons of Vancouver – were two-deck, turbine-driven ships, several of which were bought by cargo liner operators. These builders had previously specialised in structural steel work.

Of the single-deck ships built in Canada for British account, the most numerous were of 261 ft overall, from five different yards with all but two given triple-expansion machinery. *War Isis* was built and engined by Port Arthur Shipbuilding Co Ltd in Ontario, where size was constrained by dimensions of Welland Canal locks. Completed in May 1918, she was sold to France in 1920 as *Claudegallus*. She went to the recently independent Estonia as *Torni* in 1929 and managed to escape German or Soviet requisition during the war, ending up under British control. Now based in Sweden, her former Estonian owners reclaimed her in 1951, putting her under

the Panamanian flag as *Trema* and from 1957 as *Avon**. She was unloading timber in London's Surrey Commercial Docks when photographed. *Avon* was broken up in

Lübeck during 1963; among her group of twenty-four ships, she was survived only by the former *War Leveret*, built at Midland, Ontario and scrapped in 1965.

Ships built in Canada that ended up under British control were to nine different sizes, some groups comprising just one vessel. Not all were ordered by the British government: six moderate-sized, single-deck ships built and given triple-expansion engines by Canadian Vickers Ltd at Montreal originated with orders from Norwegian owner Westfal Larsen & Co A/S. The first two were launched during 1918 as *Porsanger* and *Samnanger*, but were quickly requisitioned by the Shipping Controller and allocated to Furness, Withy & Co Ltd for management. They were delivered to the Bergen company which ordered them only in 1920. Four more followed to the same length of 393 ft, completed with 'War' names, beginning with *War Earl* in August 1918.

Despite her single deck, *War Earl* spent her early career in the liner trade between New York, southern Africa and Buenos Aires. She was bought by Union-Castle Mail Steamship Co Ltd in November 1919 and, although initially renamed *Rosyth Castle*, was transferred to subsidiary company Bullard, King & Co Ltd, which operated a second-line service to South Africa and which renamed her *Umlazi** in 1921. In 1936 she reverted to tramping as *Campden Hill* with a London-Greek owner, but he received a good offer from Japan and she was sold out east in 1937 to become *Hokuju Maru*. She managed the unusual feat for a Japanese merchant ship of surviving the Second World War and lasted until 1966, when she was broken up at Osaka.

A second wave of Canadian ship building followed, because – now the country had a number of functioning shipyards – the Canadian government pursued the aim of amassing its own merchant fleet to carry the country's exports. The largest group, both in size and number, were thirty-two, two-deck ships of 413 ft in length. They began several cargo liner services under the title Canadian Government Merchant Marine, essentially the shipping arm of state-owned Canadian National Railways, which later became Canadian National Steamships. The services were gradually abandoned because they were found to be uncompetitive with existing lines that could offer faster and more economical ships.

*Canadian Scottish** was completed during August 1921 by Prince Rupert Dry Docks & Engineering Co Ltd at Prince Rupert, British Columbia. With her triple-expansion engine driving her at just 11 knots, she was slow for cargo liner services, especially for the lengthy routes of the Montreal Australia New Zealand Line, on which she was at one time employed. When the Canadian government despaired at making these lines competitive, she was sold to Greek owners in 1937 and as *Mount Parnassus* began the tramping for which she was better suited. Two years later she passed to Germany as *Johann Schulte*, but was abandoned on New Year's Day 1940 when she lost her propeller and drifted ashore on the coast of Norway. She was bound for a German port with a cargo of ore from Narvik, something of a come down for a one-time cargo liner.

The sixty-seven steel steamers built with 'Canadian' names were of five classes because, once again, individual yards built to their own capacities and capabilities. *Canadian Voyageur* completed by Canadian Vickers Ltd at Montreal in 1919 was part of a group of eight 334-ft, single-deckers of just over 3,000 grt. She remained with Canadian National Steamships until 1930, when Norwegian owners bought her and renamed her *Thuhaug*. She is seen as *Hallbjørg** following sale to P Kleppe of Oslo in 1936: note his initial 'K' on her funnel. Goalpost masts were not uncommon on ships such as these, which were intended to carry deck cargoes of lumber. *Hallbjørg* was broken up at Bremerhaven in 1954.

With the completion of the last 'Canadian' ship in April 1922, shipbuilding in Canada entered another lengthy period of inactivity, to be ended only by a further world war.

Built in Hong Kong

Two shipyards in Hong Kong and one in Shanghai were given orders for standard ships by the British government. Of the thirteen completed, nine were of the B type, which were also building in Britain, the remaining four of the smaller C type. Only one was actually completed with a 'War' name, all the others were acquired by and completed for Greek owners. However, with the vastly inflated values of ships in 1919, these owners overreached themselves and in a very few years they defaulted on payment and the ships went back on the market, fetching much reduced prices. Several British tramp owners were beneficiaries of these sales, despite the B type being two-deck ships.

The first B type built and engined by the Hong Kong & Whampoa Dock Co Ltd was intended to be named *War Sniper*, but was completed for Greek owners in August 1919 as *Meandros*, although she was quickly renamed *Iolcos*. In 1924, Haldin & Co Ltd of London acquired her for its Court Line Ltd fleet, renaming her *Ilvington Court**. She was torpedoed and sunk by the Italian submarine *Dandolo* in August 1940, while carrying iron ore from Pepel in West Africa to Glasgow. *(Ships in Focus)*

Although not an identifiable part of a standard ship construction programme, *Bur** is included to recognise the contribution of the Shanghai Dock & Engineering Co Ltd. Ordered by Norwegian owners, she was delivered in June 1919 as *Risvær*, and being built in neutral China escaped the attentions of the Allies. The British had ordered three of their somewhat larger C type standard ships from this yard, and these began to follow *Risvær* later in 1919, also fitted with triple-expansion machinery by the builder.

The 279-ft *Risvær* was soon sold to Swedish owners as *Bur*, a name carried when she was photographed at Preston, and which she retained from 1922 until 1946. She was then renamed *Sigyn*, subsequently becoming *Thetis* and *Peleus*, the latter under the Liberian flag but still under Swedish control. She was broken up in Bruges during 1964.

The two Hong Kong and one Chinese yard involved in the standard ship programme did not build on their experience to become major players in post-war shipbuilding. In the case of Hong Kong, it was content to construct and repair local craft, and the Shanghai yard was affected by turmoil in China. Although China has, of course, now become a leading shipbuilding nation, its experience contrasts strongly with that of another Asian nation that built ships during the First World War. *(J and M Clarkson)*

Japanese two-deck ships

Perhaps the greatest beneficiary of the demand for ships during the First World War was Japan. Prior to the war its steel shipbuilding industry was small, with only six yards capable of building vessels of over 1,000 grt; by the war's end this had risen to fifty-seven yards. Even by 1915 the industry had begun building standard ships, many as speculative ventures. The best yards quickly achieved prodigies of production, aided by excellent organisation and a competent workforce.

Some twenty standard ships of at least four types were bought or ordered by the British government. All were multiple deck ships, some two-deckers, others with one or two strength decks plus a shelter deck. Nevertheless, some two-deckers, such as the 462-ft *Honestas**, ended up as tramps.

She was completed at Nagasaki in January 1918 as *War Nymph* by Mitsubishi Zosen Kaisha, which also supplied her coal-burning, triple-expansion machinery. Her initial work featured mainly bulk cargoes, including coal for the Admiralty, wheat from Australia, rice from Burma and nitrates. In 1919, she was bought by Larrinaga Steamship Co Ltd of Liverpool, which renamed her *Pilar de Larrinaga*. She was sold in 1949 to the much-depleted Italian merchant fleet, first as *Delia* and converted to oil

firing. The name *Honestas* was bestowed in 1952 on sale to Genoese owners. Despite needing an expensive rebuild following grounding damage in the Elbe in 1955,

she found a further Italian buyer as *Russula* before she was broken up at La Spezia in 1958.

Despite its own large domestic production, the US government also turned to Japan for ships, giving those bought or ordered in Japan 'Eastern' names as a contrast to its locally-built 'Western' ships. *Eastern King** had been completed in July 1918 as *Yone Maru* by Harima Dockyard Co Ltd with a triple-expansion engine manufactured by Kobe Steel Works Ltd. One of her sisters had been completed a few months earlier for

British account as *War Amazon*, part of the remarkable total of 236 standard ships built in Japan during these years, giving its emerging ship construction industry an excellent fillip. Like many other Japanese-built ships of the period, these 305-ft, three-island steamers were very much based on British prototypes. One of their few distinguishing characteristics was the 'open' crosstrees, also apparent in *Honestas*.

With the United States Shipping Board having many more ships than it knew what to do with when peace had returned, many were only patchily employed, and in 1937 they were no doubt pleased to see her return to Japan, initially simply renamed *Eastern King Maru* but soon becoming *Shozan Maru*. Almost inevitably she was a victim of the hugely destructive US submarine war in the Pacific, torpedoed and sunk in July 1944 north of the Philippines.

7

Enter the Motor Tramp

Undoubtedly the greatest technological change in shipping during the period between the two world wars was the refinement and widespread adoption of the marine diesel engine. After a development period of well over twenty years, by 1939 it at last presented a serious challenge to the steam reciprocating engine for vessels with a modest requirement for speed, although it could not as yet seriously contend with the steam turbine for applications where more power was required, largely in the liner trade and particularly for passenger ships.

British owners were not as reluctant to embrace motor ship technology as is sometimes suggested, and by 1939 diesels were installed in almost 50 per cent of all British ships completed. Perhaps even more surprisingly, the United Kingdom was the world's leading producer of marine diesels during the inter-war period.

It fell to enterprising, or perhaps just highly optimistic, builders and owners to make the initial, expensive, mistakes. Innovative machinery such as the MacLagan or Fullagar engines was quickly shown to be a liability at sea, and the prize in terms of sales went to those who did not sacrifice novelty for reliability. In the UK this was Doxford, in Denmark it was Burmeister & Wain, and their efforts helped ensure that, by the late 1930s, a newly-built tramp was almost as likely to have a diesel as a steam engine.

However, not all British tramping companies eagerly embraced the motor ship, not even those such as Hain, which was backed by the mighty P&O Group. And even those that did, such as Tatem, Sutherland and Court Line, hedged their bets by ordering them in parallel with steamers, as the next chapter will tell.

The author was surprised to find that, despite the fabled conservatism of United Kingdom owners, this chapter has a disproportionate number of motor tramps built to run under the Red Ensign. The received wisdom is that the Scandinavians were eager to escape dependence on British coal as fuel, and the motor ship helped them do it. If so, relatively few tramp owners were among them, and those that did largely ordered shelter-deckers with a view to chartering them to liner companies. Particularly surprising is that few German and Dutch owners ordered motor tramps. Even with the severe economic problems of the 1930s, the British and their ships were still dominant in the tramp business. It would take another war and its aftermath to finally erode this position.

The story of the motor-driven ship designed mainly for bulk carrying begins in 1910 and in this chapter is taken up to 1939.

Note: An asterisk in a caption indicates the vessel shown in the photograph.

Motor vessels for the Lakes

The first large diesel-engined vessels to work in the bulk-carrying trades were built in the United Kingdom to navigate the Welland Canal and work on the Great Lakes.

Photographed during trials on 30 September 1910, *Toiler** (below) was the first large British-built motor ship, and the first with an internal combustion engine to cross the Atlantic. This was an innovation for which builder Swan, Hunter & Wigham Richardson Ltd has not received the credit due to it. Her twin screws were powered by two four-cylinder oil engines by A/B Diesels Motoren, Stockholm, a company better known for its 'Polar' engines.

Swan, Hunter had considerable experience of building for Canadian owners on the Great Lakes and, although completed to its own account, the 248-ft *Toiler* was clearly designed to work through the Welland Canal. Large savings in fuel consumption were expected: 1.75 tons of oil per day compared with eight tons of coal for a steam engine. However, her engines were regarded as a failure and in 1914 she was converted to steam, with a two-cylinder compound engine driving just one screw.

The owner of the vessel from 1913 was James Playfair of Kingston, Ontario and, following three more changes in registered owner, in 1918 she passed to Canada Steamship Lines Ltd, which renamed her *Mapleheath* in 1920. She was fitted with a second triple-expansion engine in 1929, after which she traded until 1960, when the machinery was taken out and she was used as a lighter. The historic ship is reported to have

been donated for use as a maritime museum in Kingston but the project did not come to fruition and her hull was broken up in 1993.

Swan, Hunter continued with innovative vessels for Great Lakes service, the single-screw *Tynemount** (small photo) of 1913 driven by an electric motor with power generated by a pair of four-stroke oil engines manufactured by Mirrlees, Bickerton & Day Ltd. This diesel-electric installation was again considered a failure and the ship, now

renamed *Port Dalhousie*, returned to the Tyne in 1914 to have conventional triple-expansion machinery fitted. She probably never returned to the Great Lakes because she was sunk by *UB 10* in March 1916 south of the Kentish Knock Light Vessel when carrying steel from Middlesbrough to Nantes.

Swan, Hunter's important and innovative development work on diesel vessels was interrupted by the outbreak of war, and its lead was lost to others. *(Ian Rae)*

British and US pioneers

With so much attention focused on *Selandia* as the first ocean-going motor vessel, the British-built *Eavestone** has been largely overlooked. Perhaps this neglect is fortuitous, because she did not cover herself in glory. The 276-ft steamer was completed for Furness, Withy by Sir Raylton Dixon & Co Ltd of Middlesbrough in June 1912, just four months after *Selandia* was delivered in Copenhagen, and a month before the completion of Barclay, Curle's *Jutlandia*, often claimed as the first ocean-going motor ship built in the United Kingdom. *Eavestone*'s engine was a two-stroke, more highly stressed the than four-strokes in the Danish ships, but offering greater power for a given weight of machinery. The design was by Carel Frères of Ghent, which delivered the four cylinders, valves and camshaft to Richardsons, Westgarth & Co Ltd, Middlesbrough, which assembled the engine. The exhaust was led up a narrow pipe that can just be seen amidships.

Almost inevitably with new and untried machinery, *Eavestone* suffered problems and at one time was held up in the Azores awaiting spares. The outbreak of the First World War, with the consequent need for reliable ships, is blamed for the suspension of development work on her

machinery and for a conventional triple-expansion engine made by Richardsons, Westgarth being fitted in 1915.

Even as a steamer, *Eavestone* herself was not

fortunate, and in February 1917 was captured, shelled and sunk by *U 45* west of Fastnet while on voyage from Barry to Gibraltar with a cargo of coal.

With much of Europe at war, development of internal combustion engines for merchant ships was not a high priority for the combatants. However, work proceeded in neutral Denmark, Sweden, Switzerland and the Netherlands, where builders were to reap the rewards of their efforts in post-war years.

During the war, two little-known but sizeable motor vessels were built in the United States. Launched as *Ada* and *Motor I*, they were completed in September and October 1917 by Manitowoc Ship Building & Dry Dock

Co in Wisconsin. Among vessels ordered from Great Lakes yards by Norwegian owners, as discussed in chapter 6, they were quickly requisitioned by the United States Shipping Board. To drive their twin screws, two four-cylinder, two-stroke engines were supplied from Sweden by J & C G Bolinders Co Ltd, one of the most successful early builders of small marine diesels.

The 261-ft *Ada* and *Motor I* never reached their intended Norwegian owners, entering US service as *Lake Oneida* and *Lake Mohonk*. They found commercial buyers

during 1920 and as the clumsily-named *Astmahco IV* and *Astmahco III* were almost immediately re-engined with locally-built diesels. The former *Motor I* became *Ormidale** in 1923 and worked in the gravel trade. Re-engined once again in 1938, she went under the Honduran flag and later the Nicaraguan flag as *Jupiter* and *Bluefields*. The owners seem to have been genuine residents of these countries, whose ensigns became early flags of convenience. *Bluefields* was torpedoed and sunk by *U 576* in July 1942 during a voyage from New York to Havana. (*Eric Johnson*)

Great British failures

Failures among early motor ships such as *Eavestone* discouraged British owners from ordering diesel-driven tramps, and several of those brave enough to try also had disasters. Hitherto successful ship owners of Cardiff, Owen and Watkin Williams had interests in both middle-distance tramping and a Mediterranean service run as the Golden Cross Line. From 1922 the brothers ordered motor vessels for the two arms of their business. The 314-ft shelter-decker *Margretian* was delivered by Charles Hill & Sons Ltd of Bristol in November 1923 with a pair of four-stroke, hot-bulb engines made by William Beardmore & Co Ltd, a highly respected ship building and heavy engineering concern.

Two Tosi diesel engines built by Beardmore under licence were put into the 431-ft, twin-screw *Silurian**,

completed almost a year later by Blythswood Shipbuilding Co Ltd, Glasgow. As a single-deck ship with engines aft and king posts, she was a precursor of the modern bulk carrier. Indeed, she was notable as the largest single-deck motor ship yet built, and also for her all-electric auxiliaries. The photograph (left) shows her in a somewhat distressed condition at Hamburg in November 1925.

Despite Beardmore's reputation, neither of the engines was a success. Breakdowns of *Margretian* disrupted the Golden Cross Line schedule, and having cost her owners a massive £140,000, she was laid up on the mud at Cardiff when just over eighteen months old. In 1928 she was sold to Stewart & Esplen Ltd and renamed *Gresham**. She is seen (right) in Roath Basin, Cardiff in 1937 after her original engines had been replaced by two six-cylinder four

strokes made by Maschinenfabriek Augsburg-Nürnberg. Even with these she was unreliable, her engines failing off Lisbon in August 1936. Later, in 1937, she became the Norwegian *Balla*, whose owners were sufficiently happy with her to give her a third set of diesels in 1948 but this time driving a single screw. As the Mexican *Guadalajara* she soldiered on until broken up in 1967.

The expensive failures of *Margretian* and *Silurian* contributed to the demise of Owen and Watkin Williams as ship owners, and *Silurian* was also quickly sold, becoming *Cynthiana* in 1927. New owners Furness, Withy had some experience with diesels, and the ship motored on, at least until June 1928 when she was wrecked in Panama Bay while carrying timber from Bellingham to Grangemouth. *(National Museum of Wales)*

In 1913 Swan, Hunter & Wigham Richardson Ltd acquired another pioneer shipbuilder in the diesel field, Barclay, Curle & Co Ltd, which brought with it the North British Diesel Engine Works. After the First World War, Swan, Hunter developed its 'Neptune' range of diesels, and the North British Engine Works built a four-stroke, single-acting diesel. With the aim of producing more power, North British looked to the double-acting MacLagan diesel. A radical departure from existing ideas, its pistons were driven up and down a long cylinder by alternating combustions at each end. The pistons were attached through slots in the cylinder linings to connecting rods outside the cylinders that transmitted the reciprocating motion to the crankshaft.

Three ships were fitted with MacLagan diesels; the first was *Swanley*, delivered by Barclay, Curle in June 1924 to a company in which Swan, Hunter had a 50 per cent interest. The 412-ft standard shelter-decker was managed by London tramp operators Harris & Dixon Ltd. The two further MacLagan engines were put into a cargo liner and a tanker.

Plagued by breakdowns of the ships' engines, operators complained so strongly that the builder had to replace them at its own expense, and in 1927 *Swanley* received a Doxford engine licence-built by Barclay, Curle. In 1932, she was renamed *Hoperange** on transfer to

another ship owning subsidiary of Swan, Hunter, and in 1937 was sold to Norway. As *Hird* she was torpedoed in the North Atlantic by *U 65* during September 1940, straggling from convoy HX 72 while on a voyage from Panama City and Mobile to Manchester.

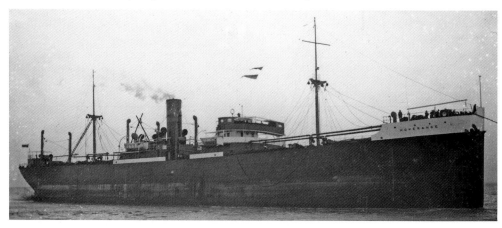

Doxford delivers

The only native, British-designed marine diesel engines to achieve success were those of William Doxford & Sons Ltd. Investing part of the income generated by its successful turret deck vessels (see chapter 4), the company began diesel engine research before the First World War, but only in 1921 did it complete its first motor ship, the Swedish cargo liner *Yngaren*. She was distinguished as the world's first ocean-going motor ship to have a single-screw. Doxford's own engines then went into cargo liners that it built for Furness, Withy and Silver Line. Its first diesel tramp was the 391-ft *Vinemoor*, delivered to William Runciman's Moor Line in September 1924, followed a month later by sister *Westmoor**. The two-stroke engines installed in this pair offered lightness, simplicity and economy compared with the better established four-stroke type, but needed to be more robustly designed and built to offer the reliability needed for marine use. Doxford's success came from achieving this reliability.

The Newcastle-based Runciman sold *Westmoor* in 1947 to London Greeks, who renamed her *Akri Hill*. In 1950 she passed to Italian owners as *Montegiove*, and just one year later she was sold on to a German owner in the process of rebuilding its fleet. The new owner commemorated her original name by calling her *Westsee*. In May 1958 she was delivered to breakers at Bremerhaven, still with her original Doxford three-cylinder engine, which was now thirty-four years old.

The Sperling Group, which had bought the Doxford company from the founding family in 1919, failed in 1924, and after the completion of *Westmoor* the yard remained closed for three years. On reopening, deliveries were split almost equally between diesel- and steam-driven ships, including both dry cargo vessels and tankers. The motor-driven tramps were all for either Runciman's Moor Line or for William Reardon Smith & Sons Ltd of Cardiff.

Sir William Reardon Smith had asked his engineering superintendents to consider the merits of the two leading British diesel engines – those designed and built by Doxford and the Burmeister & Wain type built under licence by Harland & Wolff Ltd. On paper there was little to choose between them, so one ship with each engine type was ordered. The 401-ft *East Lynn** was delivered by Doxford in August 1928 and the similar *West Lynn* by Napier & Miller Ltd with the B & W engine in October. In service, the Doxford engine proved superior, and Reardon Smith took delivery of seven more of the type before 1939.

Both pioneer motor ships were put into a cargo liner service that Reardon Smith instituted to the West Coast of North America, and in recognition of this *East Lynn* was renamed *Santa Clara Valley* in 1931. She was to become a war casualty, bombed and sunk in Nauplia Bay in April 1941 while carrying materiel for the ill-fated defence of Greece. This was not quite her end, because she was refloated in October 1952 and towed to Trieste for scrapping.

British successes

After its disappointments with fitting other makes of diesel engine, Swan, Hunter achieved modest success with its Lenfield*, delivered in December 1924. The 370-ft single-decker was powered by one of the builder's four-cylinder, two-stroke engines, to which it gave the 'Neptune' name from the Wallsend shipyard. As it was still in the hull when the ship met its end sixteen years later,

this must be counted as success but, on the other hand, few further engines of this type were ever built.

Lenfield was operated, not by a company in which Swan, Hunter had equity, but by independent Newcastle-based operator E J Sutton & Co. However, once the market did improve in the late 1930s, Sutton sold her to Norwegian owner Leif Erichsen of Bergen, who renamed

her Lenda in 1937. In Allied service during the Second World War, Lenda was torpedoed, shelled and sunk by U 47 on 27 June 1940, 160 miles south west of Fastnet while on voyage from Halifax, Nova Scotia to Hull with lumber.

Enormous faith was shown in the motor ship, and particularly in Harland & Wolff's licence-built four-stroke diesel, by Bank Line's owner Andrew Weir, by now known as Lord Inverforth. In the early 1920s, he placed orders for no fewer than twenty-four diesel-driven shelter-deckers. The first three had accommodation for thirty-two cabin passengers plus 400 unberthed for a service between Rangoon and South Africa. Bank Line was distinctly unusual in successfully operating both in the

liner and tramp trades, the latter often seeing its vessels heading off from home ports for voyages of up to three years' duration. The remainder of the order was for larger ships without passenger accommodation, suitable for either arm of the owner's trade. Interestingly, Weir's faith in diesel propulsion was not unlimited as he specified twin-screws for the second batch of twenty-one ships.

The 434-ft Comliebank* was the fifth of the second batch, completed in December 1924 by Harland & Wolff's

Glasgow yard (as were the other twenty-three), and is seen here in New Zealand waters during August 1952. In her case and others that survived the Second World War, Weir's faith in the design appears to have been fully justified. Although probably not as economical as the contemporary, two-stroke-diesel-powered Doxford products, Comliebank motored on until March 1959 when, at almost thirty-five-years-old, she took herself off to a Tokyo scrap yard. (World Ship Society New Zealand Branch)

Refreshingly, the motor ship *Oakworth** (left) did not follow the traditional split superstructure design. However, her tall, upright funnel was hardly necessary – it will be seen later in this chapter how Scandinavian designers relegated the exhaust to little more than a stovepipe. Builders for Dalgliesh Steam Shipping Co Ltd of Newcastle in 1925 were Archibald McMillan & Son Ltd of Dumbarton. This yard was managed by Harland &

Wolff Ltd, so it is not surprising that her six-cylinder four-stroke diesel was a Harland & Wolff-built machine. The McMillan yard was one of many to fall victim to the Depression, ceasing to build ships in 1930 and dismantled two years later.

The 404-ft *Oakworth* was sold in 1947 to Valdemar Skogland A/S of Haugesund, Norway, which renamed her *Carrier**. Seen (right) discharging timber in the Surrey

Commercial Docks, London, with her own, comprehensive set of cargo gear, her major modifications since the earlier photograph are an enclosed wheelhouse, faced with wood, and the elimination of the cabs at the extremities of the bridge. The motor ship had a satisfyingly long life, and when broken up at Villanueva y Geltru, Spain in 1967 had been in service for forty-two years. (*J and M Clarkson*)

King Line's first motor ships, *King James* and *King Malcolm* of 1925, are described in chapter 4. These were the last flowering of the Monitor concept, dating from before the First World War. They were followed from Harland & Wolff, Belfast, by nine conventional ships with six-cylinder, Harland & Wolff license-built Bumeister & Wain diesel engines. King Line's founder was one Owen Philipps, who came to prominence, and eventually notoriety, through his control of, and ultimately destruction of, the Royal Mail Group. An early champion of diesel technology,

Philipps' close links with the Belfast builder ensured a competitive price for the nine ships and a loan from the Northern Ireland government to finance them.

*King William** was the last of the batch of nine, delivered in July 1928. With the collapse of the Royal Mail Group and the trial of Philipps (now Lord Kylsant) and his subsequent imprisonment on charges of deceitful accountancy, King Line ordered no further ships until 1941, by when it was under different ownership. Undoubtedly the economy of the motor ships helped

King Line survive, and these proved particularly valuable on longer trades, such as carrying wheat from Australia or the Pacific to north west Europe.

Just like the Bank Line near-contemporary *Comliebank*, the 417-ft *King William* tramped on until reaching a Tokyo scrap berth in 1959. She was one of three of the group that survived the war; the others were *King Neptune* and *King Stephen*, this attrition rate sadly typical of the generation of tramps built between the wars. (*J Y Freeman*)

Doxford 'Economies'

The 1920s and the 1930s were not easy times for Doxford, nor for shipbuilding in general, and the Sunderland yard closed again in March 1931. But this time, managing director J Ramsay Gebbie took the opportunity to get his drawing office to design a ship combining a shelter-deck hull with Doxford's three-cylinder, opposed-piston, two-stroke diesel engine, which offered maximum efficiency. The design became the 'Economy' type. Three years of idleness ended

for the yard when the first ordered, yard number 612, was laid down for Newcastle ship owner Sir Arthur Sutherland, to be completed in January 1935 as *Sutherland*.

The owning company, B J Sutherland & Co Ltd, eventually took six 'Economies', and later bought a seventh. This is the fifth, the 439-ft *Peebles** of 1936. She was sold in 1951 to Australian owners as *Swanstream*, and finished her days in Hong Kong ownership, first as

San Fernando and finally *Phoenician Star*. She was broken up in Hong Kong during 1967.

Orders for Doxford 'Economies' were helped by the British government's 'Scrap and Build' scheme of 1935, which gave owners cheap loans to build new ships if they scrapped old tonnage, even that which they bought abroad simply to break up. Ten 'Economies' were financed in this way. *(Ships in Focus)*

The 'Economy' embraced some novel construction methods, with the hull plates electrically welded, although decks were still riveted. At £100,000 it was not as cheap as a new steam tramp, but offered much lower operating costs because it burned just 6.5 tons of fuel per day at 10 knots. The 'Economy' design successfully rebuilt Doxford's order book, eighteen of the first nineteen hulls taking consecutive yard numbers and a total of thirty eventually built with the three-cylinder engine.

The basic design, exemplified by *Peebles*, was

distinctive if not particularly attractive aesthetically, with its composite superstructure set well aft. The principles of standardisation were not enforced, however, and there were several variations in length and design. The flush-deck arrangement was not adopted for *Lady Glanely**, the only example taken by W J Tatem Ltd and the first motor ship in this important Cardiff-based fleet. *Lady Glanely* had a 43-ft forecastle, and was slightly longer than the standard Economy at 447 ft overall. It seems Tatem was not totally convinced by its first motor ship, and it

continued to order steamers from the Sunderland yard of William Pickersgill & Sons Ltd. Even post-war it hedged its bets with delivery of one more Doxford diesel and one Pickersgill steamer.

Lady Glanely had but a short life. Delivered in May 1938, in December 1940 she was torpedoed and sunk in the North Atlantic by *U 101* while on a voyage from Vancouver to London. No fewer than fourteen of the thirty 'Economies' were lost during the Second World War.

'Improved Economy'

In 1938, Doxford introduced an improved version of the 'Economy', with capacity raised and the three-cylinder engines uprated from 1,800 to 2,500 bhp to improve speed from 10 to 12 knots at the cost of increasing fuel consumption from 6.5 tons to 9.5 tons per day. A retrograde step was the split-superstructure profile, with the third hold positioned between the bridge and the engineers' accommodation. In a coal-burning steamer, such an arrangement ensured the bunkers were close to the boilers, but in a motor ship its sole justification seems to have been that it kept the deck officers and engineers apart. The design appears more dated than its predecessor.

The 'Improved Economies' were even more successful than the originals, with at least eighty-five built and construction extended over the remarkable period

of sixteen years from 1938 to 1954. First was the 448-ft Starstone*, delivered in August 1938 to Alva Steamship Co Ltd of London. The company had an unusual provenance, in that it was founded by Alexandre Vlasov, a Russian émigré, who in 1937 set up Navigation & Coal Trade Co Ltd in London to manage ships under the

British, Greek, Italian and Romanian flags. Starstone survived the war, although bombed and damaged in an attack by German aircraft west of Ireland in October 1940. She was transferred in 1958 to another Vlasov subsidiary, nominally based in Bermuda, and was broken up in Japan during 1963. (Fotoflite incorporating Skyfotos)

Diesels rising

By 1939 the internal combustion engine had almost reached parity with steam machinery in terms of numbers of installations in new British ships. Largely due to Doxford's efforts and example, by the late 1930s the diesel was accepted by many, but by no means all, tramp owners.

Lithgows Ltd, perhaps the Clyde's foremost builder of tramps, completed Darlington Court* in June 1936 for United British Steam Ship Co Ltd and shortly after delivery was transferred to the registered ownership of the restyled company, which was renamed Court Line Ltd (although it never ran liner services). The London company was managed by Haldin & Philipps Ltd. Founder P E Haldin was originally Haldenstein, changing his name in 1915 in the face of anti-German feeling, while L R Philipps was a brother of Owen Philipps of the King Line.

The 431-ft shelter-decker had six-cylinder four-stroke

machinery made by J G Kincaid & Co Ltd of Greenock. Once again, the split superstructure and broad funnel go some way to disguising her nature as a motor ship, while the upright stem is anachronistic for a ship built in 1936.

Darlington Court was yet another war loss, torpedoed and sunk by U 556 in the North Atlantic during May 1941 while on voyage from New York and Halifax to Liverpool with a cargo of wheat below and aircraft on deck.

Apart from Doxford, only a few of the Wearside tramp builders fully embraced the motor vessel in the 1930s, doubtless because those that placed orders preferred steam ships. An isolated example of a motor ship from the yard of William Pickersgill & Sons Ltd was the shelter-decker Hylton*, completed in January 1937. She was managed by W A Souter & Co Ltd of Newcastle and, given that she did not carry one of the company's 'Sheaf' names nor its funnel colours, it is likely that her owner, Hebburn Steamship Co Ltd, was an arms-length venture, largely financed by a loan of over £95,000 under the British government's 'Scrap and Build' scheme. To obtain the loan, the company had to scrap older vessels, and – hardly in the spirit of the legislation – it bought three ageing steamers, two from foreign owners, and had these scrapped, one in Blyth, one in Ireland and one in Germany.

Hylton's machinery was a six-cylinder four-stroke by the Newcastle works of North Eastern Marine

Engineering Co Ltd.

The 445-ft, 11-knot Hylton was torpedoed and sunk by U 48 during March 1941 south of Iceland while in convoy

HX 115 on the final leg of a voyage with timber and wheat from Vancouver to the Tyne. The entire crew of thirty-six – a typical number for a tramp of her day – was rescued.

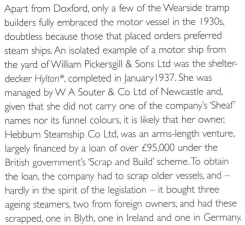

Danish shelter-deckers

To correct any impression this chapter might give that Burmeister & Wain had a monopoly of building motor vessels in Denmark, this is *Nordkap**, completed by A/S Nakskov Skibsværft in November 1930. Nevertheless, she does have Burmeister & Wain engines – two six-cylinder four-strokes driving her twin screws. Her funnel is positioned well back on the engine casing to line up with

the exhausts of these engines. Owner of this 401-ft shelter-decker was D/S Norden A/S, which was managed by P Brown Jr & Co of Copenhagen.

Her career was broadly typical of contemporary motor ships. Sold in 1955 to Basse & Co in Copenhagen as *Elke Basse*, there is photographic evidence of her on a liner company charter, running between South Africa and

Europe. In 1961 she was bought by Navigation Maritime Bulgare, Varna, which gave her the minimalist name *Mir*. Five years later she was scrapped at Split, Yugoslavia, which was almost alone in the European communist bloc in having a thriving shipbreaking industry. *(Fotoflite incorporating Skyfotos)*

Denmark had produced the world's first successful ocean-going motor ship in *Selandia*, completed and engined by Burmeister & Wain in Copenhagen. An awning-deck vessel, she was built for the East Asiatic Company's cargo liner services, and many of the motor ships that followed her also had multiple decks. But undoubtedly some of the Danish-built shelter deck motor ships were intended for tramping. *Skagerak** and *Kattegat*, a 402-ft pair completed for Olaf Ditlev-Simonsen Jr of Oslo in 1936, betray this

with masts and derricks set at the extremities of their hatches, suiting them for carrying deck cargoes of timber. In contrast to many long bridge-deck designs built in Scandinavia, they have just a forecastle. Both ships were fitted by Burmeister & Wain with its own, six-cylinder, double-acting, two-stroke machinery, potentially the most economical type of diesel but also the most complex.

Both ships were in Allied service during the Second World War, but only *Skagerak* came through the war to be

returned to Ditlev-Simonsen service. In 1954 the firm sold her to Finnish owners, who renamed her *J W Paulin* and who would have found work for her in their country's timber trade. Final owners were Greek, renaming her *Sofia T* in 1965 and amending this to *Capetan Andreas T* a year later. The letter 'T' indicates ownership by the Tsourinakis family, who traded as Cretan Shipping Company. She went for scrap at Whampoa, mainland China, in 1970. *(Fotoflite incorporating Skyfotos)*

Burmeister & Wain single-deckers

Most ocean-going motor ships built in Denmark between the two world wars were multi-deck vessels, reflecting the importance of liner services to national owners. Norwegian owners, however, were mostly interested in the tramping business for which single-deck ships had advantages. In October 1929, Boe & Pedersen of Oslo took delivery of the single-deck *Hallingdal* from Burmeister & Wain, who fitted her with one of its well-tried six-cylinder four strokes. Despite this modernity, her 334-ft hull was distinctly anachronistic, with its long bridge deck design that was now obsolescent and a counter stern.

These features did nothing to detract from her longevity. Wartime service she survived in Norway's Hjemmeflåte, under German direction. In 1951 she was sold to John Larsson of Stockholm, who renamed her *Nordanbris**, as seen here at Cape Town during the three years she spent under this name. Her later years were under a variety of Hong Kong owners, at least four of which were under the management of John Manners & Co Ltd as either *North Breeze* or *San Antonio*. Her last name was *Pacifico*, still owned in Hong Kong, which is where she was broken up in 1969. *(Ships in Focus)*

Ownership of *Tureby** leaves little doubt of her owner's trading intentions. Manager A Reimann of Stensbygaard, Denmark registered her in the name of A/S Motortramp: note the letter 'M' on her funnel. She was completed by Burmeister & Wain in January 1936, as the first of a relatively compact, 382-ft design aimed at the tramping market. With her clear deck spaces, and particularly the long hold between bridge and engine room casing, she is reminiscent of *Skagerak* and *Kattegat*, and similarly

configured to carry timber deck cargoes. Unusually for this date, she was fitted with twin screws, each driven by one of her builder's four-cylinder two-strokes. These had been built in 1931, five years prior to the hull: were they experimental engines, which only now were found a use?

Seeking to evade wartime employment by either side, *Tureby* put into Rekjavik on 10 April 1940. But within a month Iceland had been occupied by the British, and *Tureby* fell into its hands, sailing for the Clyde in July. The

Ministry of War Transport then became her formal owners until she was returned to Reimann in 1945.

In 1960 she was sold to owners in Sardinia, who renamed her *Taloro*, within a few years passing to other Italians who renamed her *Silverfir* under the Panamanian flag. Final ownership from 1968 was Greek as *Stella* and as such, still under the Panamanian flag, she arrived at Hamburg for breaking up in August 1969. Her engines were now thirty-eight years old.

Swedish shelter deckers

Like those in Denmark, Swedish shipyards were active before the First World War mainly in building relatively small steamers. And as with their Danish equivalents, the introduction of the motor ship brought a blossoming of deep-sea ship construction. Much of this comprised multi-deck ships intended for the liner trades because Sweden, although without any significant overseas outposts, built up an important network of liner routes. Among these ships are some that spent their lives tramping, including this shelter-decker.

Builder of this 346-ft hull in 1931 was Eriksbergs Mekaniske Verkstads A/B of Gothenburg, which also supplied her six-cylinder four-stroke diesel. The compact superstructure gives her a modern look, which is somewhat belied by her vertical stem. Note too that the funnel is positioned very well aft on the engine casing to suit the location of the exhaust. Among so many Scandinavian ships with forecastles she was unusual in being flush decked.

Built for owners in Slite, Sweden as *Dalhem*, in 1956 she was purchased by a company controlled by O M Thore of Jonstorp – note the letter 'T' visible on her funnel – which renamed her *Mongolia**. The photograph

was taken in the London dock system, probably in the Surrey Commercial Docks where, judging by the upright poles at the edge of her decks, she has just delivered a timber cargo. She was sold on to Greek owners in 1963 as *Ais Georgis* and was broken up in 1973 near Istanbul.

An example of how modern Swedish-built motor ships could look is provided by *Vito** of 1937, although in this post-war view at Cape Town her modernity is exaggerated by the tall radar mast perched on the lip of her funnel. The additional kingposts abaft the superstructure supplementing her already generous outfit of derricks suggests she was built with a view to charters. She is not in the funnel colours of her Oslo owner Olaf Ditlev-Simonsen Jr, indicating that she is working for a liner company, possibly Wilhelmsen if the bands on her

black funnel are indeed light blue.

The arrangement of her 443-ft hull is similar to that of *Mongolia*, although it has an even more compact superstructure. The design was repeated, and in 1942 the builder, A/B Götaverken, launched an externally identical *Viljo*. Alas, as a result of wartime conditions she was not completed until August 1945. No doubt the Ditlev-Simonsen family were delighted to take delivery of her while freight markets were still buoyed up by the post-war shortages of ships. Both near sisters had six-cylinder two-

stroke engines erected by A/B Götaverken, and while those in *Vito* were double-acting, *Vilja*'s were single-acting, the more powerful machinery in *Vito* giving her a speed of 14 knots compared with 12.75 knots for her near sisters.

Returning to *Vito*, her further career involved multiple renamings. An owner in Narvik renamed her *Stella Nova* in 1964. From 1966 she passed through the hands of four Italian owners, all of which registered her in Panama as, in sequence, *Althea*, *Maja*, *Iolanda* and *Coralba*, before sending her to breakers at Split in 1978.

Swedish single decks

Swedish yards also built single-deck motor ships, although the usual recipients were Norwegian owners. In June 1926 A/B Öresundsvarvet at Landskrona delivered the 357-ft *Saga* to H Waage of Oslo. She was built under subcontract from Götaverken at Gothenburg, and fitted with one of the latter's six-cylinder, four-stroke diesels. In 1931, she was sold to A E Reimann of Stensbygaard, Denmark, who was met with earlier managing A/S Motortramp, and was renamed *Lundby** to fit with that company's naming scheme.

Reimann might have instructed his ships to seek neutral ports when Denmark was invaded, because *Lundby* put into New York in April 1940 and was laid up. Lay-up turned to requisition by the US Maritime Commission in July 1941, and a month later she was given the rather ridiculous name *Pink Star* and placed under the Panamanian flag. At this time there were considerable numbers of seamen from occupied Denmark and Norway in United States ports, and strict manning laws meant they could not be allocated to US-flag ships, even in wartime. To get round this, suitable ships were placed under the Panamanian flag. But the career of *Pink Star* was to be woefully short. On what was her initial voyage under this name, from New York to Liverpool, she was torpedoed and sunk by *U 552* on 19 September 1941. (*J and M Clarkson*)

Although delivered in October 1926, just four months after *Saga*, the 395-ft single-decker *Brønnøy** looks decidedly older, with her long bridge deck and the apology for a funnel which Scandinavian builders, especially, fitted to many of their early motor ships. Builders were, once again, Götaverken, and machinery comprised two of the builder's six-cylinder four-strokes driving twin screws. The owner of *Brønnøy* was Gunnar Knudsen of Borgestad, Norway.

Brønnøy survived Allied service during the Second World War and after return to her owners was sold to an Oslo company as *Maur*. It did not keep her long, and she went to help rebuild the Japanese fleet that had been massacred during the Pacific War. As *Yasukawa Maru* she spent several years in Tokyo and later Kobe ownership before being broken up at Yokosuka in March 1962. (*J and M Clarkson*)

Intermediate in design between *Lundby* and *Brønnøy* is this 1930 product of A/B Götaverken, seen in later life as the rather unkempt *Rinoula**. Although not as long as that in *Brønnøy*, her bridge deck begins just ahead of the superstructure and is extended aft to leave just a short well ahead of the poop. What appears to be damage in this region is, in fact, simply dark paint.

The 370-ft motor ship began life as *Elg* and she was delivered to Norwegian owner Thorvald Hansen of Oslo. A single screw ship, in contrast to *Brønnøy*, she made do with one Götaverken-built six-cylinder, four-stroke, which gave the modest speed of 10 knots.

However, this machinery was sufficient to get *Elg* through the war, when she was under British management, and she plodded on for Hansen until 1959. Even at twenty-nine years old she could find a buyer, a Greek company managed by Lemos & Pateras renaming her *Rinoula*. After a satisfyingly long life she was broken up at Bremerhaven in 1967.

Composite superstructure Swedes

The contrast between the earliest Scandinavian motor ships and vessels such as *Aggi** of 1937 is considerable; the latter with her raked stem, counter stern and composite, gently rounded superstructure presaging the post-war tramp. The 454-ft single-decker was a product of A/B Öresundsvarvet, Landskrona, and was propelled by four two-stroke oil engines made by Atlas Diesel of Stockholm, the output of which was geared to a single screw and gave her the impressive speed of 14 knots.

This speed, plus a good outfit of cargo gear including a heavy lift derrick at her foremast, suggests that she was intended for charter to the liner trade. Her original owner was Rederi A/B Pulp, while her original name of *Dagmar Salén* reveals her management by one of Sweden's best known shipping companies, which with reefers and large tankers was eventually to overreach itself.

Dagmar Salén suffered a catastrophic fire in July 1948 off Delaware and although towed into Baltimore was declared a constructive total loss. But the world's need for ships was such that a Norwegian owner bought the motor vessel and put her back into service as *Mosnes*. The name *Aggi* was carried between 1962 and 1969 when owner Trygve Eriksen of Haugesund appears to have kept his ageing ship in immaculate condition. Her final Greek ownership as *Defteron* ended when she was towed into Bilbao on the last day of 1972, to be demolished.

Smaller and slower than *Aggi*, yet with similar machinery, were a pair of motor vessels completed by A/B Lindholmens Varv, Gothenburg, for Erik Brodin of Stockholm: *Astri* of 1937 and *Anita* of 1938. Two Atlas Diesel engines with a total of ten cylinders sufficed to drive them at 12 knots. Constructionally, they were unusual in having a combined forecastle and bridge contributing 191 ft to their overall length of 331 ft: the difference in levels of the forward and aftermost pairs of hatches is apparent in this aerial view.

As sisters sometimes do, in 1952 and 1953 they passed in a joint sale, with new owner E B Aabys Rederi A/S of Oslo renaming them *Pan* and *Peik**. Although they both spent many later years in Finnish ownership, their careers then diverged, and *Peik* first became the German *Vogelsberg* in 1956, then successively *Johanna*, *Saana* and *Haana* (all Finnish), and finally *Ouranoupolis II* (Cyprus flag, Greek owners) before she was broken up in Greece in 1980. The former *Astri* motored on for another four years.

Kockums' contribution

Some Swedish ships of this period combined a state-of-the-art diesel with the anachronistic feature of a counter stern. Completed in May 1938, the shelter-decker *Ivaran* was not even the last with this feature, because Rederi-A/B Nordstjernan (Johnson Line) of Stockholm was taking delivery of cargo liners with such sterns until after the Second World War. *Ivaran*'s machinery made by

Kockums was a five-cylinder, double-acting, two-stroke, a powerful machine which drove her at a creditable 13 knots. Despite this installation, she has a substantial funnel, in a motor ship more important for displaying her owner's colours than providing a draught.

The original owners of the 420-ft *Ivaran* was A/S Ivarans Rederi, managed by S Holter-Sørensen of Oslo,

and she returned to that company after war service for the Allies. In 1955 she was sold to Montan Transport GmbH, managed by Unterweser Reederei AG, of Bremen, in whose colours she was photographed in the Thames Estuary as *Kelkheim**. In 1963 she made her last voyage, out to Hong Kong to be broken up.

Swedish yards having produced some distinctive ships, it is surprising to find Kockums M/V A/B at Malmö turning out a vessel which could be mistaken for a contemporary British split-superstructure tramp. The 410ft shelter-decker *Lidvard* was completed for Klosters Rederi A/S of Oslo in January 1939. Kockum's machinery was the same as that in *Kelkheim*, and indeed there are similarities in

hull design, although *Lidvard* did have a cruiser stern and raked stem.

Lidvard was unfortunate enough to find herself at Dakar in June 1940 when France fell, and the Vichy-sympathising authorities detained her as being in enemy, that is, British, service. However, in what sounds like an interesting adventure, the master and crew slipped her

away from Dakar in July 1941.

She is shown in the Thames as *Brede**, a name carried from 1954 to 1965 while owned by Dagfin Henriksen of Oslo. Her final owner was the Bulgarian state, under several different titles and two names, *Opal* until 1970 and then *Tzanko Tzerkovski* until she was broken up at Split in 1976.

Bremer Vulkan motor ships

Given how impressively Germany rebuilt its merchant fleet after it had been taken by the Allies as reparations following the First World War, it is surprising that little of the new tonnage built was for the deep-sea tramp trades. Effort and money was put into cargo liners for Hapag and Norddeutscher Lloyd, while the tramping and coasting sectors were largely reliant on buying second-hand British steamers or Dutch and Scandinavian motor ships.

Even those ships built in German yards were often for non-German owners, some resulting from the Nazi government's policy of blocking expatriation of profits earned by foreign concerns. A way of releasing this money was to build ships in Germany, and a number of oil companies and others such as Palm Line used this method. It is not known whether A/S Borgestad of Porsgrunn made use of this possibility when having Sønnavind* built at Vegesack in 1935. The 414-ft shelter-decker was driven by a five-cylinder, double-acting, two-stroke diesel made by Bremer Vulkan giving her a respectable speed of 12.5 knots and, notably, she was built with a Maierform bow. In this photograph, when leaving South Africa, she has evidently just discharged a timber cargo.

Escaping German control during the war, Sønnavind gave her owner lengthy service, and only in 1963 did he

sell her. A series of London-based agencies then managed her for a variety of nationals under several flags. First she became Argolis, Greek-owned but Panama-registered. In 1973 she shifted to the then fashionable flag of Somalia and was registered in Mogadiscio as Topaz III. Breakers in mainland China cut her up in 1974.

A near sister of Sønnavind was Anna Odland*, completed by Bremer Vulkan and delivered to J Odland of Haugesund in October 1939, when Germany and Norway were not yet at war. In this photograph, subtle differences to Sønnavind are apparent, especially around the bridge. Whereas Sønnavind has an open bridge with cabs at either end – highly anachronistic for a ship built in

1935 – Anna Odland has a wheelhouse and her superstructure has been redesigned.

Machinery was similar to that of Sønnavind, as was the progression of her career: wartime under Allied direction, and post-war service for her original owner until 1964, by when she had been renamed Prosper.

An owner based in Skudeneshavn then ran her as

Soldrott until 1971, when she was sold out of Norwegian ownership to become Elissavette for a Cypriot-based, Greek-run company. A final Greek owner renamed her Interamity in 1977, but two years later she found herself demolished at Gadani Beach.

Coal ships to cargo liners

A group of six remarkable ships built in Germany in the late 1930s exemplify the difficulties of classifying ships as tramps or cargo liners. All were single-deckers intended for the coal trade, but four of them were placed on a liner service.

They were built between 1935 and 1939 for the Hugo Stinnes Group of Hamburg by Flensburger Schiffsbau-Gesellschaft, Flensburg and named *Clare Hugo Stinnes 1**, *Johannes Molkenbuhr*, *Mathias Stinnes*, *Mulheim-Ruhr**, *Flensburg* and *Welheim*, in order of completion. Their single screws were driven by two eight-cylinder MAN oil engines through single-reduction gearing giving a service speed of 13 knots. Unusually for ships intended as colliers, electric cranes served the four hatches.

Soon after completion the first four were taken up on a charter for the cotton export trade from the US

Gulf to the United Kingdom by the Transocean Coal and Transport Corporation of New York. Under the name Transocean Transport Line, this developed into a fortnightly service to Liverpool, Manchester and London. Comfortable accommodation was offered for a limited number of passengers, five in the first two ships and eight in the next two. Declaration of war in September 1939 brought the service to an abrupt end.

Johannes Molkenbuhr was making a run for home when intercepted on 3 September 1939 off the Orkneys by a British destroyer and scuttled by her crew to avoid capture. *Clare Hugo Stinnes 1* (left hand photograph) was torpedoed by a British submarine off Bjornefjord on 2 May 1940. Salved in 1943, she was attacked by Allied aircraft off Jaeren and sunk in September 1944.

Found intact in Norway at the end of the war,

Mulheim-Ruhr (right hand photograph) was taken over by the Norwegian government in 1946 and renamed *Falkenes*. In 1947 she became *Brynje* and in 1951 hoisted the Danish flag as *Danfjord*, eight years later becoming the Liberian flag *Theologos*. Lebanese flag operators acquired her in 1966, giving her the name *Universal Pride*. In September 1966 fire broke out in her engine room while on passage from Antwerp to Shanghai. She was taken in tow but foundered in the South China Sea on 16 September 1966.

Apart from *Welheim*, sunk off Norway during November 1944, the others survived the war to enter service in Norwegian, Danish and Soviet ownership to end their days, as was intended all along, as tramps. (*Clare Hugo Stinnes 1: J and M Clarkson*)

Dutch-built for charter

Remarkably few examples can be found of the Dutch building tramp-type motor vessels in the interwar period. Indeed, evidence suggests that even the 434-ft shelter-decker *Merwede** was built with the intention of chartering her to liner companies, and photographs of her exist with Palm Line and United Netherlands Navigation funnel colours. The aerial view shows her in the colours of her manager, Vinke & Zonen of Rotterdam.

Her start in life could hardly have been more dramatic. While fitting out at the yard of A Vuijk & Zonen at Capelle a/d Yssel in January 1941 she was seized by the Germans and entered service for them as *Gotha*. This service included a spell as a target for training U-boat crews, but she was later employed as a transport in the Baltic and in this role was damaged by a Soviet submarine in April 1945. This meant that, although returned to her owners in October 1945, *Merwede* could not be put back into service until May 1946.

Her registered owner under the Dutch flag was NV Houtvart, implying an interest in the timber trade. When sold in 1963, she took a series of names under Greek ownership and Panamanian registration which suggested she was still in this business: *Bork Logger*, *Sielt Logger* and *Ivo Logger*. When broken up at Whampoa in 1972 she still had her original six-cylinder, two-stroke built by Gebroeder Stork & Co, of Hengelo.

Red diesels

Soviet shipbuilding in the 1930s produced an odd mix of the modern and traditional. The 1930-built *Friedrich Engels** combines a compact superstructure with enclosed wheelhouse with a rather anachronistic three-island hull with straight stem and counter stern. She was a product of the Severney Ship Building Yard at Leningrad, although her double-acting two-stroke engine came from Maschinenfabriek Augsburg-Nürnberg in Germany. The photograph was taken in July 1932.

In 1950 she was transferred to Romania to help build up this Soviet satellite's depleted merchant fleet, although initially she kept the name. Only in 1962 was she renamed *Mamaia* by NAVROM, the Romanian state shipping organisation. Under this name she worked on the country's shipping services to western Europe, and appearances in Liverpool during the late 1960s showed that she had been superficially modernised, with a 'streamlined' funnel and shorter topmasts, although still recognisable as a veteran. This probably coincided with the replacement of her original engine by a six-cylinder unit made by Sulzer Brothers Ltd at Winterthur,

Switzerland in 1943, although the date of this modification is not known. She is reported to have been scrapped at Sulina in 1991, but presumably she had been

out of service for some time, as by then her hull was over sixty years old. (*F W Hawks*)

From the same Leningrad yard as *Friedrich Engels*, but six years later, *Chelyuskinets** presents a rather different profile and radically altered masting arrangements, although high bulwarks alongside her holds mask the fact that this 381-ft motor ship has a three-island hull. Her rather massive superstructure hints at post-war rebuilding, although register books do not record any change in her original engines, supplied by the 'Russian

Diesel' Engine Works in Leningrad.

She was photographed on the Mersey and, although the date is not recorded, it might be in June 1970 when the author was delighted to see the veteran berthed in his home town of Ellesmere Port, where Soviet ships were regular visitors. It might have been her last voyage, because she was broken up somewhere in the USSR later that year.

Both these Soviet motor ships had two decks, but the nature of state controlled shipping means they were effectively tramping, allocated to whatever service centralised control decided.

CHAPTER

8

Depression and Economy: Steamers 1920–1940

At the end of the First World War, the major concern of most tramp owners was to rebuild their fleets as quickly as possible to take advantage of the high demand for shipping which was a consequence of the crippling losses experienced over the last four years. With freight rates and ship values higher than they had ever been, the need was for more ships, and not for more economic ships, as for several years almost anything which would move cargo could make a profit. The practical motor ship was still just a dream of a few marine engineers, and – apart from some Scandinavians – most owners remained highly suspicious of it for at least the next decade. Their scepticism was fuelled by reports of how often promising new types of diesel engines simply failed to prove reliable in the testing conditions of a ship's engine room. In contrast, the triple-expansion steam engine was utterly reliable, even with the rough handling it sometimes got in tramp steamers.

By the late 1930s, the refusal of many owners to contemplate employing diesels was becoming harder to justify, because reliable machinery certainly was available. It had been proven by shipyards and engineering companies such as Doxford, together with owners such as Reardon Smith, which were looking for ways to survive the unprecedented depression that set in during the 1920s and continued more or less up until the next world war. True, the first cost of a motor ship was somewhat higher than that of a steamer, but its running costs calculated over its expected lifetime were much lower. Owners that continued to build steamers had many excuses: the price of oil was more volatile than that of coal and might suddenly rise. Shippers of coal might turn against ship owners who themselves did not use coal as fuel. The argument that engineers who were experienced with diesels were hard to find seems particularly fallacious, because such experience could only be gained if more owners operated motor ships. Inertia and fear of new technology were undoubtedly the major reasons why so many long-established tramp owners and builders were clinging to steam.

Serious efforts were made to improve the economy of the steam ship. These included the addition of exhaust turbines to extract some of the remaining energy from steam emerging from the low pressure cylinder. Superheating was also adopted, although it was unpopular with engineers because of the extra maintenance work it entailed. The most successful answer was reheating, enhancing the temperature of the steam as it passed from one cylinder to another. Even so, thermodynamic factors meant that the steam engine could never offer the same fuel economy as a diesel.

This chapter will also consider some improvements in hull design which made tramps more economic by reducing water resistance and hence fuel consumption, but these were equally applicable to motor ships.

Despite severe problems in the depression, the British were still the largest owners and builders of tramp ships, but in both aspects their position was being eroded, to a considerable extent by their slowness to adopt new technology. In particular, British shipbuilders were slowly losing their export market. The growing number of non-British builders of tramps encountered in this chapter were very largely building for national customers, but these builders posed a threat that was to become very real in post-war years.

Note: An asterisk in a caption indicates the vessel shown in the photograph.

Time-honoured designs

Many tramp owners saw no great reason to desert traditional hull designs for their steamers, at least until the financial and trading crises that followed the Wall Street Crash of 1928 opened their eyes to the benefits of new thinking and scientific testing of hulls. *Barrdale** was a quite typical tramp of her time, built to the three-island, counter-stern design that had arisen in the 1890s, and had been second only in popularity to the long bridge deck type.

Builders in 1925 were Greenock Dockyard Co Ltd, a small but versatile yard that had been bought in 1919 by Cayzer, Irvine & Co Ltd, and which was destined to become the in-house builder for Clan Line and later the British & Commonwealth Group. The yard had no engine-building facilities, and the 400-ft *Barrdale's* triple-expansion machinery came from J G Kincaid & Co Ltd.

The registered owner of *Barrdale* was Barr Shipping Co Ltd, manager of which was Barr, Crombie & Co Ltd of Glasgow. Its modest-sized fleet originated in 1916, but was without ships during 1917–25, and *Barrdale* was the first of only two new ships it ever ordered, the slightly larger

Barrwhin following her from Greenock in 1929. Barr, Crombie sold out in 1941, its remaining ships, including *Barrdale* and *Barrwhin*, going to Sir William Reardon Smith & Sons Ltd. But *Barrdale* did not serve the Welsh company

long: she was torpedoed and sunk by *U 156* on 17 May 1942 in the North Atlantic while on a voyage from New York via Table Bay to Abadan. *(J and M Clarkson)*

Also originating in the 1890s, the long bridge-deck design proved extraordinarily enduring, *Cressdene** being completed as late as April 1936, and other examples will also be found in this chapter. The builder for subsidiaries of Dene Shipping Co Ltd, London, was William Gray & Co Ltd, West Hartlepool, and its Central Marine Engine Works supplied her triple-expansion engine. She was the first of four sisters, and was followed by *Tordene* and *Oakdene* in 1936 and *Felldene* in 1937. Each one-ship owning company had a different shareholding structure, the name of *Cressdene* being chosen because the major

shareholder in her was one F Cresswell Pyman, who also happened to be managing director of the shipbuilder. To help finance her under the British government's 'Scrap and Build' scheme, the promoters bought two elderly ships, one from a British owner and one from an Estonian owner, which were then duly sold to breakers to fulfil the conditions of the loan.

Cressdene's bridge deck extends over 237 ft of her total of 396 ft. She appears to have her bridge particularly far forward, because her poop is especially lengthy and – unusually – carries a short hatch.

The four sisters typically loaded coal in South Wales for South America, where they were handed over to Blue Star Line to load homeward with cargoes that might include grain, linseed, oilcake, wool, hides or canned meat, and were usually consigned to Avonmouth.

Cressdene was mined on 16 March 1942 near Harwich while en route from London to Methil during the first leg of a ballast voyage to Rosario. She sank the next day during salvage attempts.

Flush decks and forecastles

That there was still little consensus as to the optimum hull design for a tramp is shown by the building of flush deck steamers such as *Langleecrag** alongside three-island, long-bridge deck and forecastle-only designs. Seen on the River Scheldt, the 432-ft *Langleecrag* of 1929 was one of four sisters built on the Tyne by Palmers' Shipbuilding & Iron Co Ltd for Newcastle-based Medomsley Steam Shipping Co Ltd, managed by Frederick Carrick & Co Ltd.

The story of Palmers' is particularly unfortunate, because its original yard at Jarrow practically invented the successful bulk-carrying steamer with *John Bowes* of 1851. Initial success was such that the Jarrow site even had its own blast furnace, other yards were opened on the Tyne, vessels as large as battleships were built, and by 1920 Jarrow had twelve slipways. But Palmers' was unable to survive the Great Depression, the Jarrow yard's closure being a catastrophe for the town. Palmers' also had an engine works, but the fitting of *Langleecrag* and other ships of the Medomsley order with machinery by North Eastern Marine Engineering Co Ltd suggests all was not well.

Surviving a voyage to Juno Beach soon after D-Day, *Langleecrag* was wrecked on 15 November 1947 at the eastern end of Sacred Island, Newfoundland, while on a ballast voyage from Hull to Montreal. By then, the Medomsley company had been sold following the death of Carrick, and it was to have the unusual experience of being owned by the Van Ommeren group of Rotterdam, but continuing to trade under its old name, albeit with revised funnel colours.

A contemporary of *Langleecrag*, *Pukkastan** was delivered by Short Brothers Ltd, Sunderland in October 1929. She too was a shelter-decker, of 454 ft overall, differing mainly in having a short forecastle. Owners were Hindustan Steam Shipping Co Ltd, managed by Common Brothers of Newcastle.

The company was soon to bitterly regret *Pukkastan*, one of three ships ordered in late 1928, as being one of the worst decisions it ever made. The ships went straight into lay up after trials, and when they did trade the freight rates accepted were so low that any profit was dissipated if there were delays due to bad weather. Common Brothers felt they would have done much better to have built motor ships, but felt let down by the advice to stick to steam given by both their consultant engineers and the engine builders, John Dickinson & Sons Ltd. As a relatively small engineering company, Dickinson did not have the resources to develop its own diesel engine, nor even to tool up to build one under licence. After delivering the third of the engines for the Common Brothers ships, Dickinson kept going with repair work until the business was sold in 1939.

Pukkastan was an unfortunate ship; on 7 September 1939, just days after war had been declared, she was sunk by torpedoes and gunfire from *U 34* off Bishop Rock while inward bound from Table Bay to Rotterdam with maize. A war loss insurance payout of £130,000 for an eleven-year-old vessel that had cost a shade under £100,000 was some consolation for the owners. *(World Ship Society Ltd)*

Isherwood's Arcform hull

With straitened trading conditions in the 1930s, builders and designers of ships began to look again at hull forms. One such was Sir Joseph Isherwood, who had gained a reputation – and a knighthood – for designing a ship with longitudinal stringers and widely-spaced transverse framing. By reducing the weight of steel, carrying capacity was increased without raising registered tonnage. It proved immensely popular, especially for tankers. But Isherwood did not rest on his laurels, and in 1933, following extensive tank testing, he produced his Arcform hull. Isherwood believed that a conventional box-shaped

hull prevented a smooth flow of water over its surface. His solution was a hull rounded in cross section, the curve being continued virtually to deck level.

Three prototypes were completed during 1934 at different yards, *Arcwear** by Short Brothers Ltd, Sunderland; *Arctees* by Furness on the Tees; and *Arcgow* by Lithgows at Port Glasgow. They were registered in the ownership of individual companies managed by Isherwood Arcform Ships Ltd. They are reported to have handled well and coal consumption was lower than for a conventional ship. However, owners' enthusiasm for the

type was muted, and only fifty examples are known to have been built, thirty-one being tankers.

The 377-ft *Arcwear* had a satisfactory career, in 1936 joining the fleet of a London-Greek owner as *Lord Cochrane*, in 1950 becoming the German *Frieden*, in 1958 the Greek *Martha* and later *Boston L* and finally the Panamanian-flagged but Italian-owned *Helene*. Following grounding damage in 1968 she was broken up at Durban. (*J and M Clarkson*)

Once Isherwood had demonstrated his Arcform principle, his three prototypes were sold and in 1936 *Arctees* became the first ship of Trader Navigation Co Ltd, and was renamed *English Trader**. On only her second voyage for the new owners, she went aground off Dartmouth on 23 January 1937. The pounding strained her hull so badly that she showed signs of breaking up between numbers one and two holds and it was decided to complete the job by cutting away the fore part. In the photograph of the refloated ship, the Arcform hull cross section shows to good effect.

English Trader was eventually taken to the Tyne for a new bow section to be fitted by Middle Docks Engineering Co Ltd at South Shields. Work proceeded briskly: despite the fact that, because of her Arcform hull, almost every plate had to be rolled, the new bow was

plated up within three weeks.

On 26 October 1941, *English Trader* left London for Table Bay and Mombasa with general cargo. But she got no further than Hammond Knoll on the Norfolk coast where, in a full north-north-east gale, she drove ashore and her situation became desperate. Five men were lost overboard, and the rescue of the remaining forty-four became one of the epics of the lifeboat service. The redoubtable coxswain of the Cromer lifeboat, Henry Blogg, perhaps the most decorated lifeboatman ever, said that *English Trader* was the worst problem he had ever faced. No fewer than four attempts were made before the lifeboat *H F Bailey* could take off the survivors, Blogg and his crew being undaunted by their lifeboat capsizing on the third attempt.

Bows functional and fancy

There were other attempts besides the 'Arcform' to reduce underwater hull resistance, one resulting in the Maierform hull, popular with Continental builders but which saw several British manifestations. The photograph of a lightly-laden *Egton** approaching a Bristol Channel port shows the characteristic Maier bow, the curve continuing beneath the waterline.

The Maierform bow was a slightly surprising feature to be chosen by the rather conservative Whitby-based Headlam & Son, who managed her owner, Rowland & Marwood's Steamship Co Ltd. The innovative bow was coupled with a long bridge deck, almost the last time this anachronistic hull form was adopted. The bow meant a considerably disparity between her length of 398 ft between perpendiculars and her 412 ft overall length. The builder in 1938 was William Pickersgill & Sons Ltd of Sunderland, and the triple-expansion engine came from the nearby establishment of George Clark (1938) Ltd.

Headlam & Sons was the last of several tramp ship owners and managers based in Whitby, and who were not fazed by the inability of its home port to accommodate ocean-going ships, nor by Whitby's insignificance as a deep-sea port. *Egton* remained in its small fleet until 1957, when she was replaced by a motor ship of the same name, which became famous for its longevity and latter-day inactivity. The 1938-built steamer was sold to Yugoslavia as *Dubrava*, and even at the age of

thirty-one could find a further buyer, a Venice-based owner that put her under the Somali flag as *Joker*. She returned to Yugoslav waters to be broken up at Split in 1976.

The Maierform bow went out of fashion with the outbreak of war, but at least it had the honourable intention of reducing water resistance. There could be no such justification for the shape of the bow on the 1928-built *Parracombe**, politely described as a 'teapot bow', which was purely a whim of the Pyman family, who owner her. Photographic evidence confirms that such a feature had been appearing on ships built for Pyman since at least *Canford* of 1888. It persisted until the 425-ft *Parracombe*'s slightly larger running mate, *Welcombe*, was

completed as the last ship built for the family in 1930. *Parracombe*'s builder was William Gray & Co Ltd, West Hartlepool, which provided her machinery from its Central Marine Engine Works.

When the Pymans gave up ship owning in 1940, *Parracombe* and *Welcombe* were sold to the Stanhope Steamship Co Ltd, London. Manager of the new owning company was a Jack Billmeir, who had enjoyed much financial success from running the blockades into republican ports during the Spanish Civil War. This

success persuaded the British Admiralty to engage Billmeir in 1941 to mastermind attempts at making unescorted voyages to a besieged Malta. *Parracombe* was nominated by Billmeir, as her master had Spanish Civil War experience, and an enlisted Spanish pilot helped ensure her disguise as a neutral Spanish steamer was satisfactory. Although hugging the coast of North Africa, *Parracombe* was targeted by Italian aircraft and on 2 May 1941, a mere 60 miles from Malta, she was sunk with the loss of thirty of her crew of forty seven.

Exotic machinery

The development of the triple-expansion engine, with its significant economies over compound machinery, helped the tramp steamer to dominate the ocean carriage of bulk commodities and defeat even the big steel vessels which were the sailing ship owners' last throw of the dice. Refined and developed into utterly reliable machinery, even in unsympathetic hands, the triple-expansion engine then enjoyed almost a complete monopoly as long as tramp ship owners specified steam propulsion. The principle of extracting even more power from the boiler steam had given rise to the quadruple-expansion engine, but very few tramp owners thought the extra first cost and greater complexity were worth the relatively modest savings in fuel. One exception was J & C Harrison of London, although even this careful and creative company fitted quadruple-expansion machinery

to just three of the exceptional sequence of twenty-five steamers they built during 1930–36 – Hartington of 1932, Hartlepool* of 1932 and Hartismere of 1933. In each case the builder was William Gray & Co Ltd, West Hartlepool and its Central Marine Engine Works supplied the engines. The long bridge deck hulls were 442 ft in length. Hartlepool is seen with a timber cargo that had probably been loaded at Vancouver, where Harrison's ships were frequent callers.

All three sisters attracted torpedoes during the Second World War; Hartington and Hartismere were both sunk during 1942. Hartlepool was damaged on 5 May 1940 by a German E-boat south west of Portland Bill while on voyage from the Tyne to Sydney, Nova Scotia in ballast. The torpedo hit aft, blowing off her propeller and exploding the stern magazine, which killed three of her

crew. Beached near Weymouth, she was refloated and towed to Southampton, where the forepart awaited the fitting of a new after half.

Thus renewed, Hartlepool steamed on until late 1951 when J & C Harrison began clearing its fleet of pre-war steamers, making way for a much smaller fleet of motor tramps. New owners of Hartlepool were Hong Kong based, who renamed her Zuiko. This was soon altered to Zuiko Maru when owners in Amagasaki, Japan bought her in 1952. In 1958, they decided her twenty-year old, West Hartlepool-built hull was still in good enough condition to merit investment in a new engine, and a Japanese-built diesel was installed. This lasted through several further changes of Japanese owner until 17 January 1968 when Zuiko Maru stranded off Yakeyama Saki, Aomori while on a voyage from Toyama to Nakhodka. (Warwick Foote)

.If a quadruple-expansion engine was rare in a tramp, steam turbines were a positively exotic choice of machinery. Two such sisters were built for companies managed by Sir Robert Ropner & Co, the 441-ft, long bridge-deck Clearpool in 1935 and Hawnby* in 1936. Builders were again William Gray & Co Ltd, neighbours of the Ropner headquarters in West Hartlepool. Its versatile Central Marine Engine Works supplied the steam turbines, a pair of which was geared to the single screw in each ship to give a service speed of 11.5 knots. Ropner is one of the few tramp companies for which detailed histories have been published, but these do not offer an explanation of the choice of machinery or any evaluation of its success. The company also ordered two Doxford 'Economy' type motor ships at the time and continued to build conventional steamers, so it was probably conducting a comparison. If so, the turbines were not judged as particularly successful because, once Ropner began ordering ships to its own specification again after the war,

Doxford diesels were the company's choice.

Neither turbine sister survived the war. Hawnby was mined and sunk in the Thames Estuary on 20 April 1940 while on voyage from the Tyne to Gibraltar with coal.

Clearpool survived aircraft and torpedo attacks, only to be lost through stranding in the River Humber. On 4 June 1944 she went on to Skitter Sands, off King George Dock, Hull, while outward bound for Algiers, also with coal.

Economical steamers

With her long bridge deck, *Eskdalegate** of 1930 may not look like she represents a new era in tramp ship design, but her builder, Burntisland Shipbuilding Co Ltd, was a pioneer in improving the ordinary cargo ship. If they were to stay in business during the next decade of depression, other tramp ship builders had to follow suit.

The Burntisland 'Economy' type had a redesigned propeller and streamlined rudder to improve efficiency. The engine, supplied by David Rowan & Co Ltd of Glasgow, incorporated superheating and additional insulation to improve its efficiency. Burntisland made claims based on typical tramp voyages that their 'Economy' design could manage 11.5 knots if required, but would steam at 9 knots on 19 tons of coal per day, compared with the 25 tons needed by conventional tramps. London-based Turnbull, Scott & Co ordered three single-deck, 383-ft steamers incorporating these ideas – *Eskdalegate*, *Skeldergate* (both delivered 1930) and *Waynegate* (1931).

In 1950 *Eskdalegate* was bought by Germany as the country was gradually allowed to rebuild its merchant fleet, and she was renamed *Holstein*. In 1960, with

Germany building new motor tramps, she passed to a Brazilian company with strong German connections – Empresa de Navegacion Alianca SA as *Marisa*. During July

1971, while under tow into port following an engine failure, she was wrecked on Ilha de Medo São Luis during a ballast voyage from Belem to Rio de Janeiro.

As British tramp building yards ran out of orders in the 1930s, wise managements such as that at Bartram & Sons of Sunderland kept on a nucleus of technical staff to design ships that would appeal to owners when trading conditions improved. Much of Bartram's work on refining underwater lines to improve the flow of water to the propellor involved the National Physical Laboratory at Teddington. Bartram also devised an aerofoil-shaped, semi-balanced rudder, which was integrated with a more efficient stern frame and rudder post.

As owners began to order again from 1933, Bartram's work was repaid and over the next six years the Sunderland yard launched ten ships incorporating these ideas. The ten included two 433-ft steamers for companies managed by Evan Thomas, Radcliffe & Co, Cardiff – *Llanashe** in 1936 (seen on her maiden voyage) and *Llandaff* in 1937.

Not only was their hull form novel, but also so was their machinery. Designed and built by W A White, it had two high-pressure and two low-pressure cylinders, with a

totally enclosed crankcase. Operating at 500 rpm (compared with 60–70 rpm for a typical triple-expansion engine), it was geared to the propeller. Output was supplemented by a low-pressure exhaust turbine, connected to the main engine gearbox. The White engine was eventually fitted to fifteen ships, but the outbreak of war in 1939 meant its potential was never achieved.

As to *Llanashe*, in February 1943 she was torpedoed by *U 182* while on voyage from New York to Table Bay with the loss of twenty-eight of the forty-one on board.

Composite superstructure

Joseph L Thompson and Sons Ltd, another of the great Wearside tramp builders, produced its own 'Economy' design of shelter-decker (innovative brand names were

not the style of 1930s tramp builders). Investing earlier than Bartram in this development work, 1932 was the only complete year in which Thompson was without

shipbuilding work. Its first 'Economy', *Embassage*, was a conventional split-superstructure ship, but *Starcross** of 1936 and others had a composite superstructure. Having just one erection rather than two amidships reduced construction costs as, for instance, just one set of services such as power, water and heat to cabins had to be provided. It also made the third hold, now forward of the bridge, easier to work.

The 411-ft *Starcross* was ordered by Anning Brothers, now Cardiff based but originating from south Devon and naming their ships after places in their homeland. Engines were provided by Richardsons, Westgarth & Co Ltd, Hartlepool. She was yet another 1930s tramp to become a war loss, torpedoed by the Italian submarine *Otaria* on 20 May 1941 while bound from West Africa to Hull.

With the advantages of a composite superstructure, it might be thought that the split superstructure design would soon be obsolete, especially for motor vessels. The next chapter will show just how wrong this expectation was, with the great majority of tramps built for the accounts of British or Commonwealth governments having the older design and only second thoughts preventing 2,700 Liberty ships turning out the same way.

Trader Navigation Co Ltd was registered in London in July 1936 as a subsidiary of Bunge & Co, one of the world's major grain traders. With substantial interests in the River Plate trade, during its heyday Bunge & Co was chartering six to eight ships every day to move its grain. With the world slowly coming out of recession in the 1930s, Bunge began to fear that freight rates would not remain in the charterer's favour, and decided to build up a small fleet of their own. Despite its unhappy experience with its first purchase, *English Trader* (page 102), Trader

Navigation soon ordered larger but more conventional steamers, although with a composite superstructure. *Welsh Trader** emerged from the Wearside yard of Joseph L Thompson & Sons Ltd in March 1938.

In parallel with Thompsons' improved hull design, *Welsh Trader* also benefited from work to improve the efficiency of the marine steam engine: the 'reheater' introduced in 1936 by the North Eastern Marine Engineering Co Ltd and claimed to improve efficiency by 10 per cent over normal superheating. With its proven

economy, and advantages over machinery using superheaters which was unpopular with marine engineers, the 'reheater' went on to become the leading machinery in the triple-expansion market.

The 442-ft *Welsh Trader* lived up to her name, and made several visits to Cardiff. In 1951, she was sold to Hamburg owners who renamed her *Betelgeuze*. In 1961 she passed to Italian owners, and as *Peppino Palomba* she survived until May 1970 when she arrived at La Spezia for demolition. *(William Schell)*

Dutch single-deckers

Dutch shipbuilding benefited from the opportunities presented by the First World War, which temporarily removed competition from British yards. However, the yards' emphasis was on smaller craft, which the Dutch became skilled at building and operating. Once peace returned, Dutch builders gained orders for ocean-going ships mainly from domestic tramp operators, which was itself a relatively small market.

Hilversum was a single-deck steamer completed in September 1920 by A Vuijk & Zonen at Capelle a/d Yssel for NV Stoomvaart Maatschappij Oostzee, a company managed by Vinke & Co of Amsterdam. Her steam engine was supplied by Koninklijke Maatschappij de Schelde at Vlissingen, and was fitted to burn oil fuel, in contrast to most British steam machinery which relied on coal. Few other features distinguished the 360-ft design from long bridge deck steamers built before the war in British yards.

Hilversum was under British control from June 1940,

and was not returned to Dutch control until June 1945. Five years later, she found a German buyer, and was renamed *Klaus Oldendorff** by Egon Oldendorff of Lübeck, and is seen in his ownership on the Thames while in the timber trade. Although sold for breaking up at La Spezia in January 1961, after work had started she was resold and used as a base for a crane barge. Her fate is unknown.

This aerial view of *Maiotis** shows that the short hatch between the bridge and engine room casing is nothing more than a bunker hatch, and not serving a cargo hold as in many contemporary steamers.

She began life as *Nieuwe Maas*, the first of five names she was eventually to carry under four flags. Owners were NV Hollandsche Algemeene Atlantische Scheepvaart Maatschappij of Amsterdam. She was completed in April 1919 by NV Werf Conrad at Zaandam. Although given yard number 489, it would seem the yard's previous output had been largely confined to inland or other small vessels which never made it to *Lloyd's Register*, suggesting that this yard at Zaandam was cashing in on the temporary demand for ocean-going steamers. Machinery, in contrast, came from one of the best-known Dutch engine builders, Gebroeder Stork at Hengelo.

First of a number of ownership changes came in 1922 when NV Hudig & Pieter's Algemeene Scheepvaart Maatschappij of Rotterdam gave her the unflattering name, to modern English ears, of *Berk*. In 1930, she went to German coal importers as *Poseidon*, and after the war was handed over as war reparations to the Greek government. It sold her Synodinos Brothers of Piraeus, who renamed her *Maiotis*, put the Greek letter 'S' on her funnel, and probably had the proper wheelhouse fitted. Her story is completed with a further sale within Greece during 1961, placing her under the Lebanese flag as *Evangelos*, and her beaching near Karachi for breaking up during October 1969.

Dutch shelter-deckers

Like their British counterparts, Dutch owners found it difficult to decide between single-deck ships suitable for dense cargoes, and shelter-deckers that gave reductions in tonnage and hence port dues. Hedging their bets, they invested in both.

Themisto* is an example of a Dutch-built and owned shelter-decker, completed in October 1928 by Rotterdam Droogdok Maatschappij at Schiedam, who also provided her four-cylinder compound engine. Such machinery was virtually unheard of in British ships until the White engine was developed in the 1930s (see Llanashe, page 105). The 417-ft hull is of the forecastle-only design, and appears largely devoid of sheer. Other distinguishing features are the tall kingposts topped by ventilators serving the third hatch. The provision of four derricks at each of her masts hints that the owners, NV Maatschappij Zeevaart (managed by Hudig & Veder, Rotterdam), expected to charter her for liner voyages.

Like Hilversum, she spent the war working for the British and was managed by tramp owners Hugh Hogarth & Sons Ltd from July 1940 to November 1944. Hudig & Veder kept her until 1958, when the thirty-year-old steamer found a buyer who put her under the Costa Rica flag but named her Spetsai Navigator, betraying his Greek background. Shortening her name to Navigator, and switching her flag to Panama in 1962, seems to have been a preliminary to selling her for scrap, Brodospas at Split cutting her up during 1963.

Whereas Dutch shipbuilding output in the early 1920s was largely for domestic owners, Elisavet* was unusual in that she was built in the Netherlands for Greece.

Or was she? Her first recorded owner was A & C Mazarakis of Cephalonia, but her original name was Elisabeth, not altered to Elisavet until 1923. Was she built on spec by NV Burgerhout's Machinefabriek & Scheepswerf at Rotterdam as Elisabeth, and only found a Greek buyer in September 1922 by which time collapse of the freight market had brought ship prices down to an affordable level?

Her triple-expansion engine came from her builders' own machine shops and appears to rely on natural draught given the height of her funnel. Like some British shelter-deckers, she is flush decked.

Another notable aspect of Elisavet is that she spent her entire, lengthy life with the same Greek family. Exact details changed: at one time owners were listed as A & C Mazarakis, at others Mazaraki Brothers, and from 1946 her owner was D C Mazarakis. She was still with him in October 1965 when his forty-three-year old steamer arrived at Split to be broken up by Brodospas. (Ships in Focus)

Southern European steam

Spain has long been an important maritime power, but delayed industrial development left its ship owners largely dependent on second-hand vessels, often ex-British. However, *Aritz-Mendi* was an exception, a single-decker built in a Spanish yard for a Spanish owner during 1920. Builder of this substantial, 415-footer was Compañía Euskalduna de Construccion y Reparacion de Buques of Bilbao, although it had to import machinery from Sunderland, one of the triple-expansion engines of J Dickinson & Sons Ltd.

The owner of this vessel was Compañía Naviera Sota y Aznar of Bilbao, and her Basque name testifies to the heritage of its manager. It also explains why, from August 1937, she was laid up in Barry Dock, because Bilbao and the Basque country were determinedly Republican territory during the Spanish Civil War.

When the ship returned to Spain, it was felt wise to change her Basque name, and she became *Monte Navajo**. Its two former owners had gone their separate ways, although both families remained ship owners, and she now belonged to Naviera Aznar SA. In a period when much of the Spanish fleet was state-owned, this was one of Spain's largest private ship owners, operating passenger and cargo liner services. After a life of forty-four years *Monte Navajo* was broken up at Santander during 1964. *(Fotoflite incorporating Skyfotos)*

The relative paucity of Italian-built tramp steamers for this period is perplexing, given that Italy had an important shipping industry and, for a while, harboured strong colonial ambitions. Perhaps native builders were inhibited by the ready availability of war-built tonnage from the UK, because Italian owners were major customers of the Shipping Controller.

The single-deck steamer *Mincio**, a product of Società Anonima Cantiere Cerusa at Voltri, was delivered to Navigazione Generale Italiana of Genoa in June 1921. It passed without change of name in 1929 to a company managed by the Ravano family of Genoa.

Despite her size, the 394-ft *Mincio* does not seem to have been very adventurous in her trading, and in 1938 is reported as being confined to the Mediterranean and other European waters. The photograph was taken off Gravesend in August 1933. One unusual feature is the gantry linking the two kingposts with a walkway fitted, presumably to facilitate maintenance of the gear.

However, on Italy's belated declaration of war in June 1940, *Mincio* was at large, and was captured by the Royal Navy and brought into Liverpool as a prize. The Ministry of Shipping renamed her *Empire Fusilier* and awarded her management to Watts, Watts & Co Ltd. Alas, she was to have a relatively short British career. On 9 February 1942, *U 85* torpedoed and sank her in mid-Atlantic while on a ballast voyage from the Tyne to Tampa in Florida as part of convoy ON 60. There were nine casualties among her crew. *(F W Hawks)*

Soviet steamer

Hardly typical of steamers of her period, *Pravda** is something of a curiosity, not least in having been one of the very few steamers named after a newspaper (a British owner of steam trawlers had once used this rather singular nomenclature). At 284 ft, *Pravda* just scrapes into this book's working definition of an ocean-going tramp. Her hull and triple-expansion engine were 1928 products of the Baltic Shipbuilding & Engineering Works at Leningrad, one of the small number of merchant building yards active in the Soviet Union in the inter-war years.

Although state-owned, her nominal ownership changed over the years, and a move from Leningrad to Archangel in the 1940s probably indicates an alteration in trading area from the Baltic to the White Sea. She managed the not inconsiderable feat of emerging from the Second World War intact, and was last reported as trading in 1963.

Distinctly unusual features are the substantial 'decks' alongside the two masts, and what appears to be a strengthening structure alongside the aftermost kingposts. Undoubtedly she was designed for deck cargoes of timber.

CHAPTER

9

The Second World War

Little significant happened in terms of ship design during the Second World War. The priority was to produce ships as quickly as possible to replace the horrendous war losses on all sides, and pre-war designs were dusted off and adapted. What did change was production methods and philosophy. Welding and prefabrication became widespread but, perhaps even more importantly, there was a realisation that there was nothing magical about ship building. As US industrialist Henry Kaiser showed, industrial production techniques could be readily applied to putting a ship together, and this was to have profound implications for shipbuilding in post-war years. And in many ways the whole post-war shipping scene was altered by the war, with the market for tramps partly satisfied by wartime products from US, Canadian, British and even German yards.

There was also little effort spared to improve marine engineering, the priority being to produce as many engines as possible. Almost the entire North American output was of freighters driven by basic triple-expansion engines, while the choice for British ships was governed entirely by what the engine shops could turn out, hence there was a mixture of steam and diesel, even among the same types from the same yard.

Of the combatants, the British had by far the biggest influence on the design of war-built tramps. Domestic and Commonwealth output plus the sixty US-built 'Oceans' were completed to entirely British designs. The 'Ocean' design was subtly altered to produce the 'Liberty', likely to forever remain the ship design built in the largest numbers. Of the remaining, and impressive, US wartime output, most were fast, cargo liner-type vessels or large coasters.

The basic freighters that were produced in Britain and North America were based on the shelter deck design that had become the norm for tramps. In wartime it was wisely decided that – because the shelter deck concept was all about artificially reducing measured tonnage – the small tonnage openings should be permanently closed for safety reasons. This meant that the 'Empires', 'Forts', 'Parks' and 'Liberties' were built as two-deck ships, although many post-war owners took the opportunity to open the shelter decks.

For various reasons, some misguided as it turns out, the Axis powers concentrated their shipbuilding efforts on warship production (just as the British had done early in the First World War), and for instance the few Italian merchant ships built were fast cargo liner types. Germany concentrated its wartime merchant shipbuilding effort on the small 'Hansa' A type, and produced only a limited number of the larger 'Hansa' B type. The only other combatant to produce ocean-going tramps in any number was Japan, and the relative few of the 2A type to emerge unscathed from the war are represented here.

Despite US output being massively larger, British output is dealt with in some detail in this chapter. Standardisation in British wartime shipbuilding only went so far and there were at least seven officially recognised types of tramp. There were also several variations – many quite subtle – which arose as individual yards adapted official designs to suit the dimensions of their building berths. As long as no significant design work was entailed, yards were also allowed to turn out ships to pre-war prototypes, such as Doxford's 'Improved Economies'. Unlike the US purpose-built production-lines, which turned out identical 'Oceans' and 'Liberties', British output came entirely from existing yards and marine engineering shops, with the restrictions that this meant in terms of length of available berths and, particularly, machinery supply.

Note: An asterisk in a caption indicates the vessel shown in the photograph.

British Y and X types

Having learned some lessons from the First World War, Britain prioritised merchant ship building almost immediately on the outbreak of hostilities in 1939. Yards built basic tramps (the term freighter was becoming more familiar) to government account (from September 1939 orders were placed by the Ministry of Shipping) but these were to approved pre-war designs from the builder, a sensible approach because this expedited construction. Standard types were introduced gradually, and building of these was perhaps not as widespread as many believe. The designation of X and Y type appears to have been applied to the earliest standards. The latter seems to have been the most numerous, and was broken down into several subtypes.

Belgian Sailor* is an example of the basic 448-ft Y type in wartime – she was photographed in Halifax in June 1943. She was built at the Neptune Works of Swan, Hunter & Wigham Richardson Ltd, which provided her steam engine. She was delivered as *Empire Drayton* in February 1942 but was quickly renamed and put under the Belgian flag in recognition of the Belgian government's action in ordering its entire merchant fleet to work for the Allied cause.

In 1946, Compagnie Maritime Belge SA, who had been operating her, took her over and renamed the ship *Capitaine Biebuyck*. Subsequently she sailed under the Yugoslav flag as *Kastav* and was owned in Hong Kong as *Ivory Tellus* before she was broken up in Japan in 1970. *(National Maritime Museum)*

Delivered in December 1942 as *Empire Torrent*, *Queen Maud** is another example of a Y type, seen here in commercial ownership between 1951 and 1954. External modifications have been relatively minor, essentially the removal of the floats alongside the two masts and the guns on the poop. Many British war-built ships gained topmasts post-war and lost the distinctive signal mast on the bridge, but this has not yet happened to *Queen Maud*.

Her funnel is particularly tall, but this seems to have been a modification done on behalf of her previous owner, who from 1948 to 1951 placed her in the management of Counties Ship Management Co Ltd as *Argos Hill*. Certainly dumpy funnels such as that on *Belgian Sailor* were given to *Empire Nerissa* and *Empire Gambia*, the two other Y types delivered from the same Govan yard, that of Harland & Wolff Ltd, which also built their steam engines. A more subtle change to *Queen Maud* is the elimination of the ventilator tops to the kingposts ahead of the funnel.

In 1954 *Queen Maud* was sold by her owners, companies that were managed by Thomas Dunlop & Sons of Glasgow, to Greeks, who put her under the Panamanian flag as *Scotia*. When she went under the Greek flag in 1960 her name was rendered as *Skotia*. She was broken up in Hong Kong during 1962. *(W H Brown)*

The Y type ran to at least seven sub-types, Y1 to Y7, most of which feature in the output of Lithgows Ltd. Examination of photographs suggests that only one showed major external differences, the Y1 type, numbering only two built by the Port Glasgow yard – *Empire Baffin* (delivered October 1941) and *Empire Ridley* (November 1941). The difference from the basic Y type was the flush deck, omitting the forecastle. However, internally both ships were modified in 1943 to lay pipes for the Pipe Line Under The Ocean (PLUTO) operation, successfully used to pump fuel ashore for the follow-up

to the Normandy invasion. For this they were renamed HMS *Sancroft* and HMS *Latimer*, respectively.

Reverting to their 'Empire' names in 1946, they were quickly sold. *Empire Baffin* went as *Clintonia** to Stag Line Ltd of North Shields who, among other changes, added topmasts and moved the small boat originally mounted on the bridge structure to a position alongside the funnel. Sold in 1960, she spent her three remaining years as *Aspis* for London-Greek owners. When broken up in Japan at the end of 1963, she still had the steam engines supplied in 1941 by David Rowan & Co Ltd of Glasgow.

To complete the Y1 story, after the war *Empire Ridley* was used by a contractor to help recover parts of the PLUTO pipeline. In 1947 she went to Norwegian owners who sent her to Italy for conversion into a conventional dry cargo ship. After sale to Italian owners as *Acheo* she steamed on until 1964. *Lloyd's Register* records a subtle internal modification, made when converted by Green & Silley Weir Ltd to a cable ship, in that a third deck was worked into number one hold. *(Ships in Focus)*

The designation X type seems to have been reserved for ships built to the same dimensions and external appearance as the Y type, but with diesel engines. Whether the various 'Empire' ships were fitted with steam or diesel machinery was largely determined by available capacity at engine-building works, rather than being a matter of deliberate policy. And output of an individual yard could be mixed: Lithgows for instance

turning out just one X type amid a profusion of steam-driven Ys.

As major suppliers of licence-built diesels, Harland & Wolff Ltd turned out five X types from the Queen's Island yard at Belfast. *Empire Rangoon*, completed in May 1944, had one of the builder's six-cylinder, four-stroke engines. In 1947, she was sold to the Reardon Smith Line Ltd of Cardiff, which had begun to favour motor ships in

the 1930s. Renamed *Homer City**, she was photographed looking very respectable, with 'proper' topmasts. Her boats are still mounted on the bridge structure.

Sale in 1960 saw ownership pass to Hong Kong, first as *Grosvenor Mariner* and then as the mainland China-controlled *Red Sea*. She was driven ashore during a typhoon on Lantau Island, Hong Kong in August 1971 and after refloating was broken up locally.

British B types

In 1940, the British authorities planned to build prefabricated ships, deciding on an overall length of 446.3 ft. The original design, designated PF(A) was not approved because, contrary to the concept of prefabrication, it comprised some unwieldy units that only larger yards could handle. In its place the PF(B) emerged. In essentials it was rather similar to the Y type, but sheer was restricted to the forward and extreme after parts of the hull. A useful recognition feature was that the funnel was sited further aft, leaving a large gap between it and the kingposts. As seen in the accompanying aerial view, the bunker hatch of these coal-burning steamers was situated between the kingposts and funnel, and served by a pair of derricks. The wheelhouse and the remainder of the bridge structure appeared more utilitarian than in the X and Y types.

After completing nine 'Empire' ships to its own 417-ft design, the South Dock yard of Bartram & Sons Ltd in Sunderland turned out its first B type, *Empire Rock*, in July 1943. Steam engines came from the Sunderland works of the North Eastern Marine Engineering Co (1938) Ltd.

In 1946 she was sold to a member of the Embiricos family, well-established Greek ship owners, who left her under the British flag as *Admiral Codrington**. Subsequent sales were to Italian owners in 1956 as *Sando Primo* and Dutch owners as *Amalie B* in 1959 before she was broken up at Hamburg in late 1960.

*Errington Court** is illustrated to show post-war modifications to the B type. Note that the kingposts between bridge and funnel have been doubled up. This is presumably to increase efficiency at the two hatches here because, as a result of conversion to oil fuel, the coal bunkers could be used for cargo. She also has decently tall (if not entirely upright) topmasts allowing the signal mast on the bridge to be taken down.

Her builder was Caledon Shipbuilding & Engineering

Co Ltd, who completed her as *Empire Favour* in November 1945. This was surprisingly late, because the B type had supposedly been superseded by the C and D types discussed later in this chapter. She was the last of seven B types from the Dundee yard, one of which had an oil engine. *Empire Favour*'s triple-expansion machinery was made by Duncan Stewart & Co Ltd of Glasgow.

In 1947 *Empire Favour* was sold to Watts, Watts & Co Ltd of London, a good customer of the Dundee

builders, and who renamed her *Epsom*. Sale to Court Line Ltd, renaming *Errington Court* and conversion to oil firing came in 1950. Later names under various Greek owners were *Penelope* and *Andromachi*. Under the latter name she was unfortunate enough to be lying at Suez during the 1969 Arab–Israel war and was damaged by Israeli shells, leaving her fit only for scrap.

Short's non-standard

Other ships were built to the same dimensions as the B type, but Mitchell and Sawyer – the historians of wartime merchant shipbuilding – do not classify them as such in their *Empire Ships*. These included a group built by Short Brothers Ltd at Sunderland. They had similar hulls: note how the sheer of *Cheltenham** is mostly right forward as in *Admiral Codrington*. However, there were detail differences, most notably the bridge front, which was gently rounded rather than flat. Some of this group, including *Stad Rotterdam*, the former *Empire Southey*, had a second heavy-lift derrick fitted to the mainmast, but this may be a post-war modification.

Cheltenham was completed as *Empire Envoy* in December 1942, taking the new name when bought by Thompson Steamshipping Co Ltd, London in 1946. The photograph was taken sometime between then and

1952, when she went to Buries Markes Ltd as *La Orilla*. Further names were *Ställberg* in Swedish ownership and

Verna Paulin under the Finnish flag. She was broken up at Bruges in 1969. *(Ships in Focus)*

C and D types

When it was realised that military equipment was becoming bulkier and heavier, the design of the PF(B) type was modified. Hatchways were enlarged, a 50-ton derrick added to the cargo gear and – most apparent – a composite superstructure was fitted to give greater deck space ahead of the bridge. A novel feature of what was known as the PF(C) type, and which has become much more frequent today, was the V-shaped transom stern, apparent in the accompanying photograph.

Empire Tobago was a product of Bartram & Sons Ltd, completed in October 1945 with engine by Duncan Stewart & Co Ltd, Glasgow. Sold in 1947, she was initially operated by Counties Ship Management Ltd as *Crowborough Hill*, moving in 1951 to Andrew Crawford & Co Ltd, Glasgow as *Gryfevale**. She was now in peacetime rig, with topmasts, but the 50-ton derrick originally at the foremast has been landed. Crawford's tramp fleet used the names of Scottish river valleys beginning with the letter G.

The PF(D) type was a development of the PF(C) but with a full height poop, a feature probably appreciated by crews because it virtually doubled their accommodation space, and is seen clearly in this aerial view of *Martita**. She retains the 50-ton derrick at the foremast and has a pair of small kingposts to handle stores just abaft her funnel. This aerial view also displays well the relatively narrow structure beneath the bridge, and how the bridge wings are supported.

Martita was completed in August 1946, having been launched as *Empire Gantock* but sold while building to a company managed by Kaye, Son & Co Ltd. Her builder was a branch of the Shipbuilding Corporation Ltd, formerly the Low Walker yard of Armstrong-Whitworth Ltd, which had closed in 1934 but was reopened in 1942. Her oil-fired steam engine was made by George Clark (1938) Ltd, Sunderland.

Following her sale in 1955, she traded first as *Sterling Valour* under the British flag, then as the Italian *Madda Primo* and *Madda Bozzo*, and finally as *Kriss*, still owned in

Italy but flagged out to the Somali Republic. She was broken up at Kaohsiung in 1968.

Between her sale by 'K' Steamship Co Ltd in 1960 and breaking up in Italy during 1968 she was successively

the Greek *Maroudio* and the Italian-owned, Panamanian-registered *Thalie*.

'Scandinavian' type

Two further groups of smaller, single-deck freighters were built in British yards to government account, the first dubbed the 'Scandinavian' type. The name reflected its inspiration in ships built for the Scandinavian timber trade, with unobstructed wells to accommodate deck cargoes and the cargo gear perched out of the way on the forecastle, bridge deck and poop. Overall length was 328 ft.

*Letchworth** is in very much 'as-built' condition, with a narrow funnel, no topmasts and a signal mast on the bridge. She had been completed as *Empire Caxton* in May 1942 by William Gray & Co Ltd, the West Hartlepool builder who designed this class and accounted for the hulls and engines of twenty-five of the total of thirty-five built.

Newcastle owner and manager R S Dalgleish Ltd snapped her up in 1945 and ran her in middle-distance trades as *Letchworth* until 1956, when she became *Peterland*, still British registered. In 1959, she was put under the then currently-fashionable Lebanese flag for Greek owners, first as *Pamit* and later as *Christos*. On 31 March 1967 she stranded on Kandeliusa Island while on voyage from Constantza to Hodeidah with a cargo of sugar. Although she floated off, she sank next day.

Several of the 'Scandinavian' type were fitted with additional, heavy masts in the centre of their wells carrying derricks of up to 80-tons capacity. They were sent to North Russian ports to help unload ships arriving with heavy military equipment such as tanks. The gear was removed at the end of the war.

Empire Malta type

William Gray & Co Ltd also built and engined ships similar in size to the 'Scandinavians' but with an engines-aft, bridge-amidships layout, dubbed the *Empire Malta* type after the lead ship of the class. It is reported that engines were placed aft to reduce the fire risk when case oil was carried, but this was just one of many roles for these ships, which could also work as colliers, general cargo, military vehicle carriers or heavy lift ships. Completed in March 1945, *Empire Caicos** shows signs of her former heavy-lift capability as she departs Cape Town in October 1948, with massive masts to support 80- and 50-ton derricks that have now been removed.

She is in the colours of manager Anglo-Danubian Transport Co Ltd of London, which bought two of these ships, although not *Empire Caicos* which went instead into the sugar trade as *Sugar Transporter*. Under this name she lost the heavy masts for more conventional ones with topmasts, retaining a full suit of derricks, although she was working as a bulk sugar carrier. The class of ten, which all survived the war, were widely scattered, and owners in the Far East were particularly attracted to them. After a period in Australian service as *Pattawilya*, she ended up in Hong Kong ownership, although with the decidedly homely English name of *Clovelly*. As a result of sustaining heavy weather damage in January 1967, she was broken up in Japan.

MAC grain ships

Some of the most unusual-looking dry cargo ships ever built were the grain ships completed as aircraft carriers. The merchant aircraft carrier (MAC) was conceived as a way of closing the mid-Atlantic air gap, which could not be covered by shore-based anti-submarine patrols. Fitting a flight deck required ships that had no above-deck cargo-handling gear or hatches, and in which the cargo could be either pumped out in the case of tankers (of which thirteen were built or converted) or sucked out in the case of the six grain ships. They were fitted with hangars and lifts for four aircraft and accommodation for flying and servicing crews, thus limiting cargo capacity. All were motor ships, as exhaust problems were envisaged if steam engines were fitted. Their diesel engines were uprated to give the vessels a speed of about 12.5 knots, deemed sufficient extra for them to take up flying stations or catch up with convoys after flying operations.

Such was the shortage of ships post-war that MAC grain ships went into commercial service in their wartime state, despite their limited grain capacity and lack of trading flexibility. The Lithgows-built *Empire Macrae*, completed with a Kincaid diesel in September 1943, became *Alpha Zambesi** on her sale in 1947, and is seen unloading grain. All six were eventually converted to conventional merchant ships of varying appearance. This required extensive work, including removal of the flight deck, conversion of the hangar to a hold, fitting of hatches, superstructure, masts and derricks. *Alpha Zambesi* was rebuilt during 1949–50 and emerged looking nothing like any of the standard 'Empire' ships. She

was sold to Norway as *Tobon* in 1954, and is seen in the second photograph under her final name *Despina P**. She has extensive cargo gear but, rather oddly, a split superstructure profile has been adopted. She was broken up at Kaohsiung in 1971.

The merchant aircraft carriers were essentially defensive in concept, and were soon eclipsed by the arrival of faster and better-equipped escort carriers. They are believed to have sunk at least one U-boat, and the patrols of their Swordfish aircraft must have foiled many

attacks on convoys. Their effect on morale of the merchant navy was excellent. At one convoy conference a merchant captain asked if there was to be a MAC ship present. When the reply was in the affirmative, the fifty or so masters present spontaneously applauded. They also demonstrated that the apparently almost impossible task had been achieved of designing a ship that could carry a substantial cargo of grain while functioning successfully as an aircraft carrier.

British designs, American yard

Standing alone against Germany in 1940, Britain's urgent need for more merchant ships led to a British Shipbuilding Mission visiting North America. With United States yards already busy with the beginnings of the US Maritime Commission's emergency programme, the Mission was told that there was no spare capacity in existing yards to build ships for Britain. However, the Mission also met businessmen who were quite prepared to build the ships, provided payments from Britain met the cost of both the ships and new yards to build them. Despite the inevitable resistance from the British Treasury, contracts were signed for sixty ships in December 1940. Half were to be built at the Todd-California yard near Richmond, California and half at the Todd-Bath yard in Portland Maine.

The leader of the Mission was Cyril Thompson, of shipbuilders Joseph L. Thompson and Sons Ltd. It was not surprising, therefore, that the sixty ships were to be built to plans developed at Thompson's North Sands yard for a 442-ft ship which was to become *Empire Liberty*. The major changes were that the ships would be mostly welded rather than riveted, and large sections prefabricated. Machinery was to comprise triple-expansion steam engines with coal-fired boilers, to a design of the North Eastern Marine Engineering Co Ltd, one of whose designers, Henry Hunter, was part of the British Shipbuilding Mission.

Despite new shipyards having to be laid out, the first keel was laid at Richmond on 14 April 1941 and at Portland on 24 May, and the first ship, fittingly named *Ocean Vanguard*, delivered from Richmond in October

1941. Indeed, so briskly did building proceed that she was actually finished before the British ship on whose plans she was based, delays to *Empire Liberty* being blamed on her hull being riveted rather than welded, and British yards not being able to work at night because of blackout restrictions.

*Ocean Vesper** was the sixth from California, delivered in January 1942 with engines by the General Machinery Corporation based in Ohio. In the lower photograph she is seen in the lower photograph leaving Cape Town after the war, but before being sold to Clan Line in 1951 and renamed *Clan Macqueen*. In 1954 Clan Line transferred her to their sister company Houston Line, who renamed her *Herminius*. This lasted until 1958 when she went to Hong King owners as *Egberg*. She was broken up in Japan during 1964. *(Ships in Focus)*

Seen in the upper photograph during her post-war, commercial service, although little modified, is *Alcyone Angel**. She was completed as *Ocean Angel* by the Todd-Bath Iron Shipbuilding Corporation at Portland in October 1942. Her machinery came not from a US supplier but from the Dominion Engineering Works Ltd at Montreal. Owners of *Alcyone Angel* were Alcyone Shipping and Finance Co Ltd, a London-based company managed by the Vergottis family, who bought her in 1949 and converted her machinery to oil-firing in 1951. Her final owner was a US-based, Liberian-flag outfit who renamed her *Continental*. She was broken up in Taiwan during 1970.

Of the sixty 'Oceans' built, sixteen – over a quarter – succumbed to enemy action. Although making a valuable contribution to Britain's war effort, their major significance was their contribution to a design which has been dubbed 'the ships that won the war', the Liberties.

The British Shipbuilding Mission moved on from the United States to Canada and, despite the local shipbuilding industry having contracted massively since its brief rise at the end of the First World War, signed a contract for twenty ships. Again, the drawings were those supplied for the 'Oceans', but the Canadian ships were to be mostly riveted, just like *Empire Liberty*. The initial order was subsequently increased, with the British, Canadian and even the United States governments paying for the ships. Eventually, some 450 merchant ships, not to mention 300 warships, were built in Canada.

The ocean-going cargo ships built in Canada were given names beginning 'Fort' or ending in 'Park'. *Warkworth** was completed by Burrard Dry Dock Co Ltd. at Vancouver in June 1943 as *Fort Dauphin*. She remained under this name while on charter from the British Ministry of War Transport and its successors until 1950 when bought and renamed by a company managed by R S Dalgleish Ltd, Newcastle. For a period the Forts, Parks, Oceans and British war-built standards formed the backbone of the British tramping fleet, but as their steam machinery became increasingly anachronistic

and uneconomical, they moved on to flag-of-convenience operators. One such based in Spain took *Warkworth* in 1957 and put her under the Liberian flag as *Bodoro*.

Her end came in North American waters. On 27 January 1967 she was off Chesapeake Bay en route for Baltimore with an ore cargo when she collided in fog with the US steamer *Beaver State*. Beached, she was not refloated until 24 March, but declared beyond economic repair and broken up at Portsmouth, Virginia.

Experience with the initial order for Forts led to an improved design entitled the 'Victory' type, confusingly because the United States also had a large, turbine-driven class of this name. The Canadian 'Victories' had two water tube boilers instead of three Scotch boilers and which burnt oil rather than coal. This enhanced cargo space, because oil, which unlike coal could be pumped, was stored in out-of-the-way parts of the hull not otherwise useful for cargo. Externally, the major difference was that two boats were carried abeam and just behind the

funnel, with none alongside the bridge.

The Victory *Bridgeland Park** is seen as built, with guns and floats plus bow fittings to stream paravanes to cut mine moorings. The builder was North Van Ship Repairs Ltd at North Vancouver, who completed her in 1944 for the Park Steamship Co Ltd, a Canadian government-funded venture. To fit this organisation's scheme, her name was changed from *Fort Green Lake* after she had been launched.

Her subsequent history was similar to other war-built

freighters, although her first commercial owner was the Canadian subsidiary of a cargo liner company, Elder Dempster Lines (Canada) Ltd, of Montreal, who renamed her *Cambray*; she was transferred to the parent company and British registration in 1950. Sold to a Swiss-based flag-of-convenience owner in 1960, she steamed on as *Simeto* until reaching a breaker's yard in Bilbao during May 1971. *(National Maritime Museum)*

Canadian yards also built smaller freighters, again to British plans, those of the single-deck 'Scandinavian' type built by William Gray & Co Ltd. The plans were modified several times; the first so called 'Revised' type had changes to its cargo gear. Further revisions saw the introduction of a 'tween deck into the hold; six of this type being built. *Canadian Conqueror** was of this ilk, completed as

Sutherland Park by Foundation Maritime Ltd, Pictou, Nova Scotia, in June 1945, just after the war in Europe had ended.

In an echo of events following the First World War, a one-ship subsidiary of the state-owned Canadian National Steamships bought and renamed her in 1947. *Canadian Conqueror* was used between Canada, Central

America and the West Indies, the service between the two regions stimulated by the availability of bauxite cargoes to feed the aluminium smelters of Canada, which were fuelled by cheap hydro-electricity. In 1958 she was sold to Cuba, although sources differ as to whether or not she actually worked for that country. She was broken up in Bilbao in 1965.

Liberties

By 1941 a modest, state-sponsored shipbuilding programme had been underway in the United States for some years, but was wholly inadequate to meet the needs of a country foreseeing the possibility of war on two fronts. The relatively sophisticated types designed for the Maritime Commission were not considered suitable for mass production, but – in perhaps a back-handed compliment to British ship design – the 'Oceans' were taken as a suitably simple template. Modifications were made, most obviously providing a composite superstructure (the accommodation in which was considerably improved), substitution of oil for coal firing, and some simplification of hull design. US industry then set about building them in unprecedented numbers.

Although taken in June 1947, this photograph of *Samarkand* arriving on the Mersey reflects the state of Liberties in wartime: the grey paint relieved largely by streaks of rust. Completed by Bethlehem-Fairfield at Baltimore in September 1943, she was one of 182 Liberties supplied to Britain's Ministry of War Transport under lend-lease arrangements. Although notionally returned to the United States at the expiry of these terms, 125 of these 'Sams' (prosaically, the name derived from 'superstructure aft of midships') found British buyers. Not even the most particular of companies disdained Liberties, and the Alfred Holt group made one of the largest purchases. *Samarkand* was renamed *Talthybius*, and took her turn on Blue Funnel Line sailings from 1947 to

1954 when she was transferred within the group to Glen Line as *Gleniffer*. Only in 1958 did she achieve her destiny as a tramp, first as *Dove* and later as *Patraic Sky*, both

under the Liberian flag. She was demolished at Split, Yugoslavia, in 1971.

Given their total number, surprisingly few Liberties received serious modification for civilian use. The commonest was to fit diesel engines, with Italian owners particularly keen on this change. *Laguna** had been completed as *Jesse Billingsley*. Typical of the speed of construction achieved with these ships, her keel was laid by Houston Shipbuilding Corporation on 1 July 1943 and she was delivered on 28 August. Her original triple-expansion engine came from Willamette Iron & Steel Corporation in Oregon.

Jesse Billingsley hit a stray mine in the Adriatic during May 1946 while still in US ownership. With so many ships available, she was not repaired but simply laid up at Trieste. In 1949 Venetian owner Società Italiana di Armamento (SIDARMA) bought and renamed her *Laguna* and fitted a FIAT diesel engine. The only reason for her receiving such a large funnel could be to display the owner's colours: basically yellow with a red band broken by a blue star. Otherwise her appearance is typical of the hundreds of Liberties that entered the tramp trades after the war.

Thus equipped, she saw out her life under Italian ownership, if not always the Italian flag. Genoese owners renamed her *Marilu* in 1964 and flagged her out to Panama, although sale to a Neapolitan in 1965 saw her revert to Italian registry as *Orione*. Leaks that developed during a voyage from Bourgas to Galveston in February 1969 signalled that she was getting old, or at least needed repair, and she was duly despatched to a scrap yard in Bilbao.

A handful of Liberties were lengthened, typically by inserting another hold, hatch and mast ahead of the bridge. In the case of the former *Mary Ashley Townsend*, however, modification was more profound, because she had been built as a tanker. Urgent need to transport oil, and the preference of U-boat commanders for torpedoing tankers, led the US War Shipping Administration to order the Delta Shipbuilding Co Inc to design a tanker version of the Liberty. Externally these were deliberately made almost identical to the dry cargo version, even to the extent of having dummy cargo gear

and conventional hatches. Internally they had nine cargo tanks plus pump rooms and pipework. *Mary Ashley Townsend* was one of thirty-two Liberty tankers delivered by Delta at New Orleans, mostly in 1943. Engines came from the wonderfully named Iron Fireman Manufacturing Co of Portland, Oregon.

Following lay-up from September 1946 to February 1948, *Mary Ashley Townsend* went to commercial tanker owners as *David T Wilenz* and later *Sweetville*. By the mid-1950s she had become small for a tanker, and owner Daniel Ludwig sent her to Kure Shipbuilding &

Engineering Co Ltd (a Japanese former naval yard that he leased) for lengthening to 512 ft and conversion to dry cargo. Renaming her *Berkshire* in 1956, he chose to register her in London, although owner Argyll Shipping Co Ltd was based in tax-friendly Bermuda.

Her final name was *Delos Glory*, bestowed by a Greek owner who put her under the Liberian flag from 1964 until 1968 when she was scrapped at Kaohsiung. When building Liberties, the US government foresaw them lasting no more than five years. How wrong they were. *(VH Young)*

In 1944, the US War Shipping Administration asked Delta Shipbuilding to redesign the Liberty hull to create a collier for work in the domestic coal trade between Hampton Roads and New England, supplementing an ageing fleet of colliers that had also suffered war losses. This was at the tail-end of the Liberty ship programme (preference now being given to building turbine-driven 'Victory' types), and reflected a change in emphasis to constructing ships not solely intended for wartime use.

Although recognisable as having a Liberty hull, the Liberty colliers had engines aft, necessitating some redesign of the machinery space, and also had a poop deck. Kingposts rather than conventional masts were specified, these also being fitted with gear to move the steel hatch covers. Internal changes included strengthening of bulkheads and redesign of arrangements for carrying water ballast.

The twenty-four Liberty colliers built at New Orleans were largely confined to their intended US east coast coal trade, where they proved very efficient.

Towards the end of their lives they moved out of this trade and some became rather exotic visitors to European ports, as did *Reading**. She was completed in August 1945 and named *Imboden Seam* after a coal deposit in Virginia. After working as a collier for a Boston

gas company from 1947 to 1965, she was put under the Panamanian flag by Sulpho Marine Transportation Inc of New York. The streaks on her hull are evidence she had carried sulphur when photographed. Still named *Reading* she was broken up at Santander in 1972. *(Michael Cassar)*

'Hansa' B type

Germany made plans for an emergency shipbuilding programme in autumn 1942, when it must have become apparent that, despite Germany's initial successes, the war was not going to be short. It was initially planned to build 200 ships of three sizes, the 'Hansa' A, B and C types. Because many German yards were engaged in U-boat construction, yards in occupied Belgium, the Netherlands and Denmark received a substantial proportion of these orders. There were many problems during construction, including shortages of steel, interference by the Kriegsmarine, and sabotage in yards in occupied countries, many of which were so slow in delivering that some hulls were not completed until several years after the war.

Only one of the largest 'Hansa' C types was completed during wartime and she was promptly sunk. Here we are concerned with the medium-sized B type of which sixty were planned and thirty-two actually delivered. Of 360 ft overall, they were driven by compound four-cylinder steam engines with low-pressure exhaust turbines. *Indus* was built by Flensburger Schiffsbau Gesellschaft, but when the Allies came to take over surviving German ships at the end of the war, she was incomplete and unnamed. Claimed by the British, she was finished in 1946 as *Empire Ardle*, but quickly sold to commercial owners as *Lewis Hamilton**. In 1950 she went under the Swedish flag as *Indus* for C H Abrahamsen of Stockholm, later hoisting the Finnish flag under the same name. She spent her last couple of years under Panamanian registry as *Falcon* then *Sea Falcon*, until broken up at Aviles in 1971. *(World Ship Society Ltd)*

Japanese 2A types

Of the Axis combatants, Japan had the greatest need for merchant ships when it was expanding, and later bitterly defending, its ill-gotten empire. But despite Japan having a relatively large shipbuilding industry, merchant ship construction was a low priority during wartime, naval planners being obsessed with warship building towards the decisive fleet action that they hoped would confirm Japanese control of the Pacific. Equally disastrously, the Imperial Japanese Navy largely ignored its duty to protect merchant shipping with escort vessels. In the event, US submarines targeted merchant ships to such devastating effect that Japan's scattered land forces could not be adequately supplied or reinforced.

A belated effort was made to build standard merchant ships. The largest group numerically were small, wooden vessels built in traditional Japanese yards and some of the occupied countries. Of the larger vessels, the most significant group was the 131 of the 2A type. Unlike wartime construction elsewhere, where pre-war prototypes were often adopted or their design adapted, the 426-ft 2A type were to a novel design, with engines aft and no discernible sheer.

Photographed at Adelaide, *Yamamura Maru* had received a new funnel to replace the original stovepipe and has had her wheelhouse modified. In fact, she had seen considerably internal alteration, because while building she was fitted out as a tanker, only to be converted for dry cargo in March 1945.

Yamamura Maru was completed in September 1944 by Kawaminami Kogyo KK at Koyagishima for Koun Kisen KK, Kobe, although she was operated by Yamashita Kisen KK, which ran several of the 2A type. She was broken up at Osaka in 1959. *(Ian J Farquhar)*

Of the 2A types that survived the war, a significant number were rebuilt, in some cases heroically. *Daikai Maru No 1** had been completed by Kawaminami Kogyo KK at Koyagishima in February 1945. Along with others, the apparently retrograde step was taken of moving her original steam turbine machinery to an amidships position. She emerged in 1951 with a long bridge deck, her origins as a 2A type only apparent from her hull lines.

Several others of the type were rebuilt more or less in the same way.

Daikai Maru No 1 is seen sailing from Cape Town around 1950, probably on liner services. Although in the colours of Osaka Shosen KK (original owners), she is operating for them but is now owned by Tamai Shosen KK of Kobe. The significance of the 'D006' painted on her hull is not known, although as most Japanese ships carried

numbers like these in immediate post-war years, it probably indicated that the US occupiers had licensed the ship to trade.

In 1952 *Daikai Maru No 1* was renamed *Tatsutama Maru*. In 1960, Tamai Shosen KK considered it worthwhile exchanging her turbines for diesel engines, a bad decision because, only three years later, she was broken up in her original home port of Osaka. *(Ships in Focus)*

CHAPTER

10

Last Breath of Steam

For a significant number of post-war tramp owners, it was as if the development of the diesel engine and the Second World War had not happened. Steam engines were the default option for a number of European owners, while one of the few acknowledgements of the changed world was that oil, not coal, was adopted from new for firing boilers. This rather belied the claim that steam was still specified to please the coal producers who still provided many cargoes for tramps.

Many post-war steam tramp were relatively small, those in this book falling in the 300–400 feet range, and with a single deck most were undoubtedly ordered to participate mainly in the coal trade. The majority of these were fitted with double-compound machinery – four-cylinder engines in which the steam was used just twice, although it then usually went to an exhaust turbine. The Christiansen & Meyer machinery of this type was among the final refinements of the marine reciprocating steam engine, with high working pressures, high speeds and poppet valve gear. For the larger ships, triple-expansion machinery was almost obligatory, especially for British owners. And although oil burning meant that the hatch placed amidships to serve the coal bunkers had lost its purpose, this hatch was perpetuated along with the split superstructure profile. Apart from a handful of steamers ordered in the Netherlands during the German occupation but finished for Dutch owners, the split superstructure was largely a British folly.

Although British owners again preponderate in this chapter, they were certainly not the last to build steamers. This distinction – if that is the word – goes to Spain among European countries, which completed a steam tramp in 1963. In terms of sheer numbers of steamers, Britain was also challenged by yards in Poland, East Germany and elsewhere, which built in industrial quantities to standard designs for their own and Soviet governments for whom efficient operation was not a major priority. Elsewhere, and especially in Britain, owners who clung to steam reaped the harvest in terms of uneconomic running, and in some cases it hastened their demise. However, as the next chapter will show, even the adoption of oil engines did not greatly extend the life of the classic tramp.

Note: An asterisk in a caption indicates the vessel shown in the photograph.

Small Britons

*Coulgarve** of 1949 was a shelter-decker, unusually so among four-hatch tramp steamers of her size – she was just 364 ft overall. Her builder, Lithgows Ltd of Port Glasgow, could not completely give up the split superstructure design, which with a forecastle was something of a trademark of the yard. *Coulgarve* has a narrow gap between bridge house and engine room casing and even the derricks at this position persist, used to lift stores or hoses for her oil fuel. Her engine was also unusual for a British steamer, a four-cylinder compound built by Rankin & Blackmore Ltd at nearby Greenock.

Coulgarve was ordered by Dornoch Shipping Co Ltd of Glasgow, which entrusted management to Lambert Brothers Ltd of London. Lamberts ran a remarkably diversified business. Originating in the coal business and owning a small fleet of colliers, they branched out so that they had interests in many aspects of shipping, also keeping a modest fleet of deep-sea tramps under ownership or management.

In 1954 *Coulgarve* went to another Glasgow-based company that specialised in short-distance tramp trades – Glen & Co, which renamed her *Dunolly*. In 1959, she made the big transition from European waters to the west coast of South America when sold to Valparaiso owners as *Santiago*. But she was not to remain under the Chilean flag for long. On 23 May 1960 she was driven aground by a tsunami off Isla Mocha while on voyage from Corral to Talcahuano with general cargo and was declared a constructive total loss.

It was not only British owners who specified steam engines. In April 1950, Vilhelm Torkildsen of Bergen took delivery of the 334-ft, single-deck *Fana**, propelled by oil-fired but otherwise standard triple-expansion engine supplied by North Eastern Marine Engineering (1938) Ltd at Sunderland. Her builders were a little further north – Blyth Dry Dock & Shipbuilding Co Ltd in Northumberland. *Fana* was unusual for her time in having a bridge deck extended forward to carry her second hatch.

Given her obsolescent machinery, she did not have a lengthy career under the Norwegian flag, although two Oslo owners briefly tried their hand at running her, first as *Nepos* and then as *Sunny Boy*. In 1961 she went to the People's Republic of China, where steam ships were still welcome, as long as they were cheap. Running first as *Nan Hai 154* and later as *Hong Qi 154* there is no knowing how long she lasted, except that a new ship of the latter name appeared in 1985.

Fana was photographed on the Thames where she made several visits in the 1950s, probably unloading timber in the Surrey Commercial Docks.

With her three-island hull, the 372-ft *Tynemouth** was rather more typical of small tramp steamers, although her delivery date of July 1955 made her one of the last built in the United Kingdom with triple-expansion machinery. Supplied by the builders, Smith's Dock Co Ltd of South Bank, Middlesbrough, her engines did have a low-pressure exhaust turbine coupled to the screw shaft. This turbine was a way of extracting some of the remaining energy from the steam exhausted from the low-pressure

cylinder. Becoming popular during the 1930s, it offered additional economy while avoiding the complexity and expense of quadruple-expansion machinery, which enjoyed only very short and limited popularity among tramp owners.

Owner Burnett Steamship Co Ltd of Newcastle mainly employed *Tynemouth* in trades to Canada and elsewhere in North America. She spent most of the 1950s and some of the 1960s working between there

and UK ports. She was also chartered to bring timber cargoes from West Africa. This varied work kept her busy until 1968 when she went out east, becoming *Eastern River* for Taiwanese owners. However, service here was not to be lengthy, because she stranded on 24 April 1971 off Fuga Island, north of the Philippines, while on a ballast voyage from Kaohsiung to Aparri. Declared a constructive total loss, her wreck was sold and presumably broken up.

Ironically, given that British engineers had done so much to develop the marine steam engine, some of the last British-built steamers had German machinery. *Winga** had a four-cylinder compound engine by Christiansen & Meyer of Hamburg.

The builder of the 296-ft *Winga*, which was completed in April 1957, was Alexander Hall & Co Ltd and she was one of the larger craft from this Aberdeen yard, better known for its steam trawlers and colliers. Not only was she very late to have steam engines, but also her long raised quarter deck was, at least for a ship with machinery amidships, largely obsolescent. The break in deck level forward must have been a liability in the trade of Glen & Co Ltd, who often carried Baltic timber. The layout was very similar to that of the owner's *Shuna*, built twenty years earlier in 1937, although *Winga* has significantly more cargo-handling gear. The owning company was sold to F T Everard & Sons Ltd of Greenhithe in 1961, hence the appearance of Everard's flag on the black top of her funnel in this photograph at Preston.

Winga was yet another steamer to go out East, passing to Indian owners as *Radiant* in 1967, and was

another to come to a violent end. She sank following a collision with the Greek motor ship *Altona* on 20 February 1978 in Bombay harbour while on voyage from

Port Okha and Bombay to her owner's home port of Cochin. Smit International was engaged to remove the wreck, which they cut up in situ. (*J and M Clarkson*)

Small Scandinavians

Norway had many ship owners, but relatively few ship builders, and those yards it did have seemed slow to move on from building modest-sized steam tramps. Fredriksstad Mek Verksted had an established reputation for building steam timber carriers, and after the Second World War it produced a design of 385-ft shelter-decker with a distinctive arrangement of cargo gear and

superstructure, represented here by *Folke Bernadotte**. She has three bipod masts, all with topmasts, and the first of her five hatches is mounted on an extended forecastle. A modest service speed of 11 knots was provided by machinery from her builder, the four-cylinder compound type now standard for steamers almost everywhere in Europe except the United Kingdom.

She had been completed as *Ringerd* in 1947, and in 1950 had the distinction of joining Norway's premier liner fleet, A/S Den Norske Amerikalinje, as *Trondhjemsfjord*. The name *Folke Bernadotte* was carried from 1955 to 1966 while managed by Prebensen & Blakstad of Risør. She was next owned in Italy but under the Liberian flag as *Spring* until broken up at Split in 1971.

Nordanvik was the last steam-reciprocating cargo ship built for a Swedish owner, and the seventh in a series of single-deckers built since 1943. Oskarshamns Varv completed the 297-ft ice-strengthened steamer and her triple-expansion engine in December 1954, but for such a late arrival she was to have a long and rather complex career.

Original owner Sven Rydberg of Gothenburg kept *Nordanvik* until 1958, when she was sold and renamed three times in little more than one year, becoming

Gundel* for Hjalmar Sjösten, Gothenburg, the Finnish *Sinikka* and lastly the *Malla*. Owners of *Malla* were O/Y Thombrokers A/B of Helsinki, which mainly ran her in the timber trade from Finland to western Europe, usually picking up a cargo of Polish coal during the return voyage to Helsinki. She also made two Mediterranean voyages, carrying Finnish timber to Haifa. And illustrating how difficult it is to define a tramp, from March to June 1963 *Malla* ran between Leith and Finland for Currie Line Ltd.

With freight rates falling in 1966, *Malla* and her sister

Minna (the former *Vestanvik* of 1953) were sold, *Malla* returning to Sweden, where her Estonian exile owners registered her in Panama as *Vaigu*. She steamed on until 1973 when ownership went east. Over the next eleven years she was named *Elenitsa S* (Greek owner), *Afamia Star* (Syrian), *Farid M* (Lebanese) and *Maya R* (Dubai). She was laid up for some time at Jeddah, and is believed to have been scuttled nearby, prior to 1986.

Poles for coal

One of the last trades to use steamers in Europe was coal from Poland. Here, with the ready availability of coal and the unsophisticated nature of their machinery, steam collier building persisted into the late 1950s, although even these were not the last European steamers. Although differences arose in details such as cargo gear, series building was embraced wholeheartedly, with bulk orders from the governments of the Comecon countries. The USSR took many of these designs, evidently preferring to rely on its satellites for merchant ship construction, perhaps while its own yards turned out warships.

*Gniezno** was one of the B32 series of 311-ft colliers from Stocznia Szczecinska. She was delivered in November 1957 for Polska Zegluga Morska, the aptly named Polish Steamship Company. She was the thirty-first example of the type according to her yard number, Polish builders adopting a unique but very clear numbering system, so *Gniezno* was B32/31. Her four-cylinder compound engine was of the Christiansen & Meyer type, made by Huta Zgoda of Swietochlowice. Her bipod masts retain their derricks in this photograph, although members of this class were later to lose theirs.

Surprisingly, in 1978 the twenty-one-year-old steamer could find buyers, who hid behind the title Tampa Steamship Lines Ltd, probably represented only by a brass plate in George Town, Grand Cayman. *Tulum* is last reported to have sailed from Houston in January 1981, and she was probably left to rust away in a Caribbean backwater, her owners going out of business by 1985.

The 355-ft, B31-type was even more numerous than the B32, and built mainly for the USSR. Kingposts are mounted on the forecastle, bridge and poop to facilitate loading a timber deck cargo when not carrying coal in the holds. Some later versions had a pole foremast between holds one and two, and were fitted with diesel engines. However, *Bielorussia** was a steamer, the forty-eighth example of the B31, completed by Stocznia Gdanska in December 1957 with the same type of machinery as fitted to *Gniezno* but with a low-pressure turbine. Delivered to Latvian Shipping Company, she steamed on until broken up in the USSR during 1986.

From Germany west and east

The relatively few steamers emerging in post-war years from yards in what was now West Germany were mostly relatively small. At just 329 ft, *Blidum** was unusual among these in having five rather than four hatches, that immediately in front of the bridge served by a pair of kingposts. The little shelter-decker has a good outfit of cargo-handling gear and was undoubtedly built for charter to cargo liner companies. Owners were

Nordfriesische Reederei GmbH of Rendsburg and manager Zerssen & Co, but in this photograph taken against a background of oil refineries in Rotterdam she is on charter to Harald Schuldt of Flensburg, who has insisted she fly its houseflag from her main mast.

Howaldtswerke AG of Kiel delivered *Blidum* in July 1950, and also provided her four-cylinder compound engine and a low-pressure turbine. In 1963, she was sold

to a London-based owner who put her under the Liberian flag as *Lilas*. Damaged by an engine room fire at Conakry on 9 September 1969, *Lilas* was towed all the way to Cadiz, only to be written off as a constructive total loss. Just before Christmas 1969 she was delivered to breakers at Puerto de Santa Maria.

East Germany also turned out steamers for the USSR, the long-established yard at Rostock, by now named VEB Schiffswerft Neptun, building the ice-strengthened, 355-ft *Kolomna* class. A classic three-island design, cargo gear was extensive, while the kingposts just ahead of the bridge served as ventilators, something of a characteristic of German ships. Early examples lacked the winch platforms and the distinctive cowl tops to the funnel. Engines were four-cylinder compounds with low-pressure turbines built by the Karl Liebnecht plant at Magdeburg.

Between 1953 and 1958, eighteen freighters were built to this design, while several further hulls were delivered to the USSR for naval use as repair ships or research vessels.

Balashov* emerged from Rostock in December 1955 to work for the Latvian Shipping Company of Riga. She was still with that entity almost thirty years later when sent to Spain for demolition, arriving at Aviles in September 1985. The general characteristics of the hull design were perpetuated in the even more numerous *Andizhan* type, three-island motor ships with bipod masts, turned out by Neptun from the later 1950s.

Southern Europeans

French yards turned out several very conventional steam colliers in immediate post-war years. Typical was *Béthune** completed by Ateliers et Chantiers de la Loire, Nantes in September 1948 for Société Maritime Nationale. The 323-ft, single-deck steamer had triple-expansion machinery manufactured by her builders and oil-fired boilers, enabling her to plod along at an unexciting 9 knots. Her funnel is unusually tall for a period when fans to provide a forced draught for her furnaces were usual and, despite its gently-raked bow, the hull has a totally obsolete counter stern. Cargo gear is the bare minimum: one derrick for each of her four holds.

Other French owners with very similar, basic steam colliers were Société Navale Caennaise and Compagnie Nantaise des Chargeurs de l'Ouest. Although from different builders, the former's *Dione* of 1947 and the latter's *Penmarch* of 1950 were almost identical to *Béthune*, even to the wood panelling on the rounded bridge front.

In 1961, and well into her career, *Béthune* found another owner, Bordeaux-based Robert Colombier, who renamed her *Gustave C.* She was broken up at Bilbao during 1968.

In immediate post-war years Spain's rather torpid economy tended to perpetuate the building of steamers for all but the country's fruit trade. Indeed, new buildings from Spanish yards were as yet not numerous, with many owners making do with second-hand steamers from Britain and elsewhere. The 343-ft *Santo Domingo** was delivered in July 1945 while the world was still in the closing weeks of the Second World War. Her builder – which gave her one of the four-cylinder compound engines popular further north in Europe – was Echevarrieta & Larrinaga in Cadiz, and her owner Compania Ibero-Americana de Navegacion SA of Seville. After a change of ownership in 1970, but not of name, she survived until 1974, when her demolition was completed in Bilbao.

Large Grays

Although thay had been both innovative and highly successful in their time, West Hartlepool shipbuilder William Gray & Co Ltd was definitely resting on their laurels in post-war years. But perhaps Irish Shipping Ltd of Dublin was desperate for tonnage to replace the veteran steamers that were the only ships available to a neutral country during the Second World War. Delivered in December 1949, *Irish Plane** at least had a low-pressure turbine coupled to her screw shaft, helping to increase the output from her Central Marine Engine Works triple-expansion machinery to push her along at 12 knots. The Irish company proved remarkably loyal to Gray, taking six more-or-less similar ships from the yard during 1948–53, plus two smaller steamers and a steam tanker, and following these up with a series of motor ships.

The 446-ft shelter-decker remained in the Irish fleet until 1966 when owners in Chittagong, East Pakistan bought and renamed her *Dacca City*. She arrived at Karachi in March 1971 to be broken up.

As to William Gray & Co Ltd, the West Hartlepool builder that had once been so dynamic, prospered while times were still good for British yards in the early 1950s, but then seems to have lost the will to live, and in the face of declining orders went into voluntary liquidation in 1961.

Also completed by William Gray & Co Ltd, this time in January 1951, *Seawall* could have been built any time over the previous two decades, with her shelter-deck, split superstructure and basic, triple-expansion engine made at the builder's Central Marine Engine Works. She was one of a 456-ft pair ordered by London Greeks Lykiardopulo & Co, who put both under the British flag; her sister was *Merchant Duke*.

Seawall was sold in 1955 to long-established Cardiff ship owner John Cory & Sons Ltd, and renamed *Ramillies** as seen here on the Thames. Given her basic steam machinery it is perhaps surprising she stayed in British ownership until 1966, and that she then found buyers in the liner trade, the National Shipping Corporation, Karachi, which renamed her *Surma*. She was unfortunate to be a victim of the war between India and Pakistan which led to the latter's partition and East Pakistan becoming Bangladesh. *Surma* was near Chittagong during the night of 12–13 December 1971 when sunk by Indian aircraft.

The idea of putting a steamer's boilers on deck in order to leave more room in the hull for cargo holds, is credited to a Danish designer, K G Meldahl, although a Norwegian shipyard held the rights to the design. It proved especially interesting to owners trading to the Great Lakes of North America where, until the opening of the St Lawrence Seaway, the length of ships that could reach the lakes through the Welland Canal was seriously limited. Few British owners embraced the idea, and it was criticised as detracting from the ship's stability by placing a substantial weight high in the hull. The major British owner of the type was London-based Dene Shipping Co Ltd, which between 1939 and 1953 had ten built by William Gray & Co Ltd, under licence from A/S Fredrikstad M/V. Their hold capacity was reckoned to be about 10 per cent greater than a conventional ship, but this was only an advantage with a low-density cargo such as grain, timber or coke for which the hold was filled to its volumetric capacity.

Dene's 429-ft *Hallindene** was completed and engined at West Hartlepool in December 1952. Again, building a steamer so late proved not propitious, and she was soon sold, passing in 1958 to Scindia Steam Navigation Co Ltd of Bombay as *Jalamudra*. After two further Indian owners, who renamed her *Prabhu Puni* and *Tasneem*, she was broken up in India during 1977.

Split superstructure finale

Although *Stad Alkmaar** was delivered in February 1948, her design is somewhat older: self-evidently from her split superstructure. Just how old is uncertain, although having been laid down as *Adolf Leonhardt* for Hamburg owners, the inference is that it was the German occupiers of the Netherlands who had, at least three years previously, placed the order for engines and hull with the Rotterdam yard of NV Machinefabriek & Scheepswerf van P Smit Jr. Quite when it was decided to fit a full-sized mast between bridge and engine room casing is not known, although this has echoes of pre-war Dutch cargo liner practice.

The 474-ft shelter-decker was delivered to NV Halcyon-Lijn, one of Rotterdam's best-known tramp owners. With a low-pressure exhaust turbine pushing her speed up to a heady 12 knots, *Stad Alkmaar* was found work for these owners until 1965, when buyers in Ravenna took her as *Lamone*. She was broken up at La Spezia in 1972.

Halcyon-Lijn had several other steam tramps completed in the Netherlands post-war with split superstructures, and which had also been laid down to German account including *Stad Leiden* (delivered 1948) and the turbine-driven *Stad Breda* (delivered 1949). But beyond these, it was largely British owners and builders who perpetuated the design.

The final manifestation of the split-superstructure design involved having accommodation trunked around the third hatch, exposing the crew to all the noise and disruption that accompanied working cargo at this hold. *Treglisson** was ordered from William Hamilton & Co Ltd, Port Glasgow early in 1948, and it is symptomatic of the demand for ships in immediate post-war years that she was not delivered until March 1950. The decision by Hain Steamship Co Ltd to order her, plus two other steamers from Readhead at South Shields, is odd because the eleven-ship fleet with which the company emerged from the Second World War entirely comprised motor vessels. Since 1917, Hain had been a part of the P&O Group and, while Hain's ships continued in the tramp trades, part of the rationale for its acquisition was that its ships would help out when required on the group's many liner services. The 453-ft *Treglisson* was engined by David Rowan & Co Ltd of Glasgow, and her machinery incorporated the by-now standard exhaust turbine.

Not surprisingly, these steamers were sold off within a decade, and in 1960 *Treglisson* followed a number of her British contemporaries to Pakistan, where she became *Yousufbaksh* of United Oriental Steamship Co, Karachi. Her end was violent. She was beached off Deal on 8 May 1965 after fire broke out in her cargo of jute, oil-cake and cotton which was bound from Chittagong to Boulogne. The fire was extinguished four days later and she was refloated, only to be despatched to Hamburg for demolition, work beginning early in 1966.

Completing the story of the split-superstructure steam tramp is *Baron Berwick**, delivered by John Readhead & Sons Ltd in October 1956. The South Shields yard also provided her oil-fired engines and exhaust turbine. She was the seventh near-sister completed for H Hogarth & Sons Ltd to this very attractive design, which might well have originated with Readhead. The yard built the first, *Baron Inverclyde* of 1954, and two others, but subsequent orders went to three different yards. *Baron Berwick* was the last steamer in the series, but she was followed by eight motor ships, the last of which differed only in having a 'streamlined' funnel. Lengths varied by a few feet, *Baron Berwick* measuring 456 ft overall.

Once again, within ten years of her completion steamers had virtually gone from Hogarth's fleet. *Baron Berwick* was sold in 1965 to become *Filtric* for the London-Greek Tricoglu family, who initially, and perhaps uniquely, registered her at Port au Prince in Haiti, moving her to the Greek flag in 1966. She was yet another steamer to become a total loss. Abandoned on 12 January 1970 after her wheat cargo shifted in heavy weather, she ran on to rocks near Corcubion, Spain. The partly submerged wreck subsequently broke apart. She had been on voyage from Alexandria to Copenhagen. (Ships in Focus)

Modern outside, steam inside

Split superstructure was not quite *de rigueur* among steamers, and the composite superstructure of *Reynolds** gives her a much more modern appearance. The builder of the 458-ft steamer in 1953 was William Pickersgill & Sons Ltd of Sunderland, with her oil-fired machinery (complete with exhaust turbine) also originating in Sunderland at the local works of North Eastern Marine Engineering (1938) Ltd. The owner was the long-established Bolton Steam Shipping Co Ltd of London. They might have regretted their decision to build steamers – two further such vessels coming from Smith's Dock Co Ltd in 1952 and 1954 – because all three were sold well within a decade.

Pakistan's appetite for British steamers was remarkable, and in 1961 *Reynolds* went to the United Oriental Steamship Co, Karachi and became *Imtiazbaksh*.

She lasted with that company a commendable fifteen years before succumbing to breakers at Gadani Beach, who began work in June 1976. *(J and M Clarkson)*

It might seem remarkable that in July 1963 a ship with a conventional steam reciprocating engine was delivered. However, Empresa Nacional 'Bazan' of Cartagena in Spain completed *Sac Barcelona* that month, and she was a contender for the title of the last European steam tramp ever built. The builder also supplied her oil-fired triple-expansion engine, which, aided by a low-pressure turbine, managed to push her along at a respectable 14.5 knots, a reminder that even steamers had to become faster to compete. The composite superstructure, 'streamlined' funnel and bipod masts are some concessions to modernity. Note how the upper parts of the main mast and its derricks have been painted black in anticipation that these would become discoloured by the exhaust from her engines.

As a single-decker, the 409-ft *Sac Barcelona* was intended for the coal trade of her owners, Transportes, Aduanas y Consignaciones SA, also of Cartagena, although her registry port is Barcelona. She is seen in the latter port, with two sets of hatch covers removed in anticipation of discharging by shoreside gear, and with her derricks stowed vertically out of the way. Her obsolescence is indicated by her relatively short life: in 1981 when just over eighteen-years-old she arrived at Aviles for an appointment with the ship breakers.

11

Swansong of the Tramp

The mostly diesel-driven ships in this chapter were built during the quarter century following the Second World War and are the last of the classic, engines-amidships tramp steamers. In many characteristics they are still recognisable as descendants of a type that emerged a century before, yet they show notable increases in speed – from 11 knots to 16 plus knots – and in size with several exceeding 500 feet. Cargo gear and crew accommodation were generally on a par with those of cargo liners, not least because owners were keen to grasp increasingly regular opportunities to charter to liner operators. Indeed, the distinction between the types became blurred, so that terms such as 'freighter' and 'general cargo ship' became common, the latter to distinguish them from the growing numbers of specialised ships.

Ownership and construction of these ships became more international, with British owners and – even more so – British shipyards finally losing their dominance. German yards took some of the international market, but emerging shipbuilding nations – notably Yugoslavia and Japan – made a significant impact. These years also saw the rise of the flag-of-convenience tramp, often Greek-controlled but increasingly owned in the Far East.

Perhaps surprisingly in view of this internationalisation, there was considerable consensus during this period as to what a tramp should look like – essentially it had three holds forward and two aft – although less so on details of cargo gear. Because of this, the ships in this chapter have been organised not by national origin but by design, a system having the advantage of allowing national characteristics to be compared. Organisation by masting arrangements admittedly relies on superficial characteristics, but does have the merit that cargo gear evolved over the period (in step with increases in speed and size), giving the chapter a rough chronological sequence. The single-acting, two-stroke diesel had emerged as the natural choice of machinery and, unless recorded otherwise, all the engines mentioned are of this type. The ships illustrated have been chosen partly to reflect the diversity of countries building this type.

Beauty is of course in the eye of the beholder, but the last of the classic tramps illustrated in this chapter often had an elegance that, as the two subsequent chapters will all too readily show, was soon to disappear from ship design in favour of an often ugly functionalism.

Note: An asterisk in a caption indicates the vessel shown in the photograph.

Four holds

As with the steamers in the previous chapter, the simplest tramps that could be regarded as ocean-going were four-hold vessels of between 300 ft and 400 ft, usually single-decked. Diesel-driven versions of these were built alongside the steamers although, in line with trends for larger tramps, most were shelter-deckers.

A Norwegian-built and owned version is the 355-ft *Sundove**, completed in January 1960 with a relatively conventional mix of pole masts and kingposts supporting

extensive cargo gear. The builder was Moss Værft & Dokk A/S, who fitted a Götaverken-type, eight-cylinder engine licence-built by Marinens Hovedverft to give her a service speed of 14.25 knots. Photographed in the late 1960s, she already had some history, because she was built for Oslo owners as *Mabella* and had become *Spurt* in 1963 for Lundegaard & Sønner of Farsund, which had changed her name to *Sundove* in 1964 when chartered to Saguenay Terminals. The aluminium that was the main

business of this Canadian charterer is reflected in the colour of the band on *Sundove*'s funnel.

With completion of the charter in 1969, she was sold to Empros Lines of Greece, who renamed her *Astronaftis*. Although her registered owner was altered three times, she carried this name and the Greek flag until 1985 when she was broken up at Aliaga in Turkey.

Predating *Sundove*, the 1958-built *Edwin Reith* exemplifies the more common approach to masting arrangements in the smaller freighter with her pair of bipods. The builder of *Edwin Reith* was Werft Nobiskrug GmbH of Rendsburg and machinery unusually comprised a pair of eight-cylinder, four-strokes by Maschinenfabrik Augsburg-Nürnberg AG geared to a single propellor shaft. Owner

of the 377-ft shelter-decker was 'Orion' Schiffahrt-Gesellschaft Reith & Co of Hamburg. Relatively small size was no bar to such ships roaming worldwide, and this April 1960 photograph was taken in Seattle.

Far Eastern owners were regular customers for second-hand ships of *Edwin Reith*'s size, and Hong Kong-based owners bought her in 1973 and renamed her *Sun*

Kwong, registering her in Mogadishu, when Somalia was currently enjoying some notoriety as a flag of convenience. As the attractions of the African country faded, she moved in 1979 to the Panamanian flag, as well as new owners and the name *New Hyde*. She was broken up at Shanghai in 1985. (*F W Hawks*)

Split superstructure motor ships

Previous captions have lamented that British designers of motor tramps seemed stuck in a time warp that demanded that the split superstructure, which provided a convenient bunker hatch for coal burning steamers, persisted even beyond oil-burning steamers into motor vessels. The practice continued for several owners through the 1950s, almost until the demise of the tramp ship as described in this book.

Walter Runciman of Newcastle was an early proponent of the motor tramp, and chapter 7 recorded him receiving his first diesel-driven ships from Doxford in 1924. The owner–builder relationship continued, and after the Second World War Runciman ordered a long series of tramps with split superstructure and a funnel set unusually far back on the engine room casing. Such apparently small differences, assisted by readily recognisable liveries, often gave a fleet its distinctiveness.

Exmoor* emerged from the Pallion yard on the Wear in March 1950, complete with her builder's four-cylinder machinery which gave her a modest service speed of 12.5 knots. The 448-ft shelter-decker was sold in 1962, and as Astir under the Lebanese flag gave her next owners, Greek partners named Angelicoussis and Efthimiou, a good ten years' service. This ended when she arrived at Shanghai in May 1972 to be broken up.

Although it had some innovative ideas, Silver Line Ltd, London, continued to build split-superstructure motor ships until the 1960s. Silverisle of 1960 was the last of a 452-ft series that had begun with Silverdene in 1956, also from J Crown & Son Ltd in Sunderland. They were fitted with Doxford engines, although in the case of Silverisle this had been built under licence by Hawthorn, Leslie (Engineers) Ltd at Newcastle.

Silver Line quite soon sold these ships; Silverisle was bought in 1965 by Metcalfe, Son & Co, and renamed Industria* as seen in this broadside photograph that emphasises her profile. She was kept until 1974 by Metcalfe, one of the last of a distinguished line of West Hartlepool tramp owners, who sold out to Furness, Withy in 1979.

Her further career involved Pakistani investors, which renamed her Alfaraj, after which she became the unpronounceable Annajm for owners based in Damman. This all ended predictably with her being broken up, at Gadani Beach in May 1983.

It was not just British owners and builders that perpetuated the split superstructure design well into the motor tramp era, and examples can be found in Dutch, Yugoslav and Danish practice. The Danes in particular had been building diesel-driven ships this way almost since they pioneered the ocean-going motor ship before the First World War, and were merely continuing with their pre-war layout in completing Nordhval* in November 1949. Builder of the 433-ft shelter-decker was Nakskov Skibsværft A/S and she received a Burmeister & Wain six-cylinder engine that drove her at 14 knots.

Sold in 1969, renaming involved changing half her letters to become Nordwild, Italian-owned but Panama flagged. As Gina Iuliano she later flew the Italian flag, and in 1976 ownership crossed the border into Switzerland as she became Adriastar, now under the Cypriot flag. She was broken up at Eleusis in Greece during 1983.

Among the last split superstructure ships was a class of multi-deck vessels built at Turku in Finland, mainly for the USSR with some going to Finnish owners. Commencing in 1952, completions stretched into the early 1960s, earning them the distinction of being the last of this remarkably long-lived design.

Masts and kingposts

Once the concept of a composite superstructure had, finally, become cemented in the minds of British ship designers, the obvious approach was to simply move the third hatch, plus its kingposts and derricks, forward of the bridge. The kingposts were typically placed ahead of the number three hatch, although in the case of *Kepwickhall**, they serve only this hatch. With her upright funnel, she has a slightly austere profile, although her hull lines

forward are carefully considered, with a long sweeping hance up to the forecastle, and a slight curve to her bow.

William Doxford & Sons Ltd completed her in Sunderland during October 1956 for the West Hartlepool Steam Navigation Co Ltd. A Doxford single-acting two-stroke drove her at nearly 14 knots. The letter 'G' painted on her funnel is the initial of West Hartlepool Steam Navigation's manager J E Guthe.

In 1966 she was sold to Metcalfe, Son & Co, owner of *Industria*, who gave her the name *Fidentia*. In 1972 the 469ft, shelter decker exchanged British for Maldives ownership, although flying first the Singaporean flag and later the Panamanian flag as *Premier Arctic*, a name remarkably bereft of either charm or meaning. Her end came on Gadani Beach where she was put ashore for demolition in May 1979.

Another Doxford motor ship, completed exactly two years after *Kepwickhall*, illustrates how quite subtle detail changes can substantially alter the look of a ship despite it having the same basic layout. *Fernmoor** has a less substantial superstructure, and the eye is drawn to her shapely funnel. She was built in 1958 as *Streambank* for Bank Line Ltd, which could never quite decide whether it was in the tramp trade or cargo liner trade, and as a result she has enhanced cargo gear. The pair of kingposts

forward of the bridge have derricks serving numbers two and three holds, while there is an additional pair of king posts abaft the superstructure. Note also the substantial winch platforms alongside both masts and king posts. Slightly longer than *Kepwickhall* at 487 ft, she has a similar type of Doxford diesel and is also a shelter-decker.

The name *Fernmoor* was given her in 1971 when she was bought from Bank Line by Glasgow-based owners which placed her management with Runciman of

Newcastle. She was photographed in April 1973, almost certainly on the Clyde, by which time she had only months left under the British flag. Greek owners next took her, fixing a time charter as she was initially renamed *Banglar Polyxeni*, the prefix dropped four years later for her to become *Polyxeni*. She was renamed *Intra Triumph* in 1982 but, in what was a mercifully short period given this name, in April 1983 she arrived at Gadani Beach for demolition.

When they were allowed to go back into business after the Second World War, West German owners and builders eagerly embraced the mast and kingpost design, putting their own stamp on it by making these erections particularly tall, a development that tended to hide the fact that the ships were becoming longer. That this look became familiar was partly due to the output of Nordseewerke Emden GmbH, which was particularly successful in winning orders for a class of 472-ft motor

ships. Orders came from both inside and outside of Germany, with *Karen Reed* completed in 1955 for Johs Larsen of Bergen, seen on the Thames in charter markings. Owners' individuality in this group was expressed largely in the exact details of the superstructure, in particular whether the companionways to either side were closed in or open.

Once her Norwegian owners disposed of her in 1968, she began the familiar descent into flag of convenience

registration. Initially Italian owners put her under the Liberian flag as *Primrose* and later with the somewhat pretentious name *Splendor*. On sale to Greece in 1976 she was put under the Greek flag, because the Greek government adopted policies to woo back to its flag the many Greek owners who had embraced free flags. Here she saw out her remaining days, first as *Aghios Nectarios* and later *Ais Giorgis*, before arriving at a scrap yard in Lavrion, which began demolition on New Year's Day, 1983.

Beautifully lit by the May sun as she ran trials in 1961, *Landwade* and her owners were to find the future of tramping under the British flag distinctly gloomy. The owner of this vessel was Atlantic Shipping & Trading Co Ltd, which was managed by the Cardiff-based W J Tatem Ltd, whose eponymous founder – latterly Lord Glanely – had moved from Devon sixty four years and fifty nine

ships earlier. Builders were long-standing, Sunderland tramp constructors, Bartram & Son Ltd, which were to survive largely by building SD14s. Propulsion was provided by a four-cylinder Doxford-type engine built by North Eastern Marine Engineering Co Ltd at Wallsend and which gave her a speed of 13.5 knots.

The departure from the British fleet of the 461-ft

Landwade in 1971 virtually marked the end of traditional tramping under the Red Ensign. But Greek owners would still buy such ships and work them successfully, and as the Cypriot-flagged *Marytonia*, and the Greek-flagged *Swede Tonia* and *Uniluck*, she motored on until broken up at Jamnagar in 1984.

Kingpost variations

Italian shipbuilding became significant internationally in post-war years, catching up with Italian ship owning, which had grown impressively in the inter-war years. Completed in July 1951 by Cantieri del Tirreno at Riva Trigoso, *Ercta** was an example of the more formal Italian design, with echoes of pre-war styling. She could even be mistaken for a British ship, with her relatively short masts and kingposts, a squat funnel and the companionways along the front of the superstructure. She shows a variation on the kingpost-forward design, with an extra set aft partly to serve the short number four hatch. The 480-ft shelter-decker was propelled at 12.5 knots by an eight-cylinder FIAT two-stroke.

Original owners of *Ercta* were Compagnia Siciliana di Armamento of Palermo, which sold her in 1969 to other Italian owners who put her under Panamanian registry as *Kilima*. The final transaction was a 1977 sale to Greek owners who left her under the Panamanian flag as *Blue Star*. She arrived at Split in Yugoslavia to be broken up in April 1979.

Large, elegant and fast, *Albia** illustrates how the distinction between tramp and cargo liner was disappearing when she was completed in March 1959. Her timber deck cargo, protected by tarpaulins, is indicative of her employment as a tramp, as is ownership by the de la Sota family, exiles from the Basque region of Spain and who perforce used the Liberian flag. On the other hand, she is fast at 16.5 knots, has two decks and is on charter. The king posts and masts forward have been reversed, an extra set added aft, and all have the additional height common to Dutch and German designs.

The builder of *Albia* was NV Koninklijke Maatschappij 'De Schelde' at Vlissingen, but her start in life was rather ignominious. She was ordered by Greek manager A Lusi as part of a project to build twenty-one tramps for Greek clients in three Dutch yards, encouraged by attractive financing terms on offer in the Netherlands. After five had been launched the others were cancelled, but 'De Schelde' went ahead and completed those on order, laying them up until they found buyers. The *Argo Sounion*, as she was intended to be named, was acquired by Ramon de la Sota Jr to become *Albia*. The Dutch yard had given the 517-ft ship its own licence-built six-cylinder Sulzer diesels.

In 1974 she finally hoisted the Greek flag as *Antonios C*, but spent her last few months under Panamanian registry as *Honour Five* before arriving at Gadani Beach for demolition in March 1982.

Japanese revival

As in Germany, shipbuilding was all but prohibited in Japan immediately after the Second World War, and restrictions were lifted as the US occupiers realised that Japan could be a useful ally in the troubled region of southeast Asia. Early post-war Japanese cargo ship designs were conservative, as witness the three-island, 396-ft *Burma Maru**. Completed in October 1951 as *Ginko Maru*, uniquely for this chapter she was steam turbine rather than diesel driven, the Japanese having favoured this type of propulsion even during the Second World War. The builder of the hull was Hitachi Zosen KK of Osaka and machinery came from Ishikawajima Jukogyo at Tokyo. Like the majority of Japanese freighters built post-war, she had two decks and is difficult to classify, because when she became *Burma Maru* in 1956, her owner was Osaka Shosen Kaisha, who was in the liner trade.

Sale in 1971 saw *Burma Maru* helping to build up the fleets of the southeast Asian entrepreneurs who were soon to challenge European owners as major tramp operators. She became the Taiwan-owned but Panamanian-flagged *Chieh Sheng*, retaining this name and flag when sold to Singapore a year later. Breakers at Kaohsiung took the thirty-one-year-old ship in 1982.

The Japanese were probably the last to cling to the long bridge deck design, a considerable proportion of their post-war output of general cargo ships having one or two hatches mounted on this deck. Photographed docking in London, *Hikoshima Maru** has the former layout, and the conventional mix of masts and kingposts, the latter joined with a lattice girder. This feature together with upright styling of superstructure and funnel distinguished Japanese conventional cargo ships post-war.

Hikoshima Maru was a powerful motor ship, with a service speed of 14 knots provided by her Sulzer two-strokes licence-built by Tamashima Diesel Works. Uraga Dock Co Ltd of Yokosuka completed the 449-ft hull in June 1953 for Nakano Kisen KK of Tokyo. Interrelationships in the Japanese shipping industry were complex, and *Hikoshima Maru* subsequently passed through the hands of both Mitsubishi and Nippon Yusen Kaisha.

Second-hand Japanese ships provided a source of entry-level tonnage not just for aspiring Far Eastern owners but also for Greek owners, and *Hikoshima Maru* went to one of the latter in 1970 as *Campanula*, remaining in Greek registration after 1975 as *Angy*. She reached Gadani Beach and the breakers in March 1978.

Pole masts

The Dutch *Tero** has a somewhat formal appearance. Contributing to this is her massive superstructure extending over at least three decks, a two-deck erection on the poop, plus funnel and masts which are notably upright. Rotterdam Droogdok Maatschappij delivered the 452-ft shelter-decker to NV Maatschappij Vrachtvaart, also of Rotterdam, in February 1949. However, her machinery was a generation older, Burmeister & Wain-type engines completed in 1939 by NV Machinefabriek & Scheepswerven P Smit and presumably unused because of the war.

Unusually, *Tero* has heavy lift derricks on both her forward masts, enabling them to work together. Another unusual feature are the light arms extending beyond the cross trees on each mast.

Despite her ageing engines, *Tero* served her

Rotterdam-based owners until 1967 when V Tricoglu bought her and placed her on the Greek registry as

Adytric. Five years later she was broken up at Kaohsiung, work beginning in March 1972.

German yards were building three-masted tramps alongside the kingpost-type, Lübecker Flender-Werke turning out a number of examples, including *Karpfanger** in May 1958. She continued the German tradition of tall masts, and had what was by now the norm in terms of the comprehensive cargo gear that a charterer would expect. A five-cylinder, two-stroke by Maschinenfabrik Augsburg-Nürnberg AG gave *Karpfanger* a speed of 12.75 knots. Owners of this big (498-ft) shelter-decker were Hanseatische Reederei E Offen & Co of Hamburg, whose funnel markings dramatically displayed a Teutonic cross.

Sale in 1970 saw her pass to owners based in Lugano, Switzerland, but who used various flags-of-convenience, and not a few names, as she became progressively *Providentia*, *Efor*, *Emar* and *Bonita 1*, all with different registered companies but the same beneficial owner. Under a sixth name, *Maysun II*, she was broken up in China during 1984.

Once the idea took root among British builders that tramps might have full height pole masts rather than kingposts, this configuration became the norm. In *Houston City** of 1963, Sir William Reardon Smith & Sons Ltd and builders Doxford embraced this idea wholeheartedly, giving her particularly tall masts, and for good measure a pair of kingposts aft of the centre castle. She is also unusual for the period in having a full height poop deck. This three-quarters stern view reveals her registration at Bideford, a device adopted by Devon-born but Cardiff-based William Reardon Smith when Cardiff registration became a byword for maritime fraud during difficult years in the early twentieth century.

In the 1960s, speeds of tramps increased significantly. Partly this was due to the development of more powerful diesels, and partly because owners recognised that the shipping industry was becoming more competitive. Speed was also a factor in gaining charters from liner companies, an important consideration for

owners as the classic tramp began to lose out in traditional trades to larger and more efficient bulk carriers. The 500-ft *Houston City* could give a good account of herself, her Doxford machinery driving her at 15.5 knots, compared with the 11 knots that was the norm for tramps just ten years earlier.

Sale in 1972 saw her owned by a merchant bank, which bareboat chartered her out as *Maria Elisa*, leaving her under Reardon Smith management. This continued until 1980 when Hong Kong owners renamed her *Alpac Africa*, as which she was demolished at Shanghai in 1984. *(Roger Sherlock)*

'Four posters'

As cargo ships grew larger, it became logical to move from a five- to a six-hatch and hold configuration, and this necessitated a further increase in cargo gear, as in the 512-ft *Johanna Oldendorff*. In the late nineteenth century a similar trend among sailing vessels had given rise to the four-masted barque rig, dubbed 'four posters', although the author has no evidence of this term being applied to motor cargo ships.

Lübeck-based Egon Oldendorff & Co GmbH favoured local yards when possible, and *Johanna Oldendorff* was completed by Lübecker Flender-Werke in August 1958. Tall masts are a particularly Germanic feature, the first of the four especially tall to carry the heavy lift derrick, which also necessitates this mast having extra guys. The shelter-decker was propelled at 14 knots by an eight-cylinder, two-stroke by Maschinenfabrik Augsburg-Nürnberg AG.

German owners were not slow to embrace flags-of-convenience to reduce running costs. Oldendorff had a number of such Liberian subsidiaries, including Westfalia Shipping Corporation, to which *Johanna Oldendorff* was transferred in 1971, without change of name or colour scheme. This ended in 1974 when she was sold to

Greece as *Aspis*. The name *Tekapo* was carried under the Panamanian flag for a few months in 1982 before she

arrived at Busan, South Korea in November to await the breakers.

The owner of *London Craftsman* was London & Overseas Freighters Ltd, set up in 1948 by London-Greek shipowners to run tramp tankers under the British flag. Nevertheless, it began with second-hand dry cargo ships, not achieving a tanker-only fleet until 1951. Encouraged by a buoyant tanker market, it had ambitious plans to expand and in 1956–7 ordered twelve large tankers. But tanker rates then dipped to an all-time low, and several tankers were cancelled while three others were changed

to orders for six dry cargo vessels, among them *London Craftsman* and three sisters from Uddevallavarvet A/B in Sweden. The four-masted design probably originated with these Swedish builders, because the two other tanker substitutes from a Dutch yard looked quite different. Delivered in November 1963, the 531-ft *London Craftsman* had an eight-cylinder, Götaverken-type engine built by Uddevallavarvet. As the photograph of her on charter to Svedel Line illustrates, she was another tramp

with comprehensive cargo handling gear and a cruising speed of 16.5 knots designed to be attractive to liner companies.

In 1976 she moved to the Greek flag on sale to a John Polemis, who renamed her *Pindaros*. Still owned in Greece, but now named *Leixoes*, in 1987 she migrated to the increasingly popular Maltese registry. Her final name, *Don*, was adopted for a delivery voyage to Chittagong where demolition commenced in November 1990.

Bipod masts

As can be seen in the photographs of ships with pole masts, these structures needed considerable staying, and the stays both required maintenance and restricted the reach of derricks used to work cargo over side. Bipod masts, although more expensive because they required additional steel, required much less in the way of stays. They also meant that the heels of the derricks could be separated; again improving the rate cargo could be handled. These considerations were more important to a cargo liner operator than to one who ran tramps, but even so a number of the latter type of ship appeared with bipods. *Ruysdael** of 1957 is also notable for having an extended forecastle on which is placed the hatch for her number one hold, again a feature more common in liner trade ships.

Owner of the 462-ft *Ruysdael* was Bolton Steam Shipping Co Ltd of London, which was last met taking delivery of the steamer *Reynolds* just four years earlier. *Ruysdael* was a product of Smith's Dock Co Ltd, Middlesbrough, who went to Hawthorn, Leslie (Engineering) Ltd for her Doxford-type oil engine. Her career was remarkably simple: sold when eleven years old (by now the norm for British tramps), a Greek owner ran her as *Aristides Xilas* for a further eleven years until she was broken up at Kaohsiung in 1979.

Mette Skou is a clear case of the owner, not the builder, influencing the design of a ship – in fact, a whole series of ships. Ove Skou of Copenhagen made the design of his motor ships almost a trademark, with their 'streamlined' superstructure and funnel, not to mention their white hulls with a blue cheat line reflecting the blue band on his funnels. His orders were not confined to one shipyard, or even solely to Danish builders, but his ships were always highly recognisable. The 417-ft, long-forecastle, shelter-decker *Mette Skou* was a 1957 product of A/B Helsingør Skibsværft & Maskinbyggeri, who also provided the eight-cylinder two-stroke diesel that rushed her along at 18 knots.

Mette Skou was soon sold, and indeed Ove Skou was not to survive until the present day. In 1962 she was sold as *Lircay* to Compania Sud-Americana de Vapores of Valparaiso, which wanted the 18-knot motor ship for its liner services. After eight years under the Chilean flag, she became the Greek-controlled *Essex*, and was broken up at Kaohsiung in 1980.

*Milora** represents a transition between the bipod-only school of ship design and those opting for kingposts. Her builder in 1958 for Yngvar Hvistendahl of Tønsberg was Sweden's A/B Oskarshamns Varv, while A/B Götaverken supplied her nine-cylinder, two-stroke machinery.

The 485-ft cargo ship is another example of a high-specification tramp – she had two decks and a 14.5 knot service speed – quickly sold to a cargo line operator, in this case Bharat Line Ltd of Bombay, who renamed her *Bharatkumar* in 1961. She served there until 1970, when an Italian owner who put her under the Liberian flag chose to

restore her original name, *Milora*, although he changed his mind in 1976 when she became *Senora*. The almost inevitable Greek ownership followed when she was renamed *Costathina* in 1976.

She ended her days tramping. On 15 July 1978 *Costathina* grounded off Senegal while on voyage from Maceio in Brazil to Basrah with a cargo of bagged sugar. Although refloated on 21 August, her twenty-year-old hull was declared a constructive total loss and taken to Cartagena in Spain to be broken up.

*Egton** was, in several respects, a rather sad story. First, delivered in 1962 she was the final ship built for what was also the last of the many tramp owners based in the ancient port of Whitby. Second, she was so far out of her time that almost half her life was spent laid up. And if a third reason is wanted, she offered a chance to preserve in superb condition a typical British tramp ship, an opportunity which was not grasped.

The owner of the 508-ft *Egton* was Rowland & Marwood's Steam Ship Co Ltd, managed by Headlam & Son. Its order went to highly-experienced tramp builder Bartram & Sons Ltd, Sunderland, which contracted with nearby Doxfords to supply a diesel engine to give her a service speed of 14 knots. Several features of her design are

noteworthy. Crew accommodation was at last given the attention it deserved and, in an extension of the superstructure, the additional cabins were trunked around the fourth hatch. Although the lack of topmasts detracts from her appearance, she is a handsome ship with the styling of superstructure, bows and combined funnel and radar mast having been carefully considered.

But the owners could not find enough paying work for *Egton*, and she lay for the latter part of her life at West Hartlepool. Reportedly she was excellently maintained, which makes it doubly unfortunate that in 1986 the only buyer she could find was a Finnish ship breaker.

Eastern Europeans

Although many communist-ruled countries in eastern Europe built up their shipbuilding industries in post-war years, most concentrated on supplying either their domestic market or others within the USSR-dominated Comecon. The major exception was Yugoslavia, a country that was perhaps the least influenced by the USSR, and which commanded a useful international market for its shipbuilding output. A large degree of standardisation was evident, with very similar looking ships turned out by several yards but to slightly differing specifications. One of the most ubiquitous designs is represented by the 499-ft shelter-decker Goranka*.

Although Goranka was built for a domestic tramp company, Splosna Plovba of Piran (the funnel markings depicted the mountainous nature of its province, the now-independent Slovenia), similar ships were sold for overseas owners, including those in Switzerland, Greece and Romania. The builder of Goranka in 1958 was Brodogradiliste 'Uljanik' of Pula, which also provided her licence-built Burmeister & Wain-type five-cylinder machinery. Brodogradiliste '3 Maj' at Rijeka built identical, long-forecastle ships, including examples for Jugoslavenska Oceanska Plovidba, Yugoslavia's major liner operator, illustrating again how the design of tramp and cargo liner was converging in post-war years. Brodogradiliste 'Split' produced a slightly longer, two-deck version without the extended forecastle but again with a full set of bipod

masts, examples including the Swiss-owned, Liberian-registered Cruzeiro do Sul.

Seen near Vancouver, Goranka spent her entire career

with a single owner (something only eastern European tramps seemed able to do post-war) and was sent to breakers in Alang, India in early 1984.

Several classes of small steamers built in Eastern Europe for the USSR were featured in the previous chapter, and this is one of their diesel successors, Sigulda* of 1962. Builder of the 342-ft, ice-strengthened single-decker was VEB Schiffswerft 'Neptun', Rostock in East Germany. Early versions of the class were given East German diesels, but for Sigulda machinery came from West Germany's prime engine builder, Maschinenfabrik Augsburg-Nürnberg AG, a six-cylinder machine giving her a service speed of 13.75

knots. Referred to as the 'Kovel' class, an estimated forty-six ships were built to this design, some joining the Soviet Navy, and a number being transferred from the USSR to Vietnam.

Sigulda was delivered to the nominal ownership of Estonian Shipping Co, Tallinn in October, and would fly the 'hammer and sickle' until 1992. Oddly, upon Estonia and other Baltic states achieving independence from the former Soviet Union, she went to the Latvian flag, owned

by the Riga Transport Fleet. There was no name change when she moved to private owner Samfa Ltd, who registered her in Malta, and she remained in Latvian beneficial ownership. A name change did come, but only for her delivery voyage to breakers when the first and last letters were cut off to make her Iguld. She arrived at Mumbai in June 1997, demolition beginning about two months later.

*Aleksander Zawadzki** is a second example of a series-built Eastern European ship that is difficult to classify. Shelter-deckers capable of 16 knots, this B41 type was used by both Poland and China on regular services as well as for tramping, the distinction becoming blurred when fleets are directed centrally by an arm of the government. Messageries Maritimes also took five B41s, while *Tirana* was one of the largest ships in Albania's tiny fleet.

Some twenty of this 501-ft type were built during 1964–74, the latter date making the final example, *Marian Buczek*, one of the last conventional, engines-amidships freighters built anywhere. *Aleksander Zawadzki* of 1966 was constructed by Stocznia im Komuny Paryskiej and,

while all were fitted out in Gdynia or Szczecin, one hull was built under subcontract at Seville and two, including *Marian Buczek*, at Lisbon. There were far from minor variations in the class, with the slightly bigger Portuguese pair having Stülcken masts and square funnels, while lacking the very distinctive treatment of the superstructure sides that made the earlier B41s instantly recognisable. All had Sulzer engines built in Poland by H Cegielski.

Aleksander Zawadzki and the dozen other Polish-owned B41s were completed for Polskie Linie Oceaniczne, Gdansk, transferring to Polskie Towarzystwo Okretowe SA in 1982. The sixth example, *Aleksander Zawadzki*, was broken up at Calcutta in 1992.

Kingposts and cranes

In complete contrast with the French *Béthune* in chapter 10 is *Leopold L D*, completed just five years later by the same builder, Ateliers et Chantiers de la Loire, but at its yard at St Nazaire. *Leopold L D* has no conventional masts, just kingposts and cranes, and only a signal post on the bridge to support aerials and from which to fly flags. An eight-cylinder, two-stroke Sulzer, built under licence by Compagnie de Construction Mécanique at St Denis, gave her a respectable service speed of 14.5 knots.

The 490-ft shelter-decker was delivered in January 1953 to Louis Dreyfus et Compagnie, Paris, the shipowning arm of a major French and international grain trader. Dreyfus kept its fleet up to date, and in 1964 sold *Leopold L D* to another French owner, which renamed her *Sauzon*. In 1976 the twenty-three-year-old ship could still find a buyer in the shape of Österreichische Reederei AG, Vienna, which renamed her *Austrian Explorer*. From 1980 changes of name and ownership came faster: *Nigerian Explorer*, *Bellerive* and *Cephalonian Wave*, were crammed in before she went to the breakers at Gadani Beach in June 1984.

Elettra Fassio of 1957 makes an interesting contrast with *Ercta* (page 140), also built in Italy but six years earlier. Bow and stern are curvaceous, and Italian styling has been extended to her superstructure and funnel, giving a harmonious feel. Kingposts have replaced masts completely, although unlike in *Leopold L D* the two main sets carry topmasts. The 492-ft shelter-decker came from the Genoa yard of Ansaldo SpA with FIAT supplying a seven-cylinder, two-stroke built at Turin. Initial owners were Villain e Fassio e Compagnia Internazionale di Genova Società Riunite di Navigazione SpA, Genoa.

The same aspirations to become major ship owners, which had spurred Pakistan to buy much ex-British tonnage, drove India, and in 1964 *Elettra Fassio* became *Vishva Pratap* of The Shipping Corporation of India Ltd, a state-owned enterprise that was rapidly displacing the longer-established Scindia as India's major ship owner. She was destined to remain in this fleet for the rest of her days, and was delivered to breakers in Mumbai in June 1982.

Specialist freighters

The concept of a specialised tramp is something of an oxymoron, as the tramp owner is best served by a vessel that can carry any bulk cargo. However, the freighters depicted here were designed for the requirements of particular cargoes and trades, and are included because they had much more in common with tramps than with cargo liners.

The steam turbine *Margaret Bowater** of 1955 and her sister *Sarah Bowater* were built and engined by William Denny & Brothers Ltd, Dumbarton as newsprint carriers. They were to trade from the mills of the Bowater Paper Corporation in Newfoundland to the United Kingdom and down the Atlantic coast of North America. Newsprint rolls are large and heavy, but also very vulnerable to damage: a one-inch tear could make a mile of paper unusable. To reduce damage, pillars were eliminated from the holds and

wherever possible other obstructions were avoided and sparring was covered with rubber. In winter the ships had to steam through ice up to eighteen inches thick, and so they were ice strengthened and had well-rounded forefoots. The 419-ft *Margaret Bowater* had accommodation for six or eight guests, and *Sarah Bowater* had an owner's suite. The former is seen on the Manchester Ship Canal: she regularly traded to Bowater's mill at Ellesmere Port.

Such specialised, turbine-driven ships had short lives. Once sold by Bowater Steamship Co Ltd in 1968, *Margaret Bowater* changed gender to become *John W Hill* and later *Grand State* for US-based owners before arriving at Kaohsiung for demolition in 1971. (*K. Cunnington*)

Grain has long been a staple of the tramp trades, but only a minority of ships have been designed specifically to carry this cargo. Much less dense than other staple cargoes such as coal or iron ore, grain could fill the holds of a tramp before it was down to its loadline, so ships dedicated to the grain trade had larger holds, and what was called a 'high cubic capacity'. Some such ships were owned by the large international grain traders, which could guarantee that their ships would be largely carrying grain.

Oregon Steamship Co Ltd of London was a subsidiary of one of the big four international grain traders, the US-based Continental Grain. At times they have maintained their own small fleet, because relying entirely on the charter market makes a trader subject to price fluctuations, especially when shipping is booming and freight rates rising. *Londoner** was delivered to Oregon by Bartram & Sons Ltd of Sunderland in July

1961, and fitted with a seven-cylinder, Sulzer two-stroke, licence-built by George Clark (Sunderland) Ltd, which gave her a service speed of 15 knots. Externally, she was similar to other tramps, with three sets of bipod masts, but internally the 499-ft hull had two decks.

Sold in 1971, she went east as *Hwa Gek*, passing through the hands of several Singapore-based owners until 25 May 1985 when she was wrecked after dragging her anchors during a cyclone in Chittagong outer anchorage. *(B Reeves)*

Ships designed for carrying ore were a strand in the development of the bulk carrier, discussed in chapter 13. However, conventional tramps were also deeply involved in the trade, and a number of fleets of these were largely dedicated to moving ore. Trafik A/B Grängesberg-Oxelösund of Stockholm was involved in the ore traffic from mines in northern Sweden, either from the Baltic or ice-free ports such as Narvik in Norway. Before the company invested in specialised, engines-aft ore carriers and some of the pioneer ore/oil ships, it built a fleet of conventional-looking motor tramps. Delivered in May 1943, *Kajtum** was one of ten or so near sisters built for the company during the 1940s, her wartime build not precluding the fitting of an elegant wood-panelled bridge front. Of 383 ft overall, they were built by A/B Götaverken at Gothenburg and given the builder's five-cylinder, two-stroke engines to drive them at 12.5 knots. An enduring feature of the company's ships, and indeed those of other Swedish owners, was the name painted on the hull picked out in yellow and shaded with blue, Sweden's national colours.

The career of *Kajtum* subsequent to her sale in 1959

suggests she was not so specialised that she could not find work beyond the ore trade. First a Swedish owner ran her as *Cetus*, then she went to Poland as *Grodziec*, and finally

had Greek owners who renamed her *Dalia A* and then *Ionian Breeze*. After a career of over forty years, she arrived at Gadani Beach during November 1984 for demolition.

Were it not for the designation 'ore carrier' alongside her entry in Lloyd's Register, the major occupation of *Bochum** would not have been apparent, especially as she had a shelter deck. Neither was she built for a company principally concerned with ore carrying, because she was delivered in April 1958 to August Bolten William Miller's Nachfolger of Hamburg as *Virginia Bolten*. Her builder, Lübecker Flender-Werke, was also closely associated with tramp ship construction. She also has a particularly complete set of derricks, two to each of her six hatches. Her impressive 511-ft length is emphasised by a comparatively compact superstructure, and makes even her unusually tall masts look in proportion. Machinery comprised an eight-cylinder, two stroke by Maschinenfabrik Augsburg-Nürnberg A.G.which gave her a fourteen knot service speed.

Only in 1960, when renamed *Bochum*, did she begin work for an ore company, Krupp Seeschiffahrt GmbH of Hamburg, a subsidiary of the major steel company and former armaments manufacturer. Following sale in 1965,

she ran for a Norwegian owner as *Anna Presthus*, then for Greeks as *Green Park*, *Nelson* and lastly *Frantzescos M*. Ship breakers at Bombay, as it was still called, took delivery of her in June 1983.

CHAPTER
12
The Last Tramps?

The 1960s saw a collapse of the international consensus as to how a tramp ship should be designed. It is hardly coincidental that during this decade began the inexorable rise of bulk and container carriers and with these a thinning out of both ship owners and builders that depended for their income on the conventional tramp ship. A further factor was that the regulations which favoured 'open' shelter-decks (which had only a token opening to the outside world) were phased out, which removed one of attractions of the two-deck, or 'tween-deck, ship. This chapter explores some of the last designs whose ancestry can be traced back to the basic, ocean-going cargo ship developed by British builders and owners a century before.

The typical freighter – a term that reflected the blurring of the distinction between tramp and cargo liner – of the last third of the twentieth century was usually series built. This was a trend begun in eastern European yards after the Second World War, learning much from wartime experience in Britain, Germany and especially the United States. From the 1960s, builders elsewhere embraced series building, often as part of 'Liberty replacement' initiatives. The elements of the shipbuilding industry that launched such programmes were driven by the realisation that the market was changing dramatically, and that owners were no longer placing small orders for expensively custom-built tramps.

The rationale for 'Liberty replacements' was that wartime standard ships were reaching the ends of their lives, and that economical replacements were needed. This was a flawed argument because those owners who could afford nothing more than twenty-year-old, war-built tonnage could hardly spare the odd million pounds to order a new vessel. Indeed, analysis of the owners that ordered some 700 'Liberty replacements' indicates that only a minority had ever owned a Liberty, and most were simply taking the opportunity of acquiring a useful vessel at an economical price.

Some of the designs got no further than the builder's drawing office or crude artists' impressions in trade journals. Around twenty builders succeeded in selling 'Liberty replacements' but only did so by paring costs to a minimum.

As these programmes ran their course and the economic collapse of Comecon began, building of recognisably conventional tramps also petered out. But as the question mark in this chapter's title implies, this was not to say that tramping ceased. As the next chapter will demonstrate, this aspect of shipping changed so that the tramp ship's natural successor, the bulk carrier, or a variety of specialised vessels, continued to carry the huge and growing amounts of bulk cargoes that mining, quarrying, agriculture, forestry and the chemical industry generated.

Note: An asterisk in a caption indicates the vessel shown in the photograph.

Born for the USSR

It is difficult to classify the wide variety of cargo ships built for communist-controlled countries as their deployment was sometimes political rather than economic, which meant that they could be tramping for one voyage and operating on a liner service the next. The two types chosen to represent these freighters were small vessels, the first of which was largely intended for the timber trade.

The 335-ft, single-deck *Vologdales** was one of a large number of this size built in Finland for the USSR. Four shipbuilders were involved and *Vologdales* was produced by the yard of F W Hollming at Rauma in 1962. Her Hallen mast-cum-crane serving the second and third holds may not have been judged successful because, after completion of ten of this type and a dozen similar-sized hulls with engines aft, bipods were substituted, and building of the revised types continued until 1971. Although not apparent in the photograph of the well-laden *Vologdales*, an ice-breaking bow was fitted and the hull ice strengthened because she was allocated to the USSR's Northern Shipping Company to work out of the White Sea port of Archangel. Her five-cylinder Burmeister & Wain-type engine was built in Finland by Valmet Oy.

After the break-up of the Soviet Union, *Vologdales*

was sold for further trading in 1992, unlike many Soviet ships which went directly for scrap. Initial owners as *Patriot* were Greeks, who unpatriotically registered her in Malta, and she later went to Syria, successively as *Zena III*, *Bransis* and *Amir A*. She was broken up at Mumbai during 2000. *(Michael D J Lennon)*

The larger of the two Comecon types illustrated was a shelter-decker built in serious numbers by VEB Schiffswerft 'Neptun' at Rostock in East Germany. The design evolved gradually over a building life of ten years, and indeed authoritative books on Soviet bloc merchant ships distinguish between two classes. The earlier 'Povonets' class is represented by the 347-ft *Gorno-Altaisk** completed in September 1963. The earliest units had three sets of goalpost masts to serve the four holds, but in *Gorno-Altaisk* two goalposts have been replaced with bipods, as they were in most of her forty or so class-mates. By 1967, all three masts had become bipods, and this was perpetuated in the similar-sized 'Pioner' type, distinguished mainly by a larger superstructure block. These began to roll off the launching ways at Rostock in 1968, eventually numbering over thirty, again all destined for USSR ownership. *Gorno-Altaisk* had a six-cylinder MAN-type engine built under licence by Dieselmotorenwerk Rostock and which propelled her at 12.5 knots – a modest speed that justifies including her in a book on tramps.

Gorno-Altaisk was destined for the USSR's Far Eastern Shipping Company based in Vladivostok, and appears to have spent her entire life in the Far East. The photograph was taken at anchor off Singapore in March 1981 and she ended her life in a Chinese shipbreaking yard at Shekou in 1987. *(Roy Kittle)*

Three-quarters aft

The 1960s saw a trend for dry cargo ships to have machinery placed right aft. This was sensible because only a short propeller shaft was needed and the shaft tunnel could be eliminated from the after holds. But there were initial reservations about how a vessel in ballast would trim with its heavy machinery right aft; there was also concern about placing the navigating bridge so far from the bows. As a result, several contemporary cargo liners and a few tramps were built to a compromised design, with machinery about three-quarters aft, and only one hold abaft the superstructure.

Baxtergate* emerged from the yard of the Burntisland Shipbuilding Co Ltd on the Firth of Forth in March 1962, destined for the fleet of Turnbull, Scott & Co, who originated in Whitby but had long been based in London. The 470-ft shelter-decker had a Doxford two-stroke engine licence-built by Hawthorn, Leslie (Engineering) Ltd on the Tyne. This gave a speed of 15.25 knots, and – with a good complement of cargo gear – indicates that she was intended for charter to liner companies. Indeed, during 1971–2 Baxtergate was renamed Mediator for such a charter, to T & J Harrison (Harrison Line), of Liverpool.

The conclusion of this charter saw her sold, going to Argentine owners as Marvaliente, and in 1981 to Greece as Bravo Nek. However, on 27 December 1981 she sank

following collision with the Chinese freighter Wu Men in Latakia Roads, where she had recently arrived with a cargo of bagged sugar from Gdynia.

The Doxford & Sunderland Shipbuilding & Engineering Co Ltd resulted from a 1961 merger of Doxford's Pallion yard with the nearby Laing and Thompson facilities, all three vastly experienced in building tramps and cargo liners. Almost their last essay in conventional freighters was a class that found particular favour in Greece. These fast, 540-ft, 'tween-deckers are exemplified by Iktinos*, completed at Pallion for Lyras Brothers in July 1969. Although Doxford had produced Britain's most successful native diesel, Iktinos had a seven-cylinder Sulzer built

locally by G Clark & NEM Ltd, giving 17.5 knots – more than adequate for charter to liner operators.

Illustrative of the convergence of tramp and cargo liner designs, one of this series was bought on the stocks by Harrison Line of Liverpool and named Benefactor. Bank Line also ordered a series of similar hulls from Sunderland, although specifying conventional masts, not bipods. Within a few years containerisation had ended the need for such 'tween-deck cargo ships such that Harrison Line had to charter out Benefactor while Bank

Line soon sold its examples. It is unsurprising that Iktinos and sisters were among the last high-class, conventional freighters built.

The Chinese were among the last to operate such vessels, and Iktinos gravitated to the Far East in 1985, when she became Fei Teng. Oddly for a Chinese ship, she was renamed Hawai Splendour in 1995, but this was almost certainly for a final voyage to breakers in Chittagong, where she arrived in January 1996.

Spanish variations

Spain was enjoying some success in shipbuilding in the 1960s, and attracted a number of international orders. A surprising order was from a British owner with a history that could be traced back to the earliest steam colliers, and which would have been expected to have been more conservative in its ordering policy. With her three-quarters aft superstructure, she certainly looked nothing like any of their previous ships.

Chatwood* of Wm France, Fenwick & Co Ltd, London, was ordered from Sociedad Española de Construccion Naval, Bilbao, and completed in April 1963. The 515-ft shelter-decker was propelled at 16 knots by a six-cylinder Sulzer oil engine made by her builders. Sadly, she was one of the last vessels to be owned by this venerable company.

She was undoubtedly aimed at the charter market and, after a short career with France, Fenwick, which ended in 1969, she spent eight years in the liner trade with Compagnie des Messageries Maritimes as Moheli. From 1977, ownership changes and renamings came thick and fast, with Sincerity, Mighty, Eternal Peace and Devi chosen by a number of Greek owners under their own and other flags. She was broken up at Chittagong in 1975.

It is interesting to compare the slightly smaller Ondarroa* with Chatwood. Hull and engines were completed by the same yard in July 1964, little more than seventeen months after France, Fenwick's swansong, yet Ondarroa has a bridge deck extended forward but truncated aft, kingposts in place of two of her masts and radically different treatment of her superstructure. Hazarding a guess, the 476-ft, 14.5-knot Ondarroa was designed by Sociedad Española de Construccion Naval, while Chatwood's concept originated with her owners. Ondarroa had two decks, and a deep tank for vegetable oil.

Owner Naviera Vizcaina SA of Bilbao was unlucky with Ondarroa. On 5 December 1971 she was attacked by Indian aircraft shortly after sailing from Chalna on voyage to Durban with jute. Her crew were taken off by an Indian warship, but Ondarroa was sunk during a further air attack on 6 December 1972.

Engines right aft

In the 1950s a few British builders and owners of full-size tramps took the bold step of moving the engines right aft, a position that had proved eminently satisfactory in tankers for over seventy years. And in accordance with contemporary tanker practice, the bridge and the deck officers' accommodation remained amidships. In 1957 *Romanby* and *Rushpool** were completed by Sir James Laing & Sons Ltd of Sunderland for companies managed by Sir R Ropner & Co Ltd of West Hartlepool. The 502-ft shelter-deckers were driven at 14 knots by five-cylinder Doxford engines built by Hawthorn Leslie (Engineering) Ltd at Newcastle. Ropner built only one further vessel to an engines-amidships design, and from then onwards all of its dry cargo ships were bulk carriers or ore ships. In *Wandby*, the next built in 1959, the bridge moved aft to join the rest of the accommodation.

Romanby and *Rushpool* were sold in 1969 and 1970 respectively, prematurely as it turned out because the freight market unexpectedly rose. Greek owners were the beneficiaries, *Rushpool* becoming first *Euthalia*, then *Eleftheros* and finally *Forum Spirit*. On 13 August 1982, she was heavily damaged by an engine room fire, 12 miles from Piraeus while on voyage from Port Said to Piraeus in ballast. Although soon extinguished, the fire meant the

twenty-five-year old motor ship was beyond economical repair and she was sold to Yugoslav breakers. This all took some time, and *Forum Spirit* did not arrive under tow at Split until March 1984. *(Ships in Focus)*

Louis Dreyfus and its London shipowning arm, Buries Markes Ltd, was certainly not afraid of innovation and from the late 1950s accepted a series of shelter-deckers with their machinery, navigating bridge and all accommodation right aft. Early versions such as the 455ft *La Pradera* of 1956 and the French-registered *Louis LD* of 1957 had joined kingposts forward. By the time the 463-ft *La Hortensia** was delivered to Buries Markes' management in January 1961, bipods had been specified, together with a full-height forecastle and a larger

accommodation block, the latter recognising that each crew member aspired to his own cabin. A feature of both designs was that the coamings to the five hatches extended almost the complete length of the deck, forming a girder that strengthened the hull.

Builder of the later batch was Société des Forges et Chantiers de la Méditerranée at La Seyne, who completed four for Buries Markes plus two more for other British owners (*Southwick* and *Skycrest*), two for Israelis and one for a Greek. The builder's engine works provided a seven-

cylinder Götaverken-type giving 14 knots.

Perhaps the design was a little small, as most were sold after less than ten years' service. From 1968, *La Hortensia* had a long series of Greek owners, which maintained her under the national flag as *Lambros M Fatsis*, *Triaena*, *Kavo Grossos* and *Apostolos M II* until 1985 when, just for a change, she became the Egyptian *Younis Gulf*. This did not last long, because in March 1986 she arrived at Gadani Beach where the breakers fell upon her almost immediately.

Liberty replacements

The distinction of completing the first 'Liberty replacement' went to Ishikawajima-Harima Heavy Industries (IHI), which delivered the *Khian Captain* from its Tokyo yard in September 1967. The ultimate owner, J C Carras, eventually ordered thirteen of what IHI – echoing the 'Liberty' name – dubbed the 'Freedom' type, including *Meliton**, delivered in May 1968. To produce a total of 168 of this two-deck ship, IHI worked with licensees in Singapore, Taiwan and in Spain (where five yards pursued a development that took the name 'Hispania' and ran to twenty-six examples). The two-deck Freedom design was developed in conjunction with Canadian consultants G T R Campbell, and the concept was further developed to produce the 'Fortune' type, a handy-sized bulk carrier, and the 'Freedom II' and 'Friendship' types. Their numbers add up to a total of 282, outnumbering the British SD14 and its variants.

A Pielstick four-cylinder Vee-oil engine built by IHI drove the 467ft *Meliton* at 14.5 knots, and did so while she tramped the world under Carras control for almost two decades. Only in 1986 did she pass out of Greek registry, first to the Cypriot flag as *Santa Ana*, then to Liberia as *Symphony* and finally *Symphonic*. After languishing under arrest from July 1992 at Calcutta, she was broken up at Mumbai, where demolition was completed in November 1993.

Of several German designs for 'Liberty replacements', the most successful was the 'Weser 36', produced by AG 'Weser' at Bremerhaven, and of which over seventy were delivered during 1970–78. Their success was dependent, as was that of other types, on offering favourable credit terms to potential owners, and only once these were available did 'Weser 36' sales take off. Of forty-nine built by yards in Vegesack, Flensburg and Bremerhaven, over half were for German owners (which had owned few if any Liberties). To tempt buyers, and in contrast to the 'Freedoms', many variations of cargo gear were available, one incorporating a large Stülcken mast and derrick for handling heavy lifts, and two versions with extended forecastles and poop decks. *Breda** had a 200-ton derrick at her conventional second mast.

She was delivered at Bremerhaven to Norwegian owner Hilmar Reksten in 1972 as *Gordian*, with a six-cylinder MAN engine. She took the name *Breda* in 1976 when she was one of two 'Weser 36L' types bought from the bankrupt Reksten by Koninklijke Nederlandsche Stoomboot Maatschappij NV, of Amsterdam. Names subsequent to 1987 were *Project Carrier*, *Beeco Europe*, *Manley Gosport* and *Mariupol Star*. Unusually for a ship of this size (she was 140 m overall), *Lloyd's Register* lost track of *Mariupol Star* and deleted her in 2002. *(David Whiteside collection)*

The 'Santa Fe' type 'Liberty replacement' was built by four Spanish yards, with Astilleros Espanoles SA at Bilbao building by far the biggest share – a total of forty-three. The total ordered was a fifty-one, although this is not quite so impressive when thirty-five ended up with just two beneficial owners. *Aegis Stoic** was one of twenty-five in the fleet of Aegis Shipping Co Ltd of Piraeus, controlled by N D Papalios. She had been completed at Bilbao in April 1971 as *Faith Euskalduna*, one of three

'Santa Fe' class ships that were intended for the British flag. Laid up for about one year, she was commissioned in May 1972 as *Aegis Stoic*, under the flag of Cyprus.

Her career was relatively short, although she packed in several changes of owner and two further names: *Rinio* from 1986 and *Margot* after 1988, mostly under ownership in Greece. She was broken up in Bangladesh in 1991, when barely twenty years old. The photograph was taken off Lagos at the end of 1975.

The rather distinctive, two-deck 'Santa Fe' class with its tall kingposts also found favour with the Argentinean state shipping line, Empresa Lineas Maritima Argentinas, which took ten examples. It is worthy of note that the lead yard, Astilleros Espanoles SA, did not put all its Liberty replacement eggs in one basket, but also built eight of the 'Hispania' type variants of the IHI 'Freedom' design. *(Malcolm Cranfield)*

The successful SD14

The single most numerous 'Liberty replacement', one of the most versatile and the only successful British design, was Austin & Pickersgill's SD14. 'SD' stood for shelter deck, and 14 indicated its 14,000 intended tons deadweight capacity, although in reality this was nearer to 15,000 tons. It owed part of its success to the Southwick shipyard on the River Wear, which had been laid out in the mid-1950s to undertake series building, and to facilitate automation and prefabrication. This, together with a 'no frills' approach to design allowed the price to be pared down to what Greek owners were prepared to pay for the earliest examples, which included *Janey**. Needless to say, credit facilities offered by the British government were an important factor in winning orders.

Ironically, Austin & Pickersgill's own yard was fully occupied with bulk carriers when the first orders were won in 1966. However, the nearby yard of Bartram & Sons Ltd came to an arrangement to licence-build the type. At one time Bartram seemed likely to deliver the first SD14, but embarrassment was avoided when *Nicola* was delivered by Austin & Pickersgill on 14 February 1968, one day ahead of *Mimis N Papalios* from Bartram.

Janey was the eighth from Austin & Pickersgill, delivered in July 1969 to a Liberian subsidiary of Mavroleon Brothers. In a satisfactory working life of almost twenty-six years, she also carried the names *Argolis, Anavissos, Mariner, Pigeon, Susan Sea, Vivari II* and *Armas* before demolition began at Chittagong in early 1995.

The SD14 design proved highly adaptable. Although aimed squarely at the market for tramps, a significant number were built with refinements for liner companies, including P&O, Ellerman and Lamport & Holt. Changing regulations and expectations saw the basic design evolve, especially in terms of machinery and cargo gear.

Construction ran to four series, with examples completed in four British yards and one each in Greece, Argentina and Brazil, until a total of 198 had been built over two decades. Even this was not the full story, because the Brazilian yard Companhia Comercio e Navegacao, which had constructed SD14s, produced a derivative named 'Prinasa-121', of which thirteen were built. Austin & Pickersgill's own attempts to follow up the design were less successful, with a solitary example of the SD15 and three SD18s ordered. Nevertheless, the SD14 programme was a very bright spot in a dismal period for British shipbuilding, demonstrating that, with the right product and credit facilities, it could successfully operate in a highly-competitive market.

Particularly impressive was how well the SD14 appealed to German operators, especially as competing German designs were on offer. *Good Faith** was completed at Southwick in September 1979 for a Liberian subsidiary of Egon Oldendorff, Lübeck. She had the largest heavy lift derricks yet fitted to an SD14, with a

lift of 100 tons and serving number four hatch. Subsequent names have been *Reedbuck, Springbok, Spring* and *He Feng* under the last of which she was still in commission in 2013.

Unfulfilled British hopes

Hopemount Shipping Co Ltd had been set up by shipbuilders Swan, Hunter & Wigham Richardson Ltd in 1904, mainly to own tramps that it built as speculations when orders were slow. The last gasp of this company was to take three shelter-deckers from the Glasgow yard of Barclay, Curle & Co Ltd, then part of the Swan, Hunter group and which was running short of work. The 501ft *Hopecrest** was the first of these, delivered in July 1961, equipped with a five-cylinder Sulzer diesel built under licence by Barclay, Curle and propelling her at 15.5 knots. Somewhat ahead of the craze to offer 'Liberty replacements', the Swan Hunter Group nevertheless hoped that a standard, series-built design would attract other orders, but in this they were unsuccessful, probably because the high specification made them too expensive. In the event, Swan Hunter group became part of British Shipbuilders, and in 1966 the Hopemount operation was sold to Common Brothers of Newcastle, which soon disposed of *Hopecrest*, along with sisters *Hopecrag* and *Hopepeak*. *Hopecrest* went, almost inevitably, to a flag-of-convenience company, becoming *Selene*, with ultimate ownership in Switzerland. Later names under Greek ownership were *Faneromeni* and *Filothei*. On 23 May 1983, *Filothei* stranded on rocks off Saba Island, 45 miles north of Hodeidah, after a steering gear failure. She was

on a voyage from La Spezia to Karachi with a cargo consisting of marble chips and powder. Although

refloated, she was sent to breakers, arriving at Gadani Beach in February 1984.

Doxford & Sunderland's attempt at entering the 'Liberty replacement' market envisaged a simple design with engines right aft. One of its five holds was extended to allow lengthy items to be carried below decks, and the 'tween-deck height was set at nine feet to stow containers or motor vehicles. The design was drawn up in the office where the progenitor of the Liberty ship had been conceived, over three decades earlier. Which makes it all the more unfortunate that the design never took off,

and the only two ships ordered had to become considerably more sophisticated to meet the needs of the Sheaf Steam Shipping Co Ltd. *Sheaf Crest* emerged from the former Laing yard in June 1968, while her sister, *Sheaf Field**, was delivered in March 1971 by the former Readhead yard in South Shields, which was now part of Swan Hunter Shipbuilders Ltd. The 462-ft ships were designed for Doxford's new four-cylinder 58J4-type engine, whose failure to impress potential buyers may

well have helped doom the 'Doxford Liberty'

Sheaf Field's later career was not entirely happy. In 1979 she was sold to Piraeus-based owners as *Mount Dirfys*, but spent some time laid up. Subsequent names were *Ultima* and *Fidelity*, but in January 1988 she put into Durban with engine problems so severe that she was deemed not worthy of repair. Her name was rather cruelly truncated to *Fidel* for her tow across the Indian Ocean to Chittagong Roads to await the attentions of Bangladesh ship breakers.

In the 454-ft 'Clyde' type standard ship, a latecomer to the market, the designers aimed principally at the liner trade, making them container-friendly and fitting twin side-by-side hatches. When carrying grain the hatches in the 'tween deck could fold to form a bulkhead so that the holds were divided longitudinally and the 'tween deck made a continuous space. Among many options, more powerful Sulzer-type engines, bulbous bows and controllable pitch propellers could be specified, improving performance to give a service speed of 16.5 knots. This versatility came at a cost, however, and the basic asking price was high at £1.8 million.

*Samjohn Pioneer** was completed at Clydebank in January 1972, one of two for London-Greek owners, John Samonas & Sons Ltd. She was to have the long list of

owners and names typical of any post-war freighter: *Trade Envoy, Gulf Trader, Vicky, Navick* and *Lady Charmain*. She was broken up at Jiangyin in 2000.

Despite their high cost, seven 'Clyde' type ships were built by the Scotstoun and Clydebank divisions of Upper Clyde Shipbuilders Ltd, and all but one for companies that could be considered as tramp owners. However, while the programme was underway the builders were declared bankrupt. This inevitably delayed completion of the ships, led to the cancellation of two further orders, and damaged the faith of potential owners. An improved version was offered by the builder's successors, Govan Shipbuilders, but no orders were forthcoming, helping doom the historic industry of shipbuilding in Glasgow. *(David Whiteside collection)*

13

Tramp into Bulk Carriers

The modern bulk carrier is a relatively simple ship, with a single deck, adequate water ballast capacity for long voyages without cargo, and large hatches to facilitate loading and discharge. It may or may not have its own cargo gear, and in its current form invariably has engines and accommodation positioned right aft. Most of these characteristics will be familiar from some of the ships in earlier chapters, and indeed were present in the pioneer steam collier *John Bowes* of 1851.

This last chapter looks briefly at how the bulk carrier evolved. The progenitors of the post-war bulk carrier include dedicated colliers, ore carriers built in Europe and the lakers of North America. Evolution was a process with several strands, including the enlargement of the British east coast collier to give vessels like *Hudson Deep* and *Camellia*. There were almost contemporary Japanese and German efforts to build large, US-financed ore carriers, plus a desire to find uses for redundant tankers in the bulk trades. Of the factors driving these developments, probably the most important was the demand of industry for ever more economical transport of raw materials, but also of significance was the ending of the farce of designating ships as open shelter deckers. The massive growth in size of bulk carriers which followed was facilitated by increases in the ability and capacity of yards to build larger ships, a willingness of terminal operators to accommodate them, and the readiness of financiers to pay for them on the security of long-term charters to industrial undertakings.

Post-war efforts to build ore and general bulk carrier are considered in this chapter, along with a several more modern examples. The chapter goes no further than this, however: subtypes of the bulk carrier, such as forest products and ore carriers, and their size-bands, are stories in themselves, and as such are beyond the scope of this book. Indeed, this breed of ship is mentioned largely to finish off the story of the classic tramp steamer, which bulk carriers of various sizes very largely replaced.

Note: An asterisk in a caption indicates the vessel shown in the photograph.

Lakers and canallers

The first large, single-deck, engines-aft steamers for carrying cargo in bulk were developed for use on the Great Lakes of North America during the last third of the nineteenth century. It is not known if their design was in the least influenced by the earlier development of steam colliers on the east coast of the United Kingdom, but the lakers provide an important strand in the bulk carrier story. By the early twentieth century, they had matured into vessels capable of carrying 12,000 tons of iron and other ores, grain, coal, stone, cement or forest products. *Augustus B Wolvin** of 1904 was regarded as the acme of the design at the time, as reflected in her owner's name, Acme Steam Ship Co of Duluth, Minnesota.

At 540 ft, this product of American Ship Building Co of Lorain, Ohio was larger than any ocean-going cargo ship yet built, and had a quadruple-expansion engine. Although the Great Lakes were not always calm, her career does not seem to have involved any major excitements. In 1912 management switched from A B Wolvin to A T Kinney. One year later she was sold to Interlake Steamship Co Ltd of Cleveland, managed by Pickands, Mather & Co.

Transfer to Montreal-based ownership in 1966 and hoisting the Canadian flag seems to have been a

preliminary to the sale of *Augustus B Wolvin* for breaking up, and she then ventured across the Atlantic to Santander to meet her end in September 1967. *(William Schell)*

Smaller cousins of the lakers were vessels built to navigate the canal system that connected Lake Ontario with the sea. The completion of the St Lawrence Canals in 1901 permitted use of craft up to 250 ft to move wheat and other bulk cargoes to sea ports during the ice-free season from April to December. These were not suited nor classed for trading elsewhere, and during the

winter months the canallers were laid up at Canadian ports including Toronto, Kingston and Port Colborne. However, during both world wars a few ventured across the Atlantic to work in European waters.

British yards dominated the building of these single-deck bulk carriers for Canadian owners, and an example was *Cedarton** completed in April 1924 by A McMillan & Son

Ltd of Dumbarton for Lake Steamship Co Ltd of Toronto. J G Kincaid & Co Ltd supplied a triple-expansion engine.

Completion of the St Lawrence Seaway in 1959 rendered the canallers redundant because sea-going ships could now trade to the Great Lakes. *Cedarton* was sold to breakers in 1962, but languished at Dorval in Quebec until broken up early in 1964.

Large colliers

While the design of the sea-going tramp steamer was crystallising around the engines-amidships, shelter-deck concept, ships dedicated to the coal trade continued to be built with a single deck and engines aft. Most were modest in size, reflecting the dimensions of ports involved in coastwise movements of coal, and the reluctance of designers to confront problems of weight distribution and trim when the boilers and engines were placed aft. The few exceptions included the extraordinary *August Belmont** of 1902. Ordered by Louisville & Nashville Railroad Co from C S Swan & Hunter Ltd, Wallsend, she was completed for Pensacola Trading Co Ltd, and managed by Watts, Watts & Co, both of London. The aim was to carry 6,800 tons of coal on a modest draught and discharge it within twelve hours. Her nine hatches were served by cargo gear consisting of grabs and transporters designed by a Philadelphia company. That this was unsuccessful is evidenced by its replacement with conventional kingposts and derricks. The objective of the Pensacola company was to operate a service from Europe to ports in the West Indies and the Gulf of Mexico, and it also took delivery of the turret *E O Saltmarsh*.

The 373-ft *August Belmont* was requisitioned by the British Admiralty in 1916 and converted to a tanker. The cylindrical tanks placed in her holds were not the most

efficient way to carry oil, and although briefly owned by Anglo-Saxon Petroleum Co Ltd as *Ancula*, her subsequent

career was short: she was demolished on the Tyne during 1924.

The 1920s saw isolated examples of large single-deckers built specifically to move coal. The best-known European examples were the thirteen 'PLMs' of 345 ft and 414 ft built on the Tees to move locomotive coal from North Sea ports to the Mediterranean for a French railway company, and featured in the sister publication *Coasters: An Illustrated History*. Large colliers were also built for the coal trade on the US east coast, which saw large tonnages mined in West Virginia and Kentucky shipped from ports such as Norfolk to New York, Boston and as far north as Maine.

An engines-aft example was the 350-ft *Berwindglen*, completed in July 1929 by Bethlehem Shipbuilding Corporation at Quincy, Massachusetts for Wilmore Steamship Co Inc of New York. Although she had a conventional triple-expansion engine, her sister *Berwindvale* was fitted with a steam turbine.

Berwindglen was photographed from a bridge on the Cape Cod Canal during a southbound ballast voyage. With engines aft, no cargo gear, and mechanically-moved hatch covers, she has most of the characteristics of a bulk carrier built a quarter of a century later.

In 1950, *Berwindglen* was sold, converted to a barge and renamed *Mary J Sheridan* but as such she survived only until 1954 when she was demolished at Baltimore. *(Eric Johnson)*

Ore carriers pre-war

Like coal, iron ore was moved in large quantities, often on predictable routes between ports that were equipped to load and unload it mechanically. Hence another strand in the bulk carrier story was the development of dedicated ore carriers.

An early but relatively small example was the 281-ft turret *Oxelösund**, built and engined in 1906 by William Doxford & Sons Ltd, Sunderland for a company managed by P Tham in Oxelösund, Sweden. Interestingly but difficult to explain, she is flying the Finnish national flag in this photograph, in which her turret deck is almost awash.

Oxelösund would normally have loaded ore at northern Swedish ports in the Gulf of Bothnia or, during winter months, in ice-free Norwegian ports such as Narvik, for delivery to iron and steel works. However, the First World War gave neutral Swedish owners other opportunities and hazards, and *Oxelösund* had been loaded at Holmsund with wood pulp destined for Northfleet on the River Thames shortly before she capsized and sank in Gefle Bay on 19 June 1916. *(Martin Lindenborn)*

Swedish experience led to the building of ore-carrying ships that were a quarter of a century ahead of their time. In 1925, Ångfartygs A/B Tirfing, managed by Dan-Axel Broström of Gothenburg, took delivery of *Amerikaland* and *Svealand** from Deutsche Werft AG of Hamburg. At 561 ft, not only were these the largest ocean-going cargo ships yet built, but also were diesel-driven, their machinery comprising two Burmeister & Wain eight-cylinder, four-strokes made by AEG of Berlin, driving twin screws. Fast turn-rounds provided limited time for engine overhaul in port, but the two engines allowed one to be shut down while at sea. To give such large, single deck vessels sufficient strength, the builders adopted longitudinal framing on the Isherwood system often preferred for tankers.

They were designed to work between the ore port of Cruz Grande in Chile and the Sparrow's Point steel works of Bethlehem Steel Corporation in Maryland via the Panama Canal. The ore was loaded into three holds, served by nine steel hatches that were moved mechanically, the gear for which can be seen on the deck of *Svealand*. Presaging other post-war developments, Broström had negotiated a long-term contract with

Bethlehem Steel that made financing the ships viable. *Amerikaland* was torpedoed in 1942, but *Svealand* continued on the service until 1949. She was then employed carrying ore out of Narvik, and in 1951 was re-engined with twin Götaverken diesels. This extended her life until late 1969, making her final voyage to China with her name truncated to *Svea*.

Given such successful examples of bulk carrying, it is indeed surprising that the ore carrier took so long to become widely accepted. *(Ships in Focus)*

Ore carriers post-war

A major stimulus to the multiplication of ore carriers was the decision of the nationalised British steel industry to offer long-term charters to owners prepared to build such vessels. Over a period of eleven years, a total of seventy-three were completed, to a variety of designs and of three sizes to suit the dimensions of the docks that received ore. The ships were highly successful, not only proving much more efficient in service than 'tween-deck tramps previously used, but also making money for their builders and owners.

Ormsary was the first, completed in January 1953 by Lithgows Ltd, Port Glasgow for Scottish Ore Carriers Ltd. This was a joint venture of the shipbuilders and J & J Denholm, which undertook management, as the Greenock firm did for the ore carriers of several other owners. *Ormsary* was one of six for this company, out of a total of twenty-four ore carrier hulls of 427 ft – the smallest size built, and which could access the docks at Port Talbot and reach the steelworks at Irlam on the Manchester Ship Canal. The six Lithgow-built vessels had

three different types of machinery: triple-expansion engines in *Ormsary* and *Gleddoch*, Doxford diesels in *Arisaig*, *Craigallian* and *Crinan*. The odd man out was *Morar*, which was initially fitted with a gas turbine installation, which even after the original machinery was replaced, survived only for nine years before it gave way to a diesel.

Ormsary went to breakers in Bilbao in 1969.

United States interests were also developing large ore carriers, although with the huge expense of building in the United States and operating under the national flag, the vessels were built in Japan or Germany, and placed under Liberian or Panamanian registry. A prime mover in this was the Daniel Ludwig-controlled National Bulk Carriers Ltd, which leased the former Kure Naval Shipyard in Japan to build large tankers, ore-oil carriers

and ore carriers. Another US behemoth, Joshua Hendy Corporation of Los Angeles, was behind *Rio San Juan**, delivered by Deutsche Werft AG, Hamburg in October 1957 to Transworld Carriers Inc, of Monrovia. At 657 ft, the ore carrier was considerably larger than contemporary European-owned vessels. Two steam turbines by AEG of Berlin geared to a single shaft gave her a creditable 14.25 knots.

In 1959, *Rio San Juan* became *Sigvik* for Berge Sigval Bergesen and in 1969 *Barvik* for Torvald Klaveness. It seems that these Norwegian owners took over the vessel and chartered her back to Joshua Hendy Corporation, which bought her back in 1968. Once more named *Rio San Juan* under the Liberian flag, she was broken up at Kaohsiung in 1975.

More typical of post-war ore carriers was the bridge right aft configuration of another of those built to supply British Steel works, the prosaically-named *Iron Ore** of 1959. Equally prosaic was her design, which made up for in practicality what it lacked in aesthetic appeal. Owner of the 517-ft motor ship was Vallum Shipping Co Ltd, a joint venture between Jardine, Matheson Ltd and Common Brothers Ltd, which managed the five ships owned by

Vallum. They were from three different builders; *Iron Age* and *Iron Barque* were completed by Austin & Pickersgill Ltd at Sunderland. Both had four-cylinder Doxford diesels manufactured by the North Eastern Marine Engineering Co Ltd at Wallsend. Common Brothers made a speciality of managing ships, and as well as two other BISCO-chartered ore carriers, looked after a fleet of tankers working for British Petroleum.

Iron Age was sold in 1969, presumably when her initial ten-year charter to BISCO expired, and was subsequently owned in Italy under the Panamanian flag as *Sirocco*. From 1981, an owner based in Monaco operated her as *Skyros* and later *Gamboa* until she was delivered to Turkish breakers at Aliaga in late 1986. (*J and M Clarkson*)

Only an aerial view can adequately depict how ore carrying ships have grown massively since the 1950s. *Sir Alexander Glen** of 1975 has been chosen because she is one of the last to be built in Great Britain. She is in fact not just an ore carrier, but an OBO, designed to carry, ore, oil or other bulk cargoes. The idea was to make such vessels as versatile as possible in terms of employment, but this considerably increased cost as facilities had to be provided to handle both dry and liquid cargoes.

The builder of *Sir Alexander Glen* was Swan Hunter Shipbuilders Ltd at Haverton Hill on the Tees for Thornhope Shipping Co Ltd. At 294 m, she was well over twice the length of *Ormsary*, with a deadweight tonnage twenty times greater. *Sir Alexander Glen* brought just one ore cargo to the UK, unloading at Port Talbot, where facilities had clearly been enlarged since nothing bigger than *Ormsary* could be handled.

With several examples suffering serious structural failure, this class of OBO was unfortunate, and even became notorious with the loss of *Derbyshire*, although her design seems to have been largely exonerated. *Sir Alexander Glen* avoided such problems, but her life was to end in failure and acrimony. From 1969 she was in Taiwanese ownership as *Ocean Monarch* and as *Ocean Mandarin*. In March 1994 her rudder fell off in the Pacific and she was towed into a South Korean port. She was arrested for non-payment of salvage money, and her next voyage was to breakers in mainland China.

Post-war bridge amidships

The strands of collier, ore carrier and perhaps laker came together in the single-deck, engines-aft, bulk carrier making its appearance in the 1950s, initially with its bridge amidships. Pioneers in Britain were owners strongly connected to bulk trades, and coal carrying in the case of Hudson Steamship Co Ltd, which belonged to Thames dock owners and coal importers, Samuel Williams & Sons Ltd. Following the nationalisation of British coal mining, gas and electricity industries after the Second World War, Hudson thought it prudent to diversify away from coal carrying, and some of its larger colliers were chartered to carry sugar. It was an obvious step to enlarge the collier's design with an extra hold, and so was built *Hudson Deep**, at 434ft the world's largest raised-quarterdeck vessel in 1952. Builder was John Readhead & Sons Ltd, South Shields, which fitted a four-cylinder Doxford engine built by North Eastern Marine Engineering Co (1938) Ltd at Wallsend to give her a modest service speed of 12 knots. After loading a coal cargo for the Thames, *Hudson Deep* sailed to Cuba to begin a three-year charter carrying sugar. It was not long before her charterer, Tate & Lyle Ltd, was building similar bulk sugar carriers for its own shipping subsidiary.

After giving Hudson twenty years of service, *Hudson Deep* was sold to Greece in 1972 and renamed *Irene's*

Hope. On 13 December 1978 she sank north of Alexandria after springing a leak in her engine room while carrying general cargo from Civitavecchia to Dammam.

Camellia of 1953 was a bold step into bulk carriers by Stag Line Ltd, a long-established, independent tramping company still run by the founding Robinson family from its base in North Shields. She was built within sight of its offices, just across the Tyne at South Shields, by John Readhead & Sons Ltd, who had now built several bulk carriers: note the resemblance to *Hudson Deep*. *Camellia* was fitted with a similar Doxford engine.

Camellia was followed in 1955 by *Cydonia* which, although having the same, 434-ft, raised quarterdeck, five-hold hull, was surprisingly given a triple-expansion engine made by Readhead. Both ships were fitted with the equipment needed to transit the St Lawrence Seaway and were among the first deep-sea ships to penetrate the Great Lakes, entering the Seaway just eight days after it opened in May 1959. Subsequent deliveries to Stag Line from South Shields were the diesel-driven *Gloxinia* and *Photinia* from Readhead, with hulls enlarged to 480 ft and with an extra mast.

Not surprisingly, *Camellia* remained with Stag Line longer than her younger, steam-driven, sister *Cydonia*, which went in 1969. *Camellia* was sold to become *Galicia* in 1972, and was broken up at Blyth in April 1977, shortly before the former *Cydonia* sank after engine room explosions in June 1977. *(G A Osbon/World Ship Society Ltd)*

Tanker conversions

In the 1950s and the early 1960s, the ranks of ore and bulk carriers were significantly increased by several conversions of tanker hulls. *Carola Schulte** was an early example; bought and converted just before the closure of the Suez Canal in 1956 would have made even an elderly motor tanker such as her highly profitable.

She had been completed in January 1938 by Deutsche Werft AG in the Finkenwerder district of Hamburg for John T Essberger as *Nord Atlantic*.

Requisitioned by the Kriegsmarine while at Vigo in September 1939, she may have been used to refuel U-boats, at least until she was damaged by stranding in August 1943. Laid up at El Ferrol for the duration of the war, in May 1945 British authorities managed to claim her as a prize, and she was repaired and returned to service under her existing name. Sale in 1948 saw her become *Southern Atlantic*, a name reflecting her use supporting Salvesen's whaling fleet in Antarctic waters.

Sale to Schulte & Bruns KG of Emden in 1955 was followed by her rebuilding as an ore carrier, as which she entered service in 1956, still with her original, six-cylinder, MAN-built, double-acting diesel engine. The 490-ft *Carola Schulte* traded until 1972 when, after a short lay-up at Emden, she was despatched to ship breakers at Bilbao.

A later conversion to a bulk carrier was the 515-ft *Cassian Mariner**. Her origin was as the Norwegian motor tanker *Buesten*, completed by Swan, Hunter & Wigham Richardson Ltd at Wallsend in September 1951, a time when British yards could still command a major share of the international market for tanker tonnage. Machinery was a five-cylinder Doxford-type diesel manufactured by

Swan, Hunter's own engine works, Wallsend Slipway & Engineering Co Ltd.

Original operators Rafen & Loennechen of Tønsberg sold her to the London-managed fleet of Emmanuel Marcou, for whom she continued working as a tanker under the Liberian flag as *Cassian Mariner*. Once the post-Suez tanker boom had blown itself out, she was rebuilt in

1961 as depicted in the photograph.

Following sale in 1973 she was simply renamed *Bulk Mariner* for a Panamanian company with Argentinean principals. Her final name was the somewhat tautological *Stella Star*, probably carried for no more than her delivery voyage to Gadani Beach where she arrived in November 1978.

Post-war all aft

British owners rather tentatively moved their ships' accommodation right aft in the 1950s, often on what were modest-sized bulk carriers such as *Macaulay**. Her builder in 1959 was Henry Robb Ltd, which fitted a six-cylinder Sulzer engine made in Winterthur, and which made the long journey from Switzerland to Leith for installation. The owner of *Macaulay* was Chine Shipping Co Ltd of London, and the letters 'AD' on her funnel markings were for its manager, Anglo-Danubian Transport Co Ltd. Seen as built, her initial length of 367 ft soon proved unduly modest, and after five years she was lengthened to 414 ft, and she gained a third mast to serve additional holds.

In 1968, *Macaulay* was sold and renamed *Jevington* by Stephenson Clarke Shipping Ltd, long-established in the London coal business and who were acquiring bulk carriers to help them venture outside of this declining trade. *Jevington* was kept until 1980, after which Greek owners traded her for another three years as *Omega Patmos*. She was broken up at Jamnagar in 1983.

Although not different in concept from *Macaulay*, the 580-foot, six-hatch *Aurora II** of 1968 is included to emphasise the rapid growth in size of the bulk carrier during the 1960s. The Piraeus-registered motor ship also highlights how concentration on bulk carriers helped both Japanese shipbuilders and Greek ship owners become dominant forces in their respective industries.

Aurora II was completed by Mitsui Zosen KK at Fujinagata and given a Sulzer-type seven-cylinder diesel made by Uraga Heavy Industries Ltd of Tamashima. When new, this propelled her at a respectable 17 knots, although in her later entries in registers, this was downgraded to 13.5 knots. Disponent owner was S Perivolaris of Piraeus, who put her with a single-ship company based in Piraeus and kept her there until she was sold to China Ocean Shipping Co as *Zhi Hai* in 1976. She was reported as broken up in China in the later 1990s.

Completed in 2011, *CMB Virginie* exemplifies the geared bulk carrier built in the second decade of the twenty-first century. Her cargo gear comprises four deck cranes, now standard in geared bulkers, and she carries grabs for these which are resting on her hatches. The upright structures along the sides of her deck are to help support deck cargoes, especially timber. With a length of 172 m, she is described as 'handy sized', in that she can use most important seaports. Her builder was Jiangsu Zhenjiang, one of the yards that have enabled China to overtake both Japan and South Korea in output of ships.

The hull and funnel markings of *CMB Virginie* show her allegiance to Bocimar Belgium NV, the dry cargo shipping arm of the old-established Compagnie Maritime Belge (CMB) of Antwerp. Manager is Anglo-Eastern Shipmanagement of Hong Kong. Ownership in Belgium but registration and management far off in south east Asia is no surprise to observers, because owners and managers balance the economies and conveniences of various flag states with their perceived status in the eyes of the bodies that inspect, classify and insure ships.

The practically new *CMB Virginie* was photographed off Gibraltar in October 2011, where she called to bunker with the low-sulphur fuel now mandatory in western European waters. *CMB Virginie* has traded worldwide, and as such is the successor, and perhaps the descendant, of the tramp steamers that first tentatively voyaged out of north eastern British yards 150 years ago. *(Roy Fenton)*

Bibliography

Anon, *A Century of Family Shipowning*, Cory, Cardiff, 1954.

Appleyard, H, 'Ropner Trunk-Deck Steamers parts 1 and 2', *Ships in Focus Record*, 2, 83–91; 3, 154–9.

Appleyard, H S, *Bank Line and Andrew Weir and Company*, World Ship Society, Kendal, 1985.

Appleyard, H S, and P M Heaton, *The Baron Glanely of St Fagans and W J Tatem Ltd*, World Ship Society, Kendal, nd.

'Archers, The', 'The Arch Deck Steamers parts 1 and 2', *Ships in Focus Record*, 29, 28–33; 30, 92–104.

Atkinson, G, *Hudson Steamship*, McCall, Portishead, 2004.

Atkinson, T, 'Richard B. Chellew; Chellew Navigation Co Ltd', *British Shipping Fleets 2*, Ships in Focus, Preston, 2007.

Barraclough, M, *Looking for the Silver Lining: A British Family's Shipowning Century 1875–1975*, Bound Biographies, Bicester, 2008.

Burrell, D, *The Thistle Boats*, World Ship Society, Kendal, 1987.

Burrell, D, *The Nitrate Boats*, World Ship Society, Kendal, 1995.

Burrell, D, 'Cardiff Hall Line', *British Shipping Fleets*, Ships in Focus, Preston, 2000.

Burrell, D, 'The Southdown Steamship Co Ltd', *Ships in Focus Record*, 34, 88–96.

Clarke, J F, *Building Ships on the North East Coast: A Labour of Love, Risk and Pain (Parts 1 and 2)*, Bewick Press, Whitley Bay, 1997.

Cooper, M, *Ritsons' Branch Line*, World Ship Society, Gravesend, 2002.

Cooper, M, 'Hain in a hundred: a British tramp fleet at work: New Year's Day 1900', *Ships in Focus Record*, 34, 104–11.

Cooper, M, *J and C Harrison: the History of a Family Shipping Venture*, Ships in Focus, Preston, 2012.

Course, A G, *The Deep Sea Tramp*, Hollis & Carter, London, 1960.

Craig, Robin, *The Ship: Steam Tramps and Cargo Liners 1850–1950*, HMSO, London, 1980.

Crowdy, M, *Lyle Shipping Co Ltd 1827–1966*, World Ship Society, Kendal, 1966.

Dear, I, *The Ropner Story*, Hutchinson Benham, London, 1986.

Fenton, R S, 'The Introduction of Steam to UK Coastal Bulk Trades: a Technological and Commercial Assessment', *International Journal of Maritime History*, XX/2, Dec 2008, 175.

Gibbs, J M, *Morels of Cardiff: the History of a Family Shipping Firm*, National Museum of Wales, Cardiff, 1982.

Goldberg, M H, *The 'Hog Islanders': the Story of 122 American Ships*, American Merchant Marine Museum, New York, 1991.

Gray, L, 'Hugh Roberts and Son', *Marine News*, 24, 1970, 323–30.

Gray, L, *The Ropner Fleet 1874–1974*, World Ship Society, Kendal, 1975.

Gray, L, and J Lingwood, *The Doxford Turret Ships*, World Ship Society, Kendal, 1975.

Greenway, A, *Comecon Merchant Ships*, Mason, Emsworth, 1989.

Greenway, A, *Soviet Merchant Ships*, Mason, Emsworth, 1989.

Hackman, R M, 'The Western Counties Shipping Company Ltd (1915–1922)', *Marine News*, 11, 1957, 207–8, 230–35.

Heal, S C, *Conceived in War, Born in Peace: Canada's Deep Sea Merchant Marine*, Cordillera, Vancouver, 1992.

Heaton, P M, 'Seafarer to Shipowner', *Sea Breezes*, 52, 1978, 631–4.

Heaton, P M, 'A Welsh Family Shipowning Venture', *Sea Breezes*, 52, 1978, 673–93.

Heaton, P M, 'Cardiff's Duncan Sisters', *Sea Breezes*, 53, 1979, 351–60.

Heaton, P M, 'A Brave Post-war Venture', *Sea Breezes*, 55, 1981, 399–404.

Heaton, P M, 'Seagers: a Cardiff Tramp Fleet', *Sea Breezes*, 55, 1981, 545–61.

Heaton, P M, *The 'Redbrook' – A Deep-Sea Tramp*, Starling Press, Risca, 1981.

Heaton, P M, 'South American Saint Line's 39 Years', *Sea Breezes*, 56, 1982, 115–24, 189–99, 243–52.

Heaton, P M, 'Graig Shipping: a Firm Foundation', *Sea Breezes*, 56, 1982, 559–68, 633–45.

Heaton, P M, *The 'Usk' Ships: History of a Newport Shipping Venture*, Starling Press, Risca, 1982.

Heaton, P M, *The Abbey Line: History of a Cardiff Shipping Venture*, Starling Press, Risca, 1983.

Heaton, P M, *Reardon Smith Line: the History of a South Wales Shipping Venture*, Starling Press, Risca, 1984.

Heaton, P M, *Welsh Shipping: Forgotten Fleets*, Starling Press, Risca, 1989.

Heaton, P M, *Jack Billmeir Merchant Shipowner*, Starling Press, Risca, 1989.

Hogg, P, and H A Appleyard, *The Pyman Story: Fleet and Family History*, Pyman, Hartlepool, 2000.

Jackson, H and M, *Holme Shipping Line Maryport – 1873 to 1913*, Hirst-Jackson, Maryport, 1991.

Jenkins, D, *Jenkins Brothers of Cardiff: a Ceredigion Family's Shipping Ventures*, National Museum of Wales, Cardiff, 1985.

Jenkins, D, 'Sir William Reardon Smith and the St Just Steamship Co Ltd, 1912–1932', *Maritime Wales*, 10, 1986, 45–62.

Jenkins, D, *Owen and Watkin Williams of Cardiff: 'The Golden Cross Line'*, World Ship Society, Kendal, 1991.

Jenkins, D, 'The Chellew Steam Navigation Company Limited: a note on some Welsh Connections', *Maritime Wales*, 15, 1992, 82–4.

Jenkins, D, *Shipowners of Cardiff: a Class by Themselves. A History of the Cardiff and Bristol Channel Incorporated Shipowners Association*, University of Wales and National Museums and Galleries of Wales, Cardiff, 1997.

Jenkins, D, *From Ship's Cook to Baronet: Sir William Reardon Smith's Life in Shipping 1856–1935*, University of Wales Press, Cardiff, 2011.

Jenkins, J G, 'Cardiff Shipowners', *Maritime Wales*, 5, 1980, 115–31.

Jenkins, J G, *Evan Thomas Radcliffe: a Cardiff Shipowning Company*, National Museum of Wales, Cardiff, 1982.

Jenkins, J G, *Maritime Heritage: the Ships and Seamen of Southern Ceredigion*, Gomer Press, Llandysul, 1982.

Jenkins, J G, and D Jenkins, *Cardiff Shipowners*, National Museum of Wales, Cardiff, 1986.

Jordan, R, 'Growth of a Cardiff Shipping Enterprise', *Sea Breezes*, 44, 1970, 233–42.

Lingwood, J, *SD14: The Full Story*, Ships in Focus, Preston, 2004.

Lingwood, J, and H Appleyard, *Chapman of Newcastle*, World Ship Society, Kendal, 1985.

Lingwood, J, and L Gray, *Stephens, Sutton Limited*, World Ship Society, Kendal, 1983.

Lingwood, J, and K O'Donoghue, *The Trades Increase: a Centenary History of Norex plc*, World Ship Society, Kendal, 1993.

Mallett, A S, *Idyll of the Kings: the History of King Line 1889–1979*, World Ship Society, Kendal, 1980.

McAlister, A A, and L H Gray, *Hogarth and Sons Ltd*, World Ship Society, Kendal, 1976.

Middlemiss, N L, *Travels of the Tramps: Twenty Tramp Fleets*, Shield Publications, Newcastle-upon-Tyne, 1989.

Middlemiss, N L, *Travels of the Tramps: Twenty Tramp Fleets Volume 2*, Shield Publications, Newcastle-upon-Tyne, 1991.

Middlemiss, N L, *Travels of the Tramps: Twenty Tramp Fleets Volume 3*, Shield Publications, Newcastle-upon-Tyne, 1992.

Middlemiss, N L, *Travels of the Tramps: Twenty Tramp Fleets Volume 5*, Shield Publications, Newcastle-upon-Tyne, 2003.

Mitchell, W H, and L A Sawyer, *British Standard Ships of World War 1*, Journal of Commerce, Liverpool, 1968.

Mitchell, W H, and L A Sawyer, *The Empire Ships*, Lloyd's of London Press, London, 1990.

Morgan, G, 'Thomas Jones of Aberystwyth, Shipowner', *Maritime Wales*, 17, 1995, 28–50.

O'Donoghue, K, and H S Appleyard, *Hain of St Ives*, World Ship Society, Kendal, 1986.

O'Donoghue, K, and P M Heaton, *Kaye Son and Co Ltd*, World Ship Society, Kendal, nd.

Orbell, J, *From Cape to Cape: the History of Lyle Shipping*, Harris, Edinburgh, 1978.

Ritchie, L A, *The Shipbuilding Industry: A Guide to Historical Records*, Manchester University Press, Manchester, 1992.

Sedgwick, S, S Kinnaird, and K O'Donoghue, *London & Overseas Freighters PLC 1948–1992*, World Ship Society, Kendal, 1992,

Smith-Hughes, J, 'John Mathias and Sons of Aberystwyth', *Sea Breezes*, 42, 1968, 223–5.

Spaldin, B G, and H S Appleyard, *The West Hartlepool Steam Navigation Company Limited*, World Ship Society, Kendal, 1980.

Spong, H C, *Irish Shipping Limited*, World Ship Society, Kendal, 1982.

Stewart, I G, *British Tramps and their Peacetime Contribution to World Shipping History*, Ian Stewart, Rockingham Beach, 1997.

Taylor E N, and P M Heaton, 'Pardoe-Thomas and Company Ltd', *Maritime Wales*, 6, 1981, 66–79.

Thomas, P N, *British Ocean Tramps* (two volumes), Waine Research, Albrighton, 1992, 1994.

Williams, D I, *Seventy Years in Shipping*, Graig and Stewart Williams, Barry, 1989.

Winter, M T, *The Portishead Coal Boats – a History of Osborn & Wallis Ltd, Bristol*, Black Dwarf Lightmoor, Lydney, 2005.

Periodicals
Archive
Marine News
Sea Breezes
Ships in Focus Record
Ships Monthly

Registers
Lloyd's Confidential Index, 1886–1914
Lloyd's Register of Shipping, *Register Book*, 1860–1914
Mercantile Navy List, 1870–1914
Miramar Ship Index
Starke-Schell Registers

Index